Brothers in Sport

GAA

Donal Keenan

MERCIER PRESS

IRISH PUBLISHER – IRISH STORY

Laois County Library
Leabharlann Chontae Laoise

Acc. No. ....10/17111....

Class No. ....796.33....

Inv. No. ....11526....

MERCIER PRESS
Cork
www.mercierpress.ie

© Donal Keenan, 2010

© Foreword: Criostóir Ó Cuana, 2010

ISBN: 978 1 85635 695 4

10 9 8 7 6 5 4 3 2 1

A CIP record for this title is available from the British Library

This book is sold subject to the condition that it shall not, by way of trade or otherwise, be lent, resold, hired out or otherwise circulated without the publisher's prior consent in any form of binding or cover other than that in which it is published and without a similar condition including this condition being imposed on the subsequent purchaser.

No part of this publication may be reproduced or transmitted in any form or by any means, electronic or mechanical, including photocopying, recording or any information or retrieval system, without the prior permission of the publisher in writing.

Printed and bound in the EU.

CONTENTS

FOREWORD

Is cúis mhór áthais dom na focail seo a leanas a scríobh don leabhar seo agus scéalta clainne bailithe ag an údar ag deánamh mionscrúdú ar roinnt de na deartháireacha is cáiliúla in ár gcluichí.

The family unit has always stood out for the unique and stand-alone contribution that it has made, and continues to make, to our association. If any one aspect of our membership encapsulates and distils what the GAA represents, it is the role of so many families who help make our club network the bedrock of the association.

Of course that unique family contribution does not stop at club level but features prominently at county level too, adding further credence to the importance of home place, identity and representation.

This book captures between two covers the incredible family ties and the contribution that so many siblings have made to all levels of the GAA and notably to the shop window that is our inter-county scene.

There is something special about a team – and especially a successful team – that includes a band of brothers. For example, the driving force role played by the Ó Sé brothers, Darragh, Tomás and Marc, has provided a fascinating strand to our games in recent years. Few other sports some close to matching this.

A glance at the family names featured in this book is enough to spark memories of the incredible exploits of so many figures who have enthralled and entertained in equal measure.

Of course it's not just about the games. This trip through the decades also charts the vast social changes that Ireland has experienced in six decades and how family life has changed over the same period.

It's not so long since the GAA library was a limited and sparsely stocked one. I am glad to say that this has well and truly changed, and the publication of *Brothers in Sport – GAA* is a valued and most welcome entry shining a light on a fascinating dimension to our association's activities.

Rath Dé ar an obair.

Criostóir Ó Cuana
Uachtarán Chumann Lúthchleas Gael

INTRODUCTION

Time and space. You never have enough of either especially when undertaking a project such as this one.

The stories here are the result of a journey this year that allowed me to revisit the four corners of Ireland, and places in between, to meet old friends and, hopefully, make some new ones. Those miles travelled and the family histories that were recounted, illustrate, in often startling fashion, just how much Ireland has changed over the last half-century.

My fourteen-year-old son was often a companion on those journeys and he listened bemused and amused as I recalled days using a wind-up telephone in a bar in Knocknagoshel to file a report on a Munster football final. That was the 1980s. Or hours spent cursing the traffic when stuck outside Kinnegad or Bray or Fermoy or countless other towns and villages. That was the 1990s and the early part of the twenty-first century. He could go through a long life without ever seeing any of those places on Ireland's new road networks. He was rewarded for patiently listening to my drift down memory lane by meeting his heroes, like Seán Óg Ó hAilpín and Peter Canavan and, with his sister, enjoying the heartiest of breakfasts in Paudge Quinn's fine hostelry on the Ballygawley Road.

Visiting the homes of great footballers and hurlers and writing about them was the easy bit. When planning this book about brothers in Gaelic games, the real problem was deciding who to leave out. Mercier Press made suggestions, but the final decision was mine and I take full responsibility. The fact that there were so many sets of brothers from which to choose is part of the story of the GAA itself.

Mercier did suggest Dermot and Paul Earley. I would have chosen them anyway and not just because I am a native of Roscommon. Growing up I had three sporting heroes. My father was one, for obvious reasons, even though I never saw him play. George Best was another and the third was Dermot Earley. I still consider him a hero. Though only ten years or so separated us in age, Dermot was a giant of my childhood in the 1960s and 1970s, and of my adulthood.

Alas, Dermot had been struck down by illness by the time I got round to researching the Earleys' story. He died at the age of sixty-two on 23 June 2010. He was my idol and friend. But his story in football and in the service of the nation, rising to the post of chief-of-staff of the Irish army, tells itself. The hours spent with his brother Paul were fascinating and thought-provoking, and I hope this is conveyed. The GAA should mine this man's flair and talent for all it is worth. I am glad to report that process has started.

Friends advised that I get the best mix of counties possible, so it was decided not to profile two families from one county. That ruled out Tony and Éamon McManus from

Roscommon and lots of others. As ever, Offaly proved to be the exception. In GAA terms, probably in others as well, Offaly has always been exceptional. In football, I could have chosen either side of the Connor family from Walsh Island, the Fitzgeralds or the Darbys. But I chose the Lowrys and hopefully the chapter explains why. The revelation by Michael that an irate Eugene McGee dumped Brian Cowen in the centre of Dublin after an ignominious defeat in the Leinster Under-21 Championship against Carlow was justification alone. There were multiple choices in hurling too, but the story of the Dooley brothers from Seir Kieran encompasses the rich modern history of Offaly hurling better than any.

In choosing the Ó Sé brothers of Kerry ahead of the Spillanes, I was conscious that the story of the Templenoe siblings has been recorded often in the past. And the compilation of this book coincided with Darragh's announcement that he was retiring from inter-county football.

Travelling to Galway, there were multiple choices in both football and hurling – the Connollys, Collerans, Donnellans, Meehans and Cannings immediately spring to mind. The Cooneys of Bullaun are also remarkable. I often wonder if Joe were not such a quiet man would he have a much greater profile today? When talking of hurling genius, the names of Ring, Mackey, Rackard, Doyle, Keating, Keher, Barry-Murphy, English, Carey and Shefflin are always mentioned. Joe Cooney belongs with them. His oldest brother Jimmy is best remembered for a big-game refereeing error, when he brought the All-Ireland hurling semi-final of 1998 between Offaly and Clare to a premature end. But he has done much more than that in hurling. And, with four other brothers, they were the spine of the first team ever to win back-to-back All-Ireland Club Championships.

The dilemma was the same in Kilkenny, Wexford and Tipperary, where there are also many potential subjects. But can anyone argue with the selection of the Hendersons, the three Bonnars and George and John O'Connor? Maybe you can. Having read the chapters here, I hope you understand my reasoning. A few hours in the company of George O'Connor is an enriching, almost exhausting, experience. The sport of hurling is in safe hands as long as George is around.

As ever, I am indebted to the hospitality and generosity of all the people written about here. From Donegal town to Dún Chaoin, Piercestown in Wexford to Glencull in Tyrone, I was received with great warmth and friendship, and I am entirely grateful.

The support received from Abbie, Dara and Aoife cannot be valued. It was, and is, priceless. The kids laugh when they recall me as 'an irritable git' during the months of production. That says everything. I was just that. Thanks to all at Mercier Press, and to Ray McManus and the Sportsfile team whose assistance was invaluable.

THE HENDERSON BROTHERS

In the sitting-room of their home on the outskirts of Kilkenny city, Pat and Mary Henderson have set aside one corner for a modest display of Pat's sporting achievements. All Star awards from the early years of the scheme stand side by side with the Texaco Hurler of the Year trophy. Above that is the poster from the 1974 Texaco Awards, with Pat standing beside other Irish sporting legends like Willie John McBride, Kevin Heffernan, Eddie Macken, rally driver Billy Coleman, athlete Neil Cusack and rower Seán Drea. Pat points out the various photographs of All-Ireland-winning Kilkenny teams. And then he lingers on The Fenians. Everything goes back to his beloved club in Johnstown, the home village in north Kilkenny from which he blazed a trail in the early 1960s that was followed by his brothers Ger and John, and is still being walked by modern giants of hurling.

It was into Johnstown that Pat Henderson was born in 1943 and where he would pick up his first hurley and learn the basic skills; from where he would travel to Thurles Christian Brothers School (CBS) for his secondary schooling and to further his hurling education. It was where he learned the values of community and fellowship that he passed on to his younger brothers and his own sons, values that are still so important at the start of a new century. It is to Johnstown that he consistently returns when looking back on his life and his sporting career as a player and coach during which Pat, Ger and John Henderson played a unique part in hurling's history.

From the day Pat first proudly pulled on the famous black and amber stripes for the opening round of the Leinster Senior Hurling Championship against Wexford in June 1964, to John's final game in the 1991 All-Ireland final against Tipperary, the Henderson brothers had a presence, and more often a dual presence, in twenty-eight consecutive Championships. Between them, they won eleven All-Ireland senior hurling titles and eight All Star awards. And they contributed substantially to a glorious era for The Fenians club, during which five county Senior Championships and a Leinster club title were won. Pat played senior hurling for Kilkenny from 1964 to 1978; Ger first appeared in 1974 and retired in 1989; John began as a sub in 1978, the only season all three were in the squad together as players, and retired thirteen years later. And Pat was the Kilkenny coach when Ger and John were members of the All-Ireland-winning teams of 1979, 1982 and 1983.

In amongst the exhaustive list of achievements is a re-markable September in 1975. Over the course of a fortnight between 7 and 21 September, John won an All-Ireland minor medal, Pat followed hours later with a senior medal and two weeks later Ger was a member of the under-21 team that captured a unique treble for Kilkenny, Johnstown and the Henderson clan. 'It was a proud day for the family,' says Pat quietly. John admits that it is only in hindsight he appreciated what had happened. 'I remember after we won he [Pat] came into our dressing-room under the Cusack Stand. He congratulated us and said, "now you've done your bit we've got to do our part".'

* * *

Gerard Henderson Senior was not a hurler. Cycling was his sport. His father, grandfather to the would-be hurlers, played cricket. But Gerard was an enthusiastic follower of hurling and encouraged his eldest son Pat from an early age. Pat recalls excursions to Semple Stadium in the late 1940s and early 1950s, being lifted onto his father's shoulders to avoid the crush or to catch a glimpse of some of the great players of the time, including Christy Ring. Back home in Johnstown Pat dreamed of emulating the feats of those players. There was no great tradition in north Kilkenny at the time. It had been in 1912 that the local team had last won the Kilkenny Championship and that was made up largely of men from Tullaroan. But there was great interest in the game. 'We played in local leagues and in a small triangular field at the national school across the road,' Pat remembers. 'We made our hurls from bits of boards, we played with anything that resembled a hurling stick. A hurling ball was very precious and it would be carefully mended until it fell apart completely. Whoever had the ball decided when a game would be played.'

For secondary school, day pupils went to Thurles Christian Brothers School (CBS) while boarders went to St Kieran's College in Kilkenny. Pat was twelve when he first made the journey across the county border into Tipperary to the CBS, and became consumed by the hurling tradition in the school. He played at every level and won Croke Cup and Dean Ryan Cup honours, losing in a Harty Cup final. 'Tipperary were going well through my school days and there was great rivalry,' he says. 'I remember when they won the All-Ireland in 1958 and one of my teachers, John O'Grady, was in goal. An ex-pupil, Tony Wall, was on the team. They brought the cup to the school and it was a great day for everybody. Naturally they rubbed our noses in it.'

In Johnstown Pat was also enjoying some success. The juvenile teams were strong and, by the time they reached minor level, they had qualified for two Kilkenny county finals. It was a watershed. 'At that time the area was not known for producing hurlers for the county team. I was fortunate that we had a bunch of very good players come along at the one time because it made sure that I was noticed. Without that team no one would ever have heard of me and I might never have played for Kilkenny.'

In 1961 Pat Henderson wore the number six jersey of Kilkenny for the first time and enjoyed his first taste of success. They beat Tipperary in the All-Ireland minor final and he marked Michael 'Babs' Keating. They had played against each other in schools' competitions and would meet often over the following decade, generating a great rivalry that developed into a good friendship.

Pat played under-21 hurling in the inaugural year of that grade, 1964, but Wexford beat them. In that same year, he made his senior debut for Kilkenny. 'The first time I was handed that Kilkenny jersey meant an awful lot to me, to the family and to Johnstown,' he says. 'Playing minor was great, but to be handed a senior jersey was special. It was unusual for someone from our area to play for the county at the time and I think that made it more important. It is one of the things that stands out for me. I cringe to this day when I hear that some-one doesn't want to play for the county. It means so much.'

He won his first Leinster Senior Championship that summer, but also suffered the first big disappointment of his career when they lost to Tipperary in the All-Ireland final. They lost to Wexford in 1965 but reached another final in 1966 when they were strongly fancied to win. They lost to a youthful Cork team captained by Gerald McCarthy. Kilkenny's success in the National League 'home' final and a subsequent visit to New York, where they played the exiles in what the GAA dubbed the 'away' final, provided some form of compensation.

By 1967 Kilkenny supporters were becoming impatient. The county reached the All-Ireland final again and this time Tipperary were the opposition. Kilkenny hadn't beaten their great rivals in the All-Ireland series since 1922. Trailing by 1–3 to 2–6 at half time, their prospects of ending that losing streak looked bleak. But Kilkenny used a strong wind in the second half to turn the game around and win the title. 'Because it was my first All-Ireland I suppose it does stand out,' says Pat. 'That and the fact that we had beaten what was a very good Tipperary team.'

Back home in Johnstown, Ger and John had watched the final on television. Pat's first final in 1964 is also a treasured childhood memory for the youngest members of the family. Another brother Michael, next oldest to Pat, was a hunting and fishing enthusiast. Their sister Margaret ensured the hurling bloodlines would remain blue when she married into the Fitzpatrick family, well known in hurling circles in Kilkenny and beyond. They shared in the family pride. Pat recalls the 1967 victory fondly for another reason. His father saw him win an All-Ireland. Two years later, at the age of fifty-nine, Gerard Henderson passed away. Ger was just fifteen years old, while John was eleven and still in national school. 'Pat became more of a father-figure to us then than a brother,' says John. 'He became a huge influence in every way. He was fourteen years older than me so I looked up to him in every way. But he didn't just influence us. He influenced the whole of north Kilkenny. As a hurler he broke the mould and many others would follow him.'

Pat himself was greatly influenced by Kilkenny's trainer at the time, Fr (now Monsignor) Tommy Maher. 'He was a great mentor. Himself, Donie Nealon and Snitchie Ferguson invented hurling coaching during the 1960s and 1970s. They spent their summers in Gormanston studying the game, working out new training and coaching techniques. It was a whole new approach and those of us lucky enough to learn from him applied all the tricks of the trade when we began coaching ourselves.' Fr Maher's legacy continues to the present day – Brian Cody was one of his students as well.

'Fr Tommy's philosophy was that the best way to train was playing hurling, but he also realised the need to prepare physically. For that he brought in an international athlete, Michael Lanigan, who showed us how to get fit. Dr Kieran Cuddihy looked after our diet and everything else relating to our well-being. He was an excellent guy who made a great contribution.'

Johnstown had been home to a number of different clubs over the decades. In 1968 the town had both St Kieran's and St Finbarr's. They decided to amalgamate and took the name The Fenians, winning their first Kilkenny Senior Championship in 1970. Pat was captain and was given the honour of captaining Kilkenny in 1971. They won another Leinster Championship and again faced Tipperary in the All-Ireland final. It was the first of five consecutive finals for the team during the period of experimentation with eighty-minute games. They were considered good enough to win all five, but were stopped in their tracks in 1971 when Tipperary won by three points in a high-scoring game, 5–17 to 5–14. They did win three of the next four Championships, the sequence being broken when they lost to Limerick in 1973.

'People talk today quite rightly about the achievements of the current Kilkenny team,' observes Ger, 'but that team from 1972 to 1975 was very unlucky not to win four Championships in a row. It was an outstanding team and, no disrespect to Limerick, but surely they would have done it if they had not got so many injuries in 1973.'

Ger had made his Senior Championship debut in the 1974 Leinster campaign, but lost his place on the team for the All-Ireland series. He was on the fringes during the 1975 campaign but was kept busy with a very talented under-21 side that won a second All-Ireland Championship that summer. Kevin and Ger Fennelly, Dick O'Hara, Joe Hennessy, Brian Cody and Billy Fitzpatrick would all graduate to senior status. They too would come under the spell of Pat Henderson, this time in the guise of coach.

At club level, Pat and Ger played side by side in the 1974 Kilkenny and Leinster Club Championship successes. They lost the All-Ireland club final to St Finbarr's of Cork, however, in the spring of 1975. But they won another title in 1977 and that meant that Ger would captain Kilkenny the following year. 'What sticks out most in my mind about my career,' explains Ger, 'was being the captain in 1978 and leading the team out for the All-Ireland final in Croke Park.

That moment was a brilliant feeling. Cork won the final, but it is still one of the highlights for me.'

Pat made an appearance as a substitute in that final in what was his final Championship game for Kilkenny. He played in the pre-Christmas schedule of League games, but over the holiday period decided that it was time to retire from the inter-county scene after a fourteen-year career in which he had adorned the game and won every honour possible. He was making his exit as John was beginning to establish himself as a regular. But their futures would be intertwined once again when Pat became joint trainer of Kilkenny with Eddie Keher for the 1979 Championship.

The system for appointing managers in Kilkenny was quite different then, with the county champions allowed the right to choose. Shamrocks of Ballyhale had won the Kilkenny title in 1978, and early in 1979 Pat received a call from Kevin Fennelly Senior asking him to take charge of the county team. Pat had been coaching informally with The Fenians, but had not seriously considered becoming involved at county level so fast. 'It happened very quickly and we had to adapt quickly.' Success was instant. With John and Ger holding down places in the back line, Kilkenny reached the All-Ireland final and comfortably defeated Galway. It brought the decade to a successful end. Kilkenny had played in seven out of ten finals and won four.

Ger won his second All Star award at the end of 1979 and also joined Pat on the Texaco Sports Star roll of honour when he was named Hurler of the Year. Just a year later the Henderson brothers experienced the other side of life. In the 1980 Leinster final they faced Offaly. An attendance of less than 10,000 created a ghostly atmosphere in Croke Park. Kilkenny supporters hardly bothered listening to the commentary on radio. It became a titanic struggle. Offaly held on grimly for a historic victory. 'We were not retained,' says Pat simply. John also paid a price. He was dropped from the panel for 1981.

The break was short-lived. At the end of 1981 Pat was again offered the position of Kilkenny trainer, this time on his own. John had enjoyed a good season with The Fenians and was rejoining the Kilkenny squad. Pat decided that with his two brothers in the squad he did not wish to be a selector. That decision was accepted by the County Board. Kilkenny were hurling in Division Two of the National League at the time. The first task was to gain promotion, and that was achieved. At the time the Division Two champions played in the knockout stages of the League proper. Kilkenny went all the way to the final and beat Wexford. It was the start of two years of domination. They won the 1982 All-Ireland, retained the League title in 1983 and secured the 'double double' when winning the All-Ireland again in 1983.

'We were very fortunate at that time because a good crop of players had emerged from the very successful under-21 teams of 1974 and 1975,' Pat reflects. 'I also had a lot of great leaders on the field. I had played with Noel Skehan for many years and he was a great help to me. Frank Cummins was another who worked very hard for me. And Ger was a leader by that time, a great ally.'

Brian Cody was the winning captain in 1982. Nickey Brennan, who later became president of the GAA, played alongside Ger and Paddy Prendergast on the half back line. Kieran Brennan, Richie Power, Liam Fennelly and big Christy Heffernan had emerged as big-time players. Christy scored 2–3 of Kilkenny's 3–18 points in the final against a Cork team that was led by Jimmy Barry-Murphy and contained household names like Martin O'Doherty, Johnny Crowley, Dermot McCurtain, Tom Cashman, Tim Crowley, Tony O'Sullivan, Pat Horgan, Seánie O'Leary, Ray Cummins and Éamon O'Donoghue.

A year later the personnel had barely changed. Harry Ryan started for Kilkenny. Kevin Hennessy had established himself with Cork. But the margin was much closer. Kilkenny had enjoyed an eleven-point victory in 1982. It was down to just two in 1983.

'I was coaching a team at the highest level with two brothers as players and I was probably tougher on them than on the others,' says Pat. 'But there was never any real issue. Both of them had earned their places, there were no question marks about it and we got on with it.' Clearly, it wasn't just the Kilkenny selectors who felt they deserved their places on the team. Ger was an All Star in 1982 and 1983. John received the same award in 1983. Ger recalls at an early stage in his career being shouted at from the sideline by one supporter: '"You're only on the team because of your brother …'" That stung me more than any belt I ever got,' he says. 'I decided there and then I would prove him wrong. Pat treated us no differently to the others. He didn't spare us, but he was fair.'

On one occasion during that period Pat did take John off during a League game against Tipperary. 'I wasn't happy at all,' recalls John, 'so I rang him up the next day and gave out yards.

'"Why did you take me off?" I demanded to know.

'"Because you were useless," he told me and he used more colourful language than that.

'I couldn't argue with that. But there was never a problem for Ger and myself. I think all the pressure was on Pat really.'

They won two more Leinster Championships in 1986 and 1987, plus a League title, but lost the 1987 All-Ireland final to Galway. 'It's a funny thing but that was my best individual performance in a final,' says John, 'and I remember it fondly even though we lost. We suffered that day because we didn't have a second free-taker.' Pat adds, 'It was a good Galway team too and they proved it when they won the All-Ireland again the following year.'

That final marked the end of Pat's involvement. He had changed jobs and stayed away from coaching for a number of years. He also underwent heart by-pass surgery and was forced to take things easy in the early 1990s before returning to coach at club level and becoming involved in under-age development squads in Kilkenny. Ger remained for another two seasons, but by 1989 realised the only place he was guaranteed was on the bench. 'At that stage of my career there wasn't any satisfaction for me sitting on the bench. I decided it would be best to give that to a young player on the way up.'

That left John. A cycle had been completed. He played in the 1991 All-Ireland final when they lost to Galway. 'It was a final we could have won. But I enjoyed playing with that team. Ollie Walsh was manager and he wanted me to stay on but I knew my time had come. I had a great relationship with my two corner backs, Bill Hennessy and Liam Simpson, and with Michael Walsh, the goalkeeper. I knew that team would win something. D.J. [Carey] was coming through. Those were good times as well.'

In 1993 there was a new twist in the family tale. Ger and John were still playing with The Fenians. Pat's sons were playing with Dicksboro and he agreed to coach their team for the County Championship. They reached the county final. Fate decreed that The Fenians would also qualify that year. Dicksboro triumphed. 'You can imagine it caused a bit of a stir,' says Pat.

The three brothers remain involved in various capacities in the game and have shared in the enjoyment of the successes of the last ten years, masterminded by their old team-mate Brian Cody. They have known Cody for most of their adult lives and are not surprised by the success he has enjoyed. Pat is full of admiration for Cody and what he has created. 'I hear Cody being asked, why are you doing it, and his answer is straightforward: "because I love the game". It's not about money or the time spent, you never hear those things mentioned, and that transfers through the whole setup. His philosophy is very simple: he tries not to complicate things. He puts an awful lot into it. He measures it by the enjoyment he gets out of it. It is his leisure time. Some people see it as a chore and talk about it in those terms, but if you do that it transmits itself all over the place as well.

'I watched Brian as a player. He was a minor in 1972 and played at centre back in the All-Ireland final. He was a lovely player, a superb athlete and he was unlucky he had damaged his knee before the final. Still he played well. He was an excellent player; he had great hands, great hand-to-eye coordination, a great physique and an enormous confidence in himself. If there is any single thing you would pick out that would be it. You could put him in to play Ray Cummins or anyone else and he went in with absolute confidence that he could win that battle, end of story, and nine times out of ten he would. He had all the other attributes as well, but confidence was his great strength. That comes through strongly with his team today.'

So, how does he rate Cody and his team? 'I regard the whole setup as exceptional. You have to look at the totality of the thing. There are a number of exceptional individuals on the team – you have class players, exceptionally good players, strength in depth and strength in depth in the management structure and team. It is very well led, things aren't taken for granted, they learn from mistakes even when they win. The fact that they have lasted so long means they are a great team.

'The greatest ever? I don't go along with those labels. The greatest team is at a moment, when you take a snapshot on the day. The All-Ireland last year [2009] is an example. Had Tipperary won they would have been entitled to be regarded as one of the greatest teams ever. Was the Kilkenny team that rolled Cork over when they were going for the three in a row the greatest team? You can go through it and examine various examples. How many of the current team were around in 2000? Only Henry [Shefflin]. But when you look at it in its totality, it is the greatest era of all time. On particular days the team stands up there with the best. It ticks all the boxes.'

Ger served as a Kilkenny selector for the first three years of the Cody era during which they won the All-Ireland in 2000. 'It was a great honour to be asked to serve by Brian. We had some great days and I have enjoyed watching them ever since. We really have been spoiled by the success of the last ten years and you have to admire everything that they have achieved.'

So what is it that allows Kilkenny to produce great teams so consistently through the decades? Pat says there is no single answer to that. There are cultural reasons as well as a lot else. 'People talk about tradition, but everyone has two hands and two legs, the same brainpower. It was Tommy Maher who said that the difference is that everyone in Kilkenny is coached from an early age, not just on the field, but on the street when an old lad will be passing by or watching and who will tell a youngster he is catching the hurl wrong or pass on some small bit of advice that makes a difference. It has been handed down over the generations. It is a head start, but that in itself will win you nothing. It has to be organised and coordinated. We went through periods when we had lots of talent but it was not organised. Over the last ten years we have improved on that. Before people frowned at coaches, now they know proper coaching is vital.

'There is a fear it could go too far. People can be too animated at under-age matches. Hurling should be fun. A young lad should go home from a coaching session loving the game and wanting to play more. They should not be discouraged by being reprimanded for doing something wrong. You can over-formalise everything too much. Here in Kilkenny we have a culture. You will see a young lad walking up the town with a hurl in one hand and a girl in the other. It's part of the way of life. We have great supporters who are very knowledgeable; we also have the odd stupid fella.'

John has lived outside Kilkenny for twenty years and wonders now if they take their hurling too seriously. 'It is expected in Kilkenny that we win things. I remember Liam

Walsh asking me one time when he was starting out if I thought we could win an All-Ireland. I told him then, and still believe it, that any year you play for Kilkenny you have a chance of winning an All-Ireland. That is a position of great privilege.'

Pat has enjoyed supporting Kilkenny for the last ten years but warns that it cannot last forever. 'We've been lucky. We have had very good players, a very good management structure and a lot of success, but it can't last forever. We must recognise there will be peaks and valleys, and we will go down and have to come back up again and rebuild. With the present structure and present commitment, they will always be competitive and you can't ask for more than being competitive. If you are competitive you will enjoy the game.'

John has played with, and coached, Wicklow hurlers since he moved to Bray. 'I suppose I did see the other side of life,' he says of his time with one of the non-traditional hurling counties. There was a core of people who were dedicated to hurling, who shared the passion that can be found in pockets throughout the country. But he found it hard to introduce the ethic that came so naturally to youngsters in Kilkenny. His last game was in the Wicklow Championship final which he won with the Glenealy club.

Ger spent four years coaching The Fenians, then decided in 2010 to take his first break from the game. But he continues to follow the fortunes of both club and county. 'Fenians means a lot to me. It is a small, rural parish and club and it has remained consistently in the top six or seven clubs in Kilkenny. That is some achievement when you consider the quality of opposition we face every year. The club consistently provides players to Kilkenny and we have P.J. Ryan, J.J. Delaney and P.J. Delaney with the current team. If you asked me to make a choice between Kilkenny winning five in a row All-Irelands or Fenians winning the County Championship, then I would go for Fenians.'

Although Pat did coach Dicksboro, it was only because of the family connection. He is still The Fenians' delegate to the Kilkenny County Board. He cannot imagine not being involved in some way with the GAA. 'The GAA has been a huge part of my life. I enjoy it; it might not appear that way all the time, but what would I be doing with myself if I wasn't involved? I found it a terrible wrench when I stopped training a team. I had to force myself to stop. There are only three teams I would ever train – my own club, my sons' club or the county team. I have been asked to do others but I wouldn't enjoy that. I like being out with lads playing, but I think I need to have a connection either with my own county or club, there has to be a relationship. I have resisted offers. Floods of fellas broke my heart for a few years coming to the door asking me to coach their teams but they finally copped on that no means no. I am involved with development squads now and it is great to see young people coming through, to see young coaches coming through, the enthusiasm they have and the skills they have. The CV of a good young coach is impressive now and it has to be. It is harder to manage young people now, expectations are higher and coaches need to be more professional and more skilled.'

Now in his late sixties, Pat remains as enthusiastic and committed to Gaelic games as ever. The Hendersons always liked their football and Pat admires the work being carried out at under-age level in Kilkenny. 'There's a lot of work being done here at under-14 and under-16 level,' he observes. 'At "B" level in south Leinster the schools from Kilkenny play good teams from Kildare, Laois, Wexford and Offaly and beat them. And then they don't enter teams at under-18 level because they want to commit to hurling,' he says with more than a hint of surprise. It is the Kilkenny way. He believes there will always be a conflict between football and hurling. Hurling will always remain strong where it is loved. 'The strong hurling counties will always survive and the game will prosper. Where there is a conflict between the codes it is difficult for young players to give hurling the proper time, because you have to put in more personal time with a hurling ball than with a football.'

Pat has conflicting emotions about hurling in the weaker counties. He looks to neighbouring Carlow and is filled with admiration for the work being done in a county where football is by far the stronger game. 'In Carlow they are making enormous strides but the mountain they have to climb is gigantic. They are doing fantastic work for a small county where football is also very strong. But there is great promise.

Will they win an All-Ireland senior title? I hope they do, but I don't think they will. They can aspire to, but I don't think they can win, a Leinster title. The whole of Carlow would need to be playing hurling. Offaly are the exception to this rule. The skill levels in Carlow have improved enormously.'

Elsewhere he worries about the discrepancies, the gulf in standards. He has watched the introduction of the Nicky Rackard, Christy Ring and Lory Meagher Cups for the lower-tier counties and accepts that there is a purpose in providing a platform for players to play at a level where they can enjoy the game and improve their skills. 'What concerns me at times is at colleges level I see some teams playing hurling from weaker areas and they are just fulfilling fixtures. That's not enjoyable. They are playing on bad pitches, in bad weather with bad equipment. By that I mean a guy is picking up a hurley and he's not used to it. They end up with sore shins; that's not enjoyable. Hurling is not like football. If you haven't a certain basic skill level in hurling you won't enjoy it. At the lower level, you have to get at least to a skill level where you are able to enjoy playing. You have to keep practising and if you are not practising you cannot enjoy it. That is a problem in a county where football is the dominant game. The players don't have the time to practise.'

His mobile phone rings as our conversation nears its end. He is needed across the city in Nowlan Park, the home of Kilkenny hurling. Just for an hour or so. Something small but important. The Henderson contribution continues.

THE EARLEY
BROTHERS

As the shrill of the final whistle drifted into the air over Dr
Hyde Park in Roscommon at the conclusion of the 1985
Connacht football final, the end of an era had been signalled.
Mayo had won the provincial title and the supporters began
to spill onto the field in celebration. In the middle of the
field, Mayo's Willie Joe Padden heard a familiar voice
offering congratulations. He turned to take the hand of his
old adversary, Dermot Earley, and they both felt the bolt of
emotion. This was Dermot's final game in a Roscommon
career that stretched back almost two decades. He deserved
more than a handshake. Willie Joe shouted to his team-
mates. They nodded approval. Dermot was hoisted on their
shoulders. The Mayo supporters halted their charge and
applauded the vanquished hero.

Paul Earley stood watching a short distance away. His
sense of disappointment at the loss of a major game was
temporarily suspended. All his life he had lived proud in the
knowledge that his eldest brother, the age gap being sixteen
years, was a hero to football followers not just in Roscommon

but all over Ireland. But this acknowledgement of his status by peers who should have been celebrating their own triumph was something extraordinary.

Back in an emotional dressing-room, where another old stalwart, Pat Lindsay, had also announced that he was retiring from the inter-county game, Paul had little time for deep thoughts. But he realised that he was lucky to have had the opportunity to play with Dermot even for a brief period in the Roscommon colours.

'Like every kid I dreamed of playing for Roscommon one day,' says Paul, 'and following Dermot all my life just added to my determination. But because of the age difference, it never really occurred to me that we would get the opportunity to play together. He had transferred to Sarsfields in Newbridge when I was still in school so we had never even played together for our club, Michael Glaveys. He had been a huge influence on me even though I had grown up at home, the youngest in the family, when Dermot had already moved away to start his army career.

'My life as a child revolved around school, going to football matches and following Dermot. And I had a special time. I was attending secondary school in Ballyhaunis between 1977 and 1981 and Roscommon never lost to Mayo in those five years in either League or Championship. So myself and a few other lads from Glaveys were going to school on Monday mornings with big smiles on our faces.'

In 1981 Paul had been a member of the Roscommon

minor team that won the Connacht Championship. It had been the first real opportunity Dermot had had to assess the potential of his youngest brother. For a number of years he had been hearing encouraging reports about Paul's ability and his dedication to football, but his life in his adopted home in Kildare and a busy career in the army meant that he never got the chance to see Paul play.

By the start of the National League campaign in October 1981, the Roscommon team manager Tom Heneghan decided an injection of new blood was needed. Paul was snatched up in the recruitment drive. The two brothers played together for the first time in a League game against Galway, watched by their proud father, Peadar. They lined out alongside one another against Sligo and Galway in the 1982 Connacht Championship before Paul was lured to a brief career in Australian Rules football during 1983 and 1984. He returned in time to be part of the final chapter in Dermot's career in 1985.

'I was only seventeen when I first played with him and I think I was in awe of him and the rest of the team because of everything they had achieved,' recalls Paul. 'The most important thing for me growing up was to emulate him by playing for the county, but the fact that we had a few years together with Roscommon was a great thrill.'

Dermot wrote of their relationship in his biography, *The Earley Years*: 'We didn't get to know one another until we played together. I enjoyed playing with him. I consider him to be a far faster and more skilful player than I could ever be, even though he was often playing in my shadow. He was a great utility player. It was great to get to know him as a person. It was good to have somebody to confide in about my frustration with my own game. He had different opinions about other players and about the game and I found this interesting. We talked about other aspects of life and this was enriching for me.'

On 23 June 2010, the entire nation was stunned when Dermot Earley died after a short illness. Though it was known everywhere that the army chief-of-staff and sporting legend had been ill for some months, it was hard for his friends and fans to come to terms with his passing. His funeral on 25 and 26 June was attended by tens of thousands of friends, admirers and contemporaries. He was buried with full military honours in St Conleth's cemetery in Maynooth. At the wishes of his wife Mary and family, an All-Ireland Championship qualifier game between Kildare and Antrim went ahead in Newbridge on 26 June. Dermot Junior played. That is the Earley spirit.

* * *

As a young married couple from Mayo setting out in life in the 1940s, Peadar and Kitty Earley had gone through a few postings during Peadar's career as a national schoolteacher. By the time their eldest son Dermot was seven years old in 1955, they were settling into what would become their permanent home in Gorthaganny, a small village in west Roscommon just a short distance from the border with Mayo. Dermot was born in Castlebar and in later years would be claimed by many a Mayo football supporter.

Peadar loved football and was a dedicated member of the GAA. Within a year of arriving in Gorthaganny he was the prime mover behind the founding of a new GAA club which he called Michael Glaveys in honour of a local man who had been a great sportsman as well as a freedom fighter and was killed in 1920. Meetings were held in the Earley household or the home of another official. Peadar served in every position – chairman for long periods and secretary for other long periods. His sons watched proceedings and got an early understanding and appreciation of the politics and administration of the GAA.

Dermot was the eldest. Deirdre, Margaret and Peter followed, and Paul was born in July 1964. By that time Dermot was a boarding student in the famous football nursery of St Nathy's College in Ballaghaderreen and was showing great promise as a footballer. He was just fifteen when he was selected to play for the Roscommon minor team in 1963. Two years later he won his first Connacht Championship when still a minor and played in Croke Park for the first time. Roscommon lost to Derry by three points and Dermot missed a penalty. But there were other highlights that year: he also played for the Roscommon under-21 team and in

October was selected on the senior team for the National League.

His rise to national attention was accelerated in 1966 when he was a member of the Roscommon team that won the All-Ireland Under-21 Championship. Now enrolled in the Army Cadet School in the Curragh, Dermot found himself preparing for the final among the opposition of Kildare. He was just eighteen, but showed a maturity beyond his years and played a major part in a rare national success for Roscommon. Three years later he played in another under-21 final, but Roscommon lost to Antrim.

With such a supply of talent being provided it was expected that Roscommon would begin to make an impact at senior level. But the 1960s proved to be a frustrating time. Dermot had to wait until 1972 for success and many observers consider his performance in the Connacht final against Mayo that year as arguably his greatest for the county. Partnering Gerry Beirne in midfield, Earley was in commanding form and crowned his display with a goal that followed a thundering solo run through the middle of McHale Park.

Hints continued to drop that the 1970s might prove to be a more lucrative decade. Roscommon reached the National League final in 1974, but were denied victory by a last-minute equalising goal from Kerry's John Egan. Kerry won the replay, but Earley's performances were rewarded when he was included on the All Stars selection at midfield alongside Kerry's Paudie Lynch. That celebration led to one of the few major controversies in his career. Selection on the All Stars at that time meant a tour to the United States the following May for a series of exhibition games. However, the All Stars rules had strict disciplinary guidelines at the time and a player who served a term of suspension was not eligible for selection. Even if a player was suspended following selection, he was not allowed to tour. For the only time in his illustrious career, Dermot Earley was sent off during a National League game in Croke Park against Dublin in February 1975. An innocuous tangle with Dublin's Jimmy Keaveney led to a scuffle. It was brought to an end when Dermot punched Bobby Doyle on the nose. He was sent to the line. 'It was the most devastating thing that ever happened to me playing football, much worse than losing the All-Ireland,' he recalled. 'As I walked back to the line the realisation of all the things that were going to happen came to me. First of all, it meant there was a blot on my career. I always wanted to be as fair as I could. Even if I fouled, I always felt it was wrong afterwards. To be warned by a referee is a blot on your copybook, but to be sent off is incredible.'

A two-month suspension meant he would miss the All Stars' tour. When an appeal failed, friends pressed him to travel even though he could not play. New York's 'Mr GAA', the famous John 'Kerry' O'Donnell, invited him to travel and offered to pay Dermot's expenses. Eventually, with the role of assistant to tour manager Seán Purcell as his official title, he did accompany the team.

Injury and overseas duty with the army in the Middle East interrupted his career, but he was back for the 1977 Championship and the most exciting period of his football career.

Dermot was one of the most experienced players with Roscommon in 1977, alongside Pat Lindsay, Harry Keegan, Tom Heneghan and Mickey Freyne. They were joined by a new batch of players that included future All Star Tony McManus, his brother Éamon, John 'Jigger' O'Connor, John O'Gara and Danny Murray. They won four Connacht Championships in a row and the National League in 1979 when Dermot won his second All Star award. They also reached the All-Ireland final in 1980 where they lost to Kerry in a game most observers believe they should have won. Conditions were tricky on the day, but Roscommon seemed unnerved about facing the All-Ireland champions, who were bidding for their third title in a row. Roscommon exploded into action and were 1–2 to no score ahead after eleven minutes, but they failed to maintain the momentum. Two brilliant saves from Kerry goalkeeper Charlie Neligan boosted Kerry's bid for another title and they held on to win by 1–9 to 1–6.

The game led to some recriminations. The Kerry manager Mick O'Dwyer was critical of what he believed was Roscommon's physical approach and some treatment he said was meted out to particular Kerry forwards. In his biography Dermot addressed those claims: 'In all our discussions and practice sessions there was never once any mention of stopping, tripping, holding or kicking an opponent. When they got the ball our job was to be as close as possible, to be absolutely committed, to harass, to chase and to contest, but always to play within the rules. When we got the ball our job was to be as elusive and creative as possible. At no stage was there even a hint that we should go out and be physical.'

That defeat marked the beginning of the end of a team considered unlucky not to have won an All-Ireland Championship. They did reach the National League final the following May but lost to Galway, despite a trademark thunderbolt goal from Dermot. Weeks later, in the biggest shock in years in Championship football, Roscommon were beaten by Sligo in the opening round of the Connacht campaign.

Throughout his playing days, Dermot also developed his career in the army, serving abroad as well as in various senior administrative positions in the Curragh. He was promoted to lieutenant colonel in 1995 and to colonel in 2001. He became major general and deputy chief-of-staff in 2004 and in April 2007 Dermot became chief-of-staff of the Defence Forces.

* * *

Paul was part of the earliest experiments between Gaelic football and Australian Rules. The two organisations were in the initial stages of discussions about potential links when the youngster from west Roscommon spotted an advertisement in the *Sunday Press* looking for interested young footballers to take part in trials in Dublin organised by the Melbourne Demons club. His sister Denise was living in Australia and that was certainly part of the attraction.

'I was a mad sportsman, I loved playing sport and you can imagine what kind of an opportunity it presented to me,' he explains. His father and guiding influence, Peadar, was ill at the time, so Paul withdrew from the trial. Seán Wight, a Kerry minor with a Scottish background, and Dubliner James Fahy were chosen to travel. Peadar Earley passed away in February 1983 and Paul took some time to decide on his future. Dermot returned from a tour of duty in Lebanon for the funeral but football was barely mentioned.

When Paul's interest was revived, after a period of mourning, a special trial was arranged for him in Artane in Dublin. A Christian Brother, Tom McDonnell, saw enough to provide a recommendation to the Demons that the young Earley had potential. By May, he had decamped to the capital of the state of Victoria and a completely new way of life. 'London had been the extent of my travels up to then so you can just imagine what it was like to travel to the far side of the world at that time,' he says.

His late arrival meant he had missed pre-season, but that merely introduced him to an even more frenetic way of life. 'They just immersed me in football for the first couple of months. It was non-stop. Even today when I am coaching here I apply some of the things I learned then. I had a football in my hands almost all the time. It is one of the things that sticks in my mind, because the coaches were constantly telling you to keep a ball in hand. If you were sitting down, they wanted you to have the ball; watching television, they expected you to work with it. You brought a ball with you when you went for a walk. They wanted the ball to become an extension of your hand, to make the ball a natural part of your movement. It was a way of preparing you for whatever situation you encountered in a game. When the ball came to you, you were expected to get it with one grab; they didn't want it to take two grabs. That was one too many.'

For most of his waking hours, he had a coach in attendance. When he wasn't training, he attended clinics. 'People think it's getting used to the oval ball that causes the greatest difficulty for players coming from Ireland but it's not. You learn the skills quickly. The biggest problem is game sense, game awareness, what to do, where to run, particularly in how you deal with the tackle. When you get the ball you have to move with pace, accelerate away from the tackle. In Gaelic football you have time to look up and see what is happening around you. If you do that in Australian Rules, you get nailed.

'The biggest thing was the emphasis on skill development. Every session started with basic skills work. You might kick a ball back and across with another player maybe fifty times

– left foot, right foot. You then work on the hand pass – right hand, left hand. They never allowed you to lose touch with the basic skills. As a professional player, they believed you should be able to perfect the skills on both sides of your body and they worked hard on that. As a coach now I put more emphasis on the skills side. Sometimes we neglect that here and we allow players to develop them themselves. We don't spend enough time on the biomechanics of kicking and catching, and running and hand passing. We spend more time on teamwork and tactics, fitness and physical preparation to the detriment of the skills. We have improved a lot, but there is still some distance to go.

'For example, when Tadhg Kennelly went out the first thing they did was to change his running technique because they felt it would cause him some difficulty long-term with injuries. That wouldn't have happened here. That's professionalism – it's about having the time and a number of different specialist coaches who can work on different aspects of the game with players. They are able to dissect the game and the players into component parts and allocate specialist coaches to work with individual players – be it a psychologist, a kicking coach, or a strength and conditioning coach. We are trying to do that here now, but with limited time it's just not possible to do it to the same extent. It's amazing how much time coaches here do put in with the players, but there are just not enough hours in the day after work to do it. Coaches have plenty of time with the players there; the players have plenty of time to do their work and to rest.'

For many reasons which he articulates well, Paul has no fears about players being recruited by the Australians. They are treated well, most come home and when they do they are better footballers for the experience. 'Most of the guys who have gone out will say they are looked after well, the environment is great, it's the great outdoor life. It's different to the soccer apprentice in England who will have to do all the menial tasks and is way down the pecking order. In Australia, the Irish are integrated very quickly. There is no class distinction of any sort. It is full-time, so you can manage your body in the right way to play at your peak all the time.

'The other difference and something that we need to learn here is that the players are incredibly flexible and their level of agility and flexibility is far superior to ours because they spend so much time on injury prevention programmes and recovery sessions. The science and knowledge has developed to the extent that they realise it's important to train hard but to train smart and to have a proper recovery. The physical make-up of the individuals is such that it allows them to play for a number of years and avoid injuries as much as possible.'

Paul had further experience of the professional game in Australia after his own playing days had ended here in Ireland. He moved to Sydney for three years between 1996 and 1998 and became involved with the Swans AFL club.

It was quickly apparent that they had made huge advances in every aspect of preparing a professional sportsman to do his job to the best of his ability at all times. He recalls their attitude towards injuries. 'They had developed what they called an SIPP, which was a Specific Injury Prevention Programme which was designed for each player. They would assess each player through the season and if somebody had a hamstring problem – if their right hamstring was at 80 per cent of the strength it would be at their peak, they would have a specific programme for that player to get back to 100 per cent. And they wouldn't let him back playing until he was 100 per cent. In an amateur context if the hamstring is deemed okay or nearly there, the next game is most important. What happens then is that a minor injury can become a chronic injury and become a problem for three or four years.'

Paul did assist in the movement of a number of players from Ireland to Australia and is well aware of the concerns among sections of the GAA over ongoing recruitment efforts which have been capturing the headlines in Ireland for a number of years. 'I don't know Ricky Nixon [the agent most publicly associated with luring Irish players to Australia] so I don't know what he is doing. I did have an involvement with Tadhg Kennelly going to Australia and I was involved with Marty Clarke going over. I haven't had any involvement in the last three or four years for a number of reasons, largely my involvement with coaching development with the Leinster Council and I haven't had the time. My only interest in doing it was to maintain the links and give some guys who are interested an opportunity to do it and to explain to them and their parents what's involved, the pros and cons. I think it's important to keep the link alive because it is the closest game to Gaelic football on the planet and because we have learned so much from them.

'I wouldn't have the same worries that others have. The stats prove the vast majority of the players come back and when they do, they add value. Anthony Tohill came back and was a top player for Derry for many years. Colin Corkery brought great value back to Cork. Brian Stynes in Dublin and Dermot McNicholl in Derry were two others who were much improved footballers when they came back and gave great service to their counties. Brendan Murphy is back and will be a big addition to Carlow. Marty Clarke is back and he will be a massive addition to Down. In many ways we have gained more than the Aussies have because they have invested a lot of time and money in the players who are now back here. Keeping the link alive is important for coaching as well, to allow us access to the most modern methodologies and practices.'

He hears the arguments about professionalism in the GAA from those who oppose the notion and those who would love to embrace it. But he would love a more coherent approach to examining how the GAA should progress in the future; what is possible within the amateur framework that currently exists or whether the GAA could support and sustain any form of professional sport. 'I don't know the answer about the way forward and I know there are polarised opinions out there,' he admits. 'I would love to see someone commissioned to do a study on it. There's a discussion every week about it – can the GAA go professional or go semi-professional. Every player, if he is being honest, will say he would love to play full-time. If they are asked in an interview they say no because it is politically the right thing to do. But all of them would love to play without the pressure of work. It is an incredibly demanding task at the moment to be a county footballer. The study would examine if it was sustainable; what impact would it have on the traditions of the GAA; is it financially feasible? It probably isn't unless there are radical changes to the way the GAA is run.'

He reflects on the tenure of Liam Mulvihill as the director general of the GAA and regrets that more heed was not taken of some of Mulvihill's musings during his term of office. 'Liam Mulvihill always had interesting stuff in his annual reports and they never were implemented. I remember particularly one report when he talked of moving away from the county system and to a cluster of teams such as Sligo and Leitrim merging, or Roscommon and Longford merging. You could call them the North West Tigers or something. You would have similar amalgamations around the country and it would be interesting to see what impact it would have.

'I know if you put it out as an idea now you would get

some very entrenched views. Some people would mock it. But look at what has happened in rugby in Ireland; look at Munster and what they have achieved. It is a modern phenomenon. Look at Leinster. It's a franchise. Leinster have started winning and they are gathering great support, something they had never experienced before. They have people from every sporting background following them and they are playing in front of huge crowds every time they play at home.

'I have no doubt if Sligo and Leitrim got together and started winning, or if Roscommon and Longford got together and started to be competitive, then they would galvanise a support base.'

* * *

There was no one in Ireland as proud as Dermot Earley when the All Star football selection for 1985 was announced in November. His own career had brought him two of the coveted awards. Now, in the year in which he had finally retired from the game, his twenty-one-year-old brother Paul joined him in the famous roll of honour when he was named the All Star full forward. Paul's career trajectory mirrored that of his illustrious older brother. He had played for the Roscommon minors for three years; he played in an All-Ireland under-21 final, though in Paul's case it was a losing experience, against Donegal. He had also enjoyed success in

1985 with Michael Glaveys when they won the Roscommon Intermediate Championship. 'That was one of the real highlights of my career,' he insists.

His senior career with Roscommon, however, was littered with disappointments in the latter years of the 1980s. He played in four Connacht finals, plus one replay, between 1985 and 1989 and lost three times to Mayo ('they paid me back in spades for those years when Roscommon beat them when I was a schoolboy') and once to Galway. The loss in 1989, after a replay, by just two points, was particularly frustrating as they watched Mayo go so close to winning the All-Ireland final against Cork.

In 1990 they finally got it right and beat Galway in the provincial final before losing to All-Ireland champions Cork in the semi-final. A year later Paul helped Roscommon to another provincial title. Meath, champions of 1987 and 1988, provided the opposition in the All-Ireland semi-final. It was a tight, tense affair, the highlight of which was a brilliant Derek Duggan goal. It was not sufficient. Brian Stafford's free-taking proved the undoing of Roscommon. 'Looking back,' says Paul, 'you realise that when you lose a number of finals and then win one, the satisfaction levels are much higher. I had lost four, so to go on and win two Connacht finals back to back was incredible.'

By then his body was showing signs of wear and tear. He played on until the mid-1990s, but it was a struggle. 'Because of the number of injuries I had I didn't enjoy it as much. If I had some of that time over again I would have retired earlier because I was in so much pain that I didn't enjoy it.'

Between 1987 and 1991, Dermot served as deputy military advisor to the secretary general of the United Nations, based in New York. Despite a schedule that brought him to the strife-torn corners of the earth, Dermot kept himself informed of events back in Roscommon and in Paul's career. On his return, he immersed himself again in the life of the Sarsfields club in Newbridge and paid close attention to Roscommon. When a managerial vacancy arose at the end of the 1992 Championship, Dermot was approached and subtle pressure was applied. Paul's presence on the panel made the decision a little easier and, though success eluded them, the Earleys enjoyed their short period together in different roles. Dermot also managed Kildare and assisted at different levels and in various roles with Sarsfields.

His eldest son David enjoyed prolific success with the club, winning county titles at minor, under-21 and senior level. Dermot Junior began to mock the supposed burden of a famous name when he won a Kildare Minor Championship in 1996 and by 1998 he was a member of the Kildare senior team under the management of Mick O'Dwyer. Despite being one of the best supported counties in football, Kildare had not won a Leinster title for thirty-two years. But the Earley family was out in force in Croke Park on 2 August when Dermot Junior played a major part in their victory over Meath. They beat Kerry in the All-Ireland semi-final and played a huge role in one of the most entertaining finals of the modern era, losing narrowly to Galway. He joined his father and uncle Paul on the All Stars roll of honour that year and won a second award at midfield in 2009. Uniquely, the youngest Earley, Noelle, was named on the Ladies' Football All Stars selection just weeks later. Dermot and his wife Mary have three other children, Conor, Paula and Anne Marie.

Paul also caught the coaching bug. He returned from Australia in 1998 and immediately became involved with the Allenwood club in Kildare. 'I had no experience at all but I tried to combine all that I had learned during my time with Roscommon with what I had learned from the professional game in Australia and I thoroughly enjoyed my three years with the club.' During that time, Allenwood reached the Kildare senior football final. Inevitably, their opponents were Sarsfields of Newbridge, for whom Dermot Junior and David Earley were playing, with Dermot Senior a selector. Sarsfields took the laurels. Paul enjoyed another three-year spell with the Celbridge club and they progressed from playing in Division Two of the League to reaching the quarter-finals of the County Championship. Now, as a Level Two coach, he is assisting the Leinster Council of the GAA in their coach development programme.

During 2008 he had his first experience of inter-county management when he took on an emergency role with Roscommon following the resignation of John Maughan.

While the Roscommon County Board sought a permanent replacement, Paul agreed to take temporary charge. 'I loved the job even though I only did it for a month, but I just did not have the time to take it on for any longer.

'I would love to be an inter-county manager and maybe some time in the future it will happen for me. But it is a full-time job and I already have one of those [he works in the financial services industry]. I have a huge interest in coaching, but I see what the commitment to the inter-county scene is and at the moment I could not give it the time. I was interviewed a few years ago for a manager's job and I told the county chairman involved at the time that I could only do it if the post was offered on a full-time basis. Of course that was not possible, but I thought I had to be honest.

'The inter-county manager's job is a sixty-hour week. I really admire the guys who are doing it at the moment. To combine it with work and a family life is really difficult. [Paul and Mairéad have three children, twins Ailbhe and Lea, and Declan]. At the moment I'm afraid I just do not have the time to give it the sort of commitment it deserves. Hopefully that will not always be the case.'

Five decades have passed since the Earley name first seeped into the public consciousness and this story is not yet completed.

THE LOWRY BROTHERS

Some days are more inspirational than others. Imagine those that immediately followed Offaly's All-Ireland Football Championship final victory in October 1972 when the players took the Sam Maguire Cup on the traditional parade of the schools of the county. The team captain Tony McTague was especially in demand, but there was no more important visit than that to the national school in Ferbane, his home place in west Offaly. Accompanying him on that visit was his twenty-year-old team-mate Seán Lowry, another former pupil at the school.

They carried the famous trophy through the familiar gates and walked the corridors from memory. They exchanged greetings with teachers they knew as friends. And they recognised in the excited faces of the children the features of their parents, many of whom Tony and Seán worked with or played with. Two of the faces among the boys from fifth and sixth classes were more familiar than others to Seán Lowry. They were his brothers, Brendan and Michael, and their smiles were as broad as any in the school and their beaming faces were full of pride for their oldest brother.

'I felt like I was ten foot tall in the classroom that day,' Michael remembers fondly. 'Seán had the cup and it looked huge, it was full of Cidona and to us it was the greatest thing in the world. I had a dream that some day in the future I would bring the cup into our school. There's no harm in a young lad having his dreams, is there?'

But even during those exciting, fun-filled and happy days when it felt absolutely as if dreams could be fulfilled, no one could possibly have imagined what the future held for the Lowry clan, the All-Ireland hero and his kid brothers. Ten years later, on 19 September 1982, Seán, Brendan and Michael Lowry would play together for Offaly in one of the most famous All-Ireland final victories of them all when they stopped Kerry's bid for a historic five consecutive Championships.

They would do it with panache and style, fierce will and possibly the most famous goal ever scored in the football Championship. 'An awful lot has happened since that day,' says Seán. 'A lot of teams have won the All-Ireland for the first time, there have been great matches and great teams, but hardly a week goes by that someone does not ask me about that final. You could go to a funeral and be in the process of commiserating with someone and they will say "I was looking at the 1982 final on TV the other night". It's amazing.'

Almost thirty years have passed and the Lowry name is back in the sporting headlines, not just in Ireland but around the world. Shane Lowry is making his exciting way in the world of professional golf, an Irish Open title won when he was still in the amateur ranks. As the world gets to know this talented youngster, the media consistently refer to him as the son of 'the famous Offaly footballer Brendan Lowry'.

* * *

Like so many young couples of their generation, Ned and Margaret Lowry left Ireland in the 1950s to find employment abroad. They based themselves in Manchester where the first few of their eleven children, including Seán, were born. They kept in close contact with their families back home, always listening for news of employment opportunities in a homeland that was embracing the modern world. The Electricity Supply Board was expanding and one of its major projects was the opening of the power station in Ferbane. Ned Lowry saw his opportunity to return to Ireland and secured employment at the plant. 'I always say that only for the power station in Ferbane I would have ended up playing for Manchester United instead of Offaly,' jokes Seán.

Ireland was changing rapidly as a country. The ESB and Bord na Móna were among the major employers. 'Without them a lot of the people in Offaly and other counties would have had to look elsewhere in the country or more likely out of the country for work,' Seán explains. 'And it is hard to imagine that Offaly would have been winning football All-

Irelands in the 1970s and 1980s if those jobs had not been made available.'

Back in Ireland and settled in Ferbane, the growing Lowry family was comfortable among family and friends. They worked hard and found respite with football and hurling. Ned Lowry was a passionate football man. His brothers Art and Joe played for Offaly. Art farmed in Clogherinkoe and his son John later played for Kildare against an Offaly team that included cousin Seán. The maternal gene also contained plenty of football DNA. The Horans of Ballycumber were a renowned football family. 'We were reared on stories of club games, the hitting and the fights. They'd call it dirt now, but then it was regarded as manly stuff,' explains Seán. 'My Uncle Johnny always told me to keep my elbows up to protect myself.'

The swinging 1960s began with Offaly winning its first ever Leinster senior football title. The county became transfixed with the fortunes of a hugely talented group of footballers who would inspire Championship-winning generations to come. They might have won an All-Ireland title themselves had they managed to avoid the crusading Down team that emerged from Ulster to claim Sam Maguire and bring his trophy across the border for the very first time in 1960. The team of Kevin Mussen, Dan and Jim McCarthan, Joe Lennon, Paddy Doherty and Seán O'Neill thwarted Offaly in the 1960 All-Ireland semi-final and the 1961 final after a replay.

But those Offaly giants awoke a county. Willie Nolan, Paddy McCormack, Greg Hughes, Phil O'Reilly and Mick Casey were just some of the heroes. Ned Lowry went to all the games. Tim Egan in Ferbane owned a car and he had a regular load to travel to Portlaoise, Croke Park or wherever Offaly were playing. Young Seán also secured a ride. 'It cost my father five shillings for himself and two and six for me.'

On summer evenings on the green in front of the terrace where the Lowrys and their neighbours made their homes, the boys learned their football skills. They played all sports, whatever was the fashion of the week, but football was dominant. They would start around 4 p.m. and might not finish until close to midnight. Those were carefree days and skills were honed during the long hours. 'We had no gear then,' Seán says. 'That led to a few problems if you came home to your mother with the toe off your shoe, a tear in the knee of your trousers or a green grass stain on your good shirt. It was a struggle for our poor mothers to keep everything right. But we were always doing something.

'Those days you wouldn't even think of being bored. There was always something to do. If we weren't on the green, we would be out in the fields with the men helping on the land. You'd get fifteen shillings for a day's work and you handed up twelve shillings and six pence to your mother.'

Among the older lads kicking football around the green were Seán Grogan and Tony McTague. The Grogans were a football-mad family and Seán Grogan was named captain of the Offaly minor team in 1964. Tony took the frees. They won the Leinster title by beating Laois by a single point. They went on to win the All-Ireland title, Offaly's first in any grade, beating Cork in the final. The seeds for success were being firmly planted.

The Lowry family was growing all the time. Éamon, Joe, Jimmy, Mary, Brendan, Michael, Eileen, Kieran and Tom joined Rose and Seán. Éamon played football with Offaly during the 1970s and was captain of Ferbane when they won the County Championship in 1974. Everyone joined in the adventures on the green. They didn't need organised sport. They managed for themselves. Under-age and schools football were not as organised as they are today. County trials were held for the minor team and clubs sent in four or five players for those trials after which a team would be picked for a Championship game the following Sunday. There were no formal training sessions. They were different times, Seán says. 'I remember when I was picked for the minors and a few days later a parcel arrived at the house. It had an O'Neill's football in it. Whoever sent it remained anonymous and to this day I don't know who the donor was. I remember pumping the ball and the whole terrace came out to play with it. It was a huge thing to have an O'Neill's ball. Of course, after two days it was kicked out on the road and a car ran over it. But it shows how times were.'

Seán also played at under-21 level for Offaly and at the age of nineteen, in 1971, he was called into the Offaly senior panel for the Championship and ended up with an All-Ireland medal as a substitute. He felt privileged just to be associated with the team that would make history by bringing the Sam Maguire Cup back to Offaly for the first time. A year later, he was wearing the number six jersey as Offaly retained that title by beating a famous Kerry team in a replay. 'I was just twenty years old and life was wonderful. I had two Leinster senior medals, two All-Ireland medals and two Leinster under-21 medals. I thought this was going to happen every year.'

He was young and happy. Life was to be enjoyed and there was no better way to enjoy it than by winning big football games. Ferbane won the Offaly Senior Championship in 1971 for the first time since 1914. It was getting better and better. The club was always a priority. 'I've always said if you haven't a passion for your club you will never make it. When I'm eyeing up a footballer I never worry too much at first about how good he is; I go back and see what kind of lad he is. You'd often hear "he doesn't bother with the club much" and that means he is no good to me.'

Seán enjoyed playing with good players and there were plenty of them on the Offaly team on which he became a regular as the 1972 Championship progressed. The quality is apparent just in reading the names: Martin Furlong, Michael Ryan, Paddy McCormack, Larry Coughlan, Eugene Mulligan, Martin Heavey, Willie Bryan, Seán Evans, Seán Cooney, Kevin Kilmurray, Séamus Darby, John Smith, Paddy

Fenning, Murt Connor, Nicholas Clavin and Mick Wright among them. It was an injury to Clavin that gave Seán his chance. He would remain in the Offaly colours for another eleven seasons.

They won the Leinster Championship by beating Meath and Kildare. They accounted for Donegal in the All-Ireland semi-final and then met a star-studded Kerry team in the final. Mick O'Connell and John O'Keeffe formed a powerful midfield partnership; Donie O'Sullivan and Micheál Ó Sé were two of the outstanding defenders; the forwards included Brendan Lynch, Dan Kavanagh, Mick Gleeson, Éamon O'Donoghue and Mick O'Dwyer. Kerry were the traditional giants but, on 24 September 1972, Offaly were the better team yet had to be satisfied at the end with a draw, 1–13 each, in front of 72,000, a new record for the reconstructed Croke Park.

The replay was fixed for 15 October. Kerry led early in the second half until a speculative ball from Paddy Fenning was allowed to fly straight into the net. Offaly seized the initiative – Bryan out-fielded O'Connell; McTague scored 0–10 of Offaly's 1–19 in a convincing victory. There wasn't a happier man in Ireland than Seán Lowry, was there? Maybe one. 'My father, Ned. It was a great time for him. He had brought me everywhere as a boy, gave me all the encouragement I could ask for. He didn't rant or rave, just had a quiet word here or there, little words of encouragement and advice that meant so much.' He was fifty-four then and died at just sixty in

1978. 'I'm so glad he saw me win an All-Ireland but it is sad that he was not around for 1982.'

Seán looks back now and reflects on how football has changed so dramatically. 'It was very direct then. Kicking skills were so much better. That was the benefit of how we played as kids on the green in Ferbane or anywhere in Ireland really. At home, I could kick the ball 150 times in an evening. Now lads go training and they mightn't see a ball at all. And then they go home to the PlayStation.'

Offaly retained the Leinster Championship in 1973 but lost to Galway in the All-Ireland semi-final. 'I think now I should have savoured those days more because there were barren years to come,' says Seán. But through those years Seán, Martin Furlong and Séamus Darby kept the faith. Their success had fired the imagination of the youth of the county in the same way as the team of 1960 and 1961 had inspired them. For six years they had to sit and watch as Kevin Heffernan's Dublin revolution brought new colour to football and Mick O'Dwyer turned to coaching and created the Kerry team many now call the greatest ever. They could not have known the part they would eventually play in the story of that team and in the history of football.

* * *

Seán Lowry was one of the senior members of the Offaly team when they finally broke Dublin's grip on the Leinster

Championship in 1980, after winning the provincial final by two points. He lined out at full back in the All-Ireland semi-final against Kerry which Offaly lost by five points. It was the dawn of a new era for Offaly. Eugene McGee had set a plan in place when coaching both the under-21 teams and the senior team, and it was beginning to bring results. For three years between 1977 and 1979 Brendan Lowry was a regular member of the Offaly under-21 team, winning Leinster titles in 1977 and 1979. For the second victory, Michael had joined him on the team. Brendan had flirtations with the Offaly seniors during the National League in 1978 and some tournament games a year later. Michael was also blooded in the League in 1979. But for the 1980 Championship the two younger Lowry brothers were absent.

Though his potential was obvious from his early teens, Brendan did have distractions. He had another sporting passion – soccer. The ban on GAA members playing other sports such as soccer and rugby had been lifted in 1971, but traces of the ban mentality lingered. Brendan doesn't recall any obvious displeasure at his other pursuit, but it did interfere with his football. He was enjoying some success with the local soccer club and that encouraged him to continue playing. He also admits that he had a difficult relationship with Offaly manager McGee in the early days. 'I didn't get on with him until I got to know him and he wasn't an easy man to get to know.'

Michael had a small problem with McGee as well, though

the reasons were more practical. He was based in Dublin at the time and would travel to under-21 games with McGee, who was also living in Dublin, and another member of the team, a law student from Clara called Brian Cowen. 'We played Carlow in the Leinster Championship and were surprisingly beaten. Eugene never spoke the whole way back to Dublin from Carlow. Brian and myself sat in the back and never opened our mouths. He dropped us in O'Connell Street and I think we were lucky we got that far. He was furious.'

For the 1980 Leinster Senior Championship Brendan and Michael decided they would take a break from inter-county football. 'I was on a course in Dublin and decided to concentrate on that for 1980,' says Michael. Brendan focused on his soccer and enjoyed it immensely. Michael was back in time for the start of the National League in the autumn of 1980 but Brendan took a little persuasion. 'It was my mother at first who began to encourage me to play again. And then Seán began to convince me that I could enjoy it and that we could be successful.'

In the summer of 1981 the Lowry brothers and Dinny Wynne travelled together to Offaly training sessions. Seán's versatility was being utilised again. He was playing at full forward that year, with Brendan on his right flank. They won the Leinster Championship again and beat Down quite comfortably to qualify for the All-Ireland final and another clash with a Kerry team going for a fourth consecutive title. It was a tough, close game played in difficult weather conditions and a goal from Jack O'Shea in the closing minutes set up by some intricate play by Eoin Liston, Mikey Sheehy and John Egan closed the game out for Kerry. Seán's prediction that Brendan would make a big impact on his return was proven correct when Brendan won an All Star award. 'I was also an Offaly Sports Star of the Year that year for soccer,' Brendan recalls with a laugh.

'Losing that final was a huge disappointment,' recalls Michael, made even worse when they faced the enormous crowds that awaited them on their homecoming to Tullamore the following evening. 'The people of Offaly must have been broke with all the games they were going to week after week following the hurlers and the footballers. Yet here they were again supporting us even though we had been beaten. You knew you just had to go out and try to win it the next time.'

Seán remembers a meeting of the players in the weeks following the final. 'We knew then that there was only one team around who could beat us and that was Kerry. We believed we had the beating of Dublin, Roscommon, Galway or whoever came out of Ulster and we were confident that we could push ourselves to another level.' A training camp in Spain in the spring of 1982 helped cement the bond between the players. They could feel a team coming together. Richie Connor was captain for a second year and provided strong leadership, feeding off the experience and strength of character of Martin Furlong and Seán Lowry, who had reverted to playing at centre half back with Connor playing at centre half forward. The squad contained five sets of brothers: the Lowrys, Richie and Matt Connor, their cousins Liam and Tomás O'Connor, Pat and Mick Fitzgerald and the Darbys, Stephen and Séamus.

They had a comfortable ride through the Leinster Championship, beating Louth, Laois and Dublin. Galway provided tougher opposition in the All-Ireland semi-final, but Offaly emerged with a one-point win. They were set up for round three with Kerry in another final – Offaly stood before the history-makers again. The country was consumed by talk of five in a row for Kerry. Songs were written, T-shirts were made. The parties had begun before the final had even been played on 19 September. At their training camp in Ballycommon outside Tullamore, the Offaly team and management were making plans of their own. Seán describes the approach: 'We decided that no matter what happened we would mark our own man at all times. At no stage would two players go for one Kerry player and leave another free. If that happened Kerry could wipe you out. We needed to be disciplined and we were. If they tried a one-two, the two was marked. If your man passed the ball, you went with him. That meant they had to kick a lot of ball from 40 and 50 yards for scores because they had no one to kick it to.'

Michael had his own worries. A hamstring injury had bothered him all summer. He had it strapped for the semifinal but found it too restrictive and cut the strapping off. He wasn't 100 per cent fit but he was selected to start at right full back. Seán was at centre back and Brendan at left full forward. Michael didn't last the game and was replaced by Stephen Darby. 'People often wonder if I was upset at being taken off, but there is no point in dwelling on it. It happened. We still won the All-Ireland. That's what matters.'

What was noticeable in the Lowry clan in the build-up to the final was the confidence of the players, especially the younger ones like Michael and Brendan. 'We had no nerves,' says Brendan. 'Those come when you're thirty. I was doing what I enjoyed.' Michael told his uncles that Offaly would win by five or six points. 'I was telling everyone I met that we would win. There was this great belief throughout the team. We were confident together. Even when we went behind in the final we felt we could win it.'

While Offaly adopted a disciplined approach defensively, they were also expansive in attack. The half back line of Pat Fitzgerald, Seán and dual player Liam Currams each briefly hiked upfield to get on the score sheet and contribute to Offaly's one-point lead at half time, 0–10 to 0–9. 'I was always confident,' says Seán 'that if we didn't concede a goal against Kerry we would win. They had a habit of scoring goals that put teams away.' Offaly's strict defensive mode kept the options to a minimum. Martin Furlong, the goalkeeper, did the rest. In the fifty-second minute, the referee, P.J. McGrath, awarded a penalty to Kerry for a foul on John Egan. Mikey Sheehy stroked the ball to Furlong's right. The goalkeeper dived and blocked it and Pat Fitzgerald cleared the lines.

The next significant moment of a dramatic game came with two minutes left when Séamus Darby, a substitute, scored the winning goal. Kerry were two points up when Seán beat Tom Spillane to the ball and passed to Pat Fitzgerald. He was fouled and took a quick free to Richie Connor, who spotted his cousin Liam running up from his position at full back and passed it to him. Liam made some yards before sending a high ball to the edge of the Kerry square. Tommy Doyle and Séamus Darby went for it. There was contact. The ball fell to Darby. 'The minute it left his boot I knew it was going in,' recalls Brendan. 'And people are still talking about it today.'

This victory was about more than the goal. Seán points to the quality of the players available. 'Just look at the full forward line we had – Johnny Mooney, Matt Connor and Brendan Lowry. They were three serious footballers. We were charmed to have them. That was as good a line as ever played football. You couldn't get three finer footballers ability-wise. Brendan's first half that day was brilliant.'

Margaret Lowry didn't attend matches and did not make exceptions for the All-Ireland final. But she greeted her sons on the Monday night when the team returned to Tullamore. And she was with them on the Wednesday night when they brought the Sam Maguire back to Ferbane. 'It was a pity dad wasn't there,' says Michael, 'but it was special to see mam when we got home.'

The three Lowry brothers did bring the Sam Maguire Cup

back to Ferbane National School. Michael also brought it to another venue a week after the final – the Bridge House Hotel in Tullamore – where it had pride of place at the top table at his wedding to Margaret. 'It is always forgotten,' he says, 'that the girls made sacrifices for football too. Seán was married to Nuala, Brendan had married Brigid and we were gone a lot of the time. You left for training around six in the evening and you might not be home until near midnight. Your weekends were never free. There was hardly time for family life. But they put up with it.'

Seán's career in the ESB brought a move from Offaly to Crossmolina in Mayo with whom he won a Connacht Championship in 1985. His daughters Rachel and Sarah were eight and six years old respectively when they moved to Mayo. Rachel married a Crossmolina man, Gerry O'Malley, and Seán and Nuala are now proud grandparents of Tom and Ella. Sarah played ladies' football with Mayo and competed in an All-Ireland minor final, but finished on the losing team. 'I think I appreciated 1982 more than the previous All-Ireland wins because I was thirty and I was coming to the end of my career. And it meant so much to have my two brothers playing with me. Brendan was a fabulous talent. It is the sign of a great player that even when he is a marked man he can still deliver. He had a great radar, great natural ability. Michael was a harder man, he was the backbone of Ferbane for many years.'

Brendan and Michael helped Ferbane to an incredible

five consecutive Offaly senior football Championships between 1986 and 1990 and won another two titles in 1992 and 1994. They were also Leinster club champions in 1986. They continued playing with Offaly until the early 1990s. One major incident involving a team-mate, however, had a massive effect on the brothers and the entire county of Offaly. During Christmas 1984 Matt Connor was involved in a serious car accident and would never walk again. 'That knocked the heart and soul out of all of us,' Brendan explains. 'If we had Matt for a few more years you wouldn't know what we might have achieved, but it didn't matter really.' Michael recalls Matt's power. 'I blocked a shot of his one day and I had pins and needles in my arm for two days. It's a pity there isn't video footage of some of the goals he scored in club matches because they were brilliant.'

Once his playing days ended, Brendan began coaching at club level and was manager of Westmeath for three years. In recent years, he and Brigid have been travelling all over Ireland and abroad supporting Shane's golfing exploits. After a brilliant amateur career, Shane is now taking the first steps in the professional ranks. 'I suppose it is a dream realised,' Brendan says proudly. 'He has worked very hard for this. It is not an easy life. It can be very lonely, but he is working hard and he will get the rewards.' Sixteen-year-old Alan is also showing promise and is playing off a handicap of four. The boys have a sister, Sinéad.

Conor Lowry, Michael's son, played minor football with

Offaly this year. His brother Eoghan is also playing with the club, Ferbane-Belmont. 'Everyone says Conor is like me and Eoghan is another Brendan. That means Conor will be doing all the work and Eoghan will be kicking points without looking at the posts,' laughs their father.

Seán has returned to live in Offaly. He was an advisor to the Offaly GAA Board in the appointment of two county team managers, Kevin Kilmurray and Richie Connor, but he has no coaching ambitions himself. 'I just don't have the enthusiasm for coaching,' he says. 'It's too stressful now.' But he still loves his football and keeps a close eye on developments. 'I have had a great life, a charmed life. There were ups and downs but you couldn't praise it enough. I lost more money through playing football, but I wouldn't change one second of it. I know people will say it is easy for me to say that because I was successful. But it was about more than success. It was about the people you met, the friends you made, the GAA family I call it.'

He wonders about the emphasis on coaches and managers today. 'I had a lot of coaches and certainly in the early days it wasn't coaching, it was match planning. In my early years with Offaly, Fr Gilooly was my first coach and I remember the 1972 All-Ireland semi-final when I was playing centre half back at twenty years of age against this great Kerry team. He brought me over to the corner of the dressing-room and said, "May Our Lord look after you and Our Lady protect you." It wasn't much by way of coaching but he knew I had the ability and when he went away I thought, he doesn't think anything bad of me, he thinks I'm good enough. In its own way it was probably the best bit of confidence building he could do.

'You got the opposite then when you were dealing with Eugene McGee. He told you everything to do. You got on the bus at three minutes past one; you got off at four minutes past two. It was that meticulous. He was a brilliant organiser; he never missed a training session or a match. Eugene was always analysing. He was so thorough, everything was planned to perfection. He wasn't a great communicator. His real forte was preparation, it was brilliant.'

Seán welcomes the embracing of the Gaelic Players Association (GPA) by the GAA and believes there is an important role for the GPA in representing the interests of the players. But he argues against the introduction of any form of professionalism. 'We don't have the money in Ireland to do it. Just look at what has happened to the soccer clubs. They are bankrupt. The country is too small. But that doesn't mean that we should not look after the players, give them perks, make sure they have holidays and do things that ordinarily they would not do. But we can't afford the consequences of paying players.

'I know that there is an argument that when you go to Croke Park on a big day with 80,000 people there and the only people who are not being paid are the ones putting on the show – all the security people, the catering people, the bar staff and GAA staff are all being paid. But I would argue that the player gets the reward for the rest of his life. He can go anywhere in Ireland and he will be known and that has its benefits. When I moved to Mayo it was as if I never left Ferbane. I saw other guys who made moves like that and it was lonely and difficult. They never knew if someone would come to visit. We had visitors from day one.'

Shane Lowry's success has given his father and uncles a new focus. Wherever he goes in the world, however, he will meet someone who will remind him of 1982.

THE DOOLEY BROTHERS

'Over the bar, Johnny. Take the point.'

The shouted words slipped through the rumble of the expectant crowd and momentarily registered with Johnny Dooley. He glanced to his right to confirm the source. Derry O'Donovan, the team trainer, acting on behalf of the team manager, Éamon Cregan. Two men not to be messed with normally. But this wasn't normal. Just over five minutes were left in the 1994 All-Ireland hurling final. Offaly had played considerably below the high standards they set for themselves and were trailing Limerick by five points, 1–11 to 2–13. It was not an insurmountable deficit if the team was playing well. It wasn't.

In the seconds after the awarding of the free for a foul on his brother Billy by Limerick's Joe O'Connor on the 20-metre line, Johnny had a decision to make. The old hurling mantra 'take your points and the goals will come' invaded his thoughts along with the advice coming from the sideline. He stood over the sliotar as if he was obeying.

Behind him to his right stood Billy willing him to go for goal, but staying quiet. The eldest Dooley, Joe, watched from the old dugout under the Cusack Stand, having been substituted ten minutes earlier, 'not thinking at all, except that the game was probably gone from us'.

Six Limerick players lined up in front of the goal at the Hill 16 end of Croke Park. With thirty minutes and five seconds showing on the clock, Johnny's decision was made. He lifted and struck the sliotar, and watched as it flew through the defensive cover and into the net to spark one of the most incredible comebacks in Championship history.

Just forty-two seconds later Pat O'Connor scored another goal for Offaly. Billy Dooley fired over three points in quick succession. Offaly supporters who had already left the ground in a despondent mood came rushing back to Croke Park. Some made it just in time to see Offaly's captain Martin Hanamy collect the Liam McCarthy Cup. Offaly 3–16, Limerick 2–13. Seán and Betty Dooley's three sons had scored two goals and eleven points of that total.

* * *

Clareen, also known locally as the parish of Seir Kieran, is a small rural community five miles east of Birr in County Offaly. Like his neighbours, Seán Dooley farmed the land to provide for his young and growing family. The work was hard, but a strong community spirit was sustained and strengthened by neighbourliness and the shared interest of agriculture and sport.

For Seán no sport could compare with hurling. Although Offaly as a county operated below the sanctified level of the premier hurling counties, there was a small pocket of the county around Birr in which the game was a real passion. Seán had played club hurling with Clareen. They might not have enjoyed anything in the way of success but they loved their hurling. In the evenings at home or when they were gathered together out in the fields doing the various bits and pieces that youngsters could help out with on the farm, Seán regaled his young family with stories of the great Cork and Kilkenny teams he had seen. He painted pictures of the exploits of Christy Ring and Eddie Keher to his five sons and four daughters, passing to a new and willing generation a fascination for the game.

Joe, Séamus, Kieran, Billy and Johnny travelled into Birr with him almost every Sunday during the summer months to watch club games. Offaly did not have ready-made heroes for the boys to worship as they grew up, but they absorbed the affection, passion and intensity of feeling for the game that the hurling people of the county exhibited at these events. The girls – Mary, Sandra, Patricia and Eilish – also came under the spell. 'The whole house revolved around hurling,' is Billy's recollection.

Though they regularly played football and soccer, hurling was the true pursuit of the young kids around Clareen. 'The hurl was like an extension of your body,' explains Johnny. 'You always carried one around with you, going up through the farm, herding cattle, the hurl was always at your side. Seir Kieran was a small parish, made up of around 400 people. The club drew from about four or five families and we all grew up playing hurling in each other's yards and haggards. We didn't realise it at the time, but we were developing skills that would stand to us later. It was a great, tight-knit community and we developed strong bonds and a knowledge of each other that would help us in our hurling in later years.'

The Dooleys, Connors, Coughlans and Mulrooneys were just some of the families that lived side by side and played hurling almost every day. Kevin Kinahan was another neighbour. As a group they became a powerful force in Offaly hurling, breaking through in the 1980s to challenge the traditionally strong clubs of Lusmagh, Kinnity, Birr, Coolderry and St Rynagh's that had dominated Offaly for the previous two decades.

When the Offaly county team embarked on the historic journey to its first All-Ireland Senior Hurling Championship in 1981, the stylish full back was Eugene Coughlan from Seir Kieran. Seven months later, in April 1982, Joe Dooley was handed the Offaly senior jersey for the first time. Thus began a Dooley presence on the Offaly hurling team that continues today in the form of Joe's son Shane.

* * *

'Sure I was only a kid when Joe started playing for Offaly, he's a lot older than me,' jokes Johnny. But he clearly recalls those early days following Joe's progress with the county and becoming a regular in the Offaly forward line for the 1984 Championship. It was the centenary year of the GAA and the All-Ireland hurling final was switched from the traditional setting of Croke Park to Semple Stadium in Thurles, the town in which the association was founded 100 years previously.

Offaly's breakthrough in 1981 had proven to be a huge inspiration to the young hurlers of the county. Men like Damien Martin, Pat Delaney, Ger Coughlan, Joachim Kelly, Mark Corrigan, Pat Carroll, Pádraig Horan and Johnny Flaherty were not just local heroes, but national heroes. To have big brother Joe playing alongside these hurling giants had a massive impact on the younger Dooleys.

Johnny and Billy were among the large family contingent that travelled to Thurles on the sunny first Sunday of September 1984 when Offaly contested the All-Ireland final against Cork. The sense of anticipation was heightened by Offaly's form in the semi-final when they had beaten Galway by fourteen points. But that form deserted them. 'It was a huge disappointment,' recalls Johnny. The story, however, was only beginning.

By 1985 it became clear to the outside world that something special was happening in Offaly hurling. The team that had failed to perform in the centenary year final, retained its

Leinster title and reached another All-Ireland final where Galway provided the opposition. Joe lined out at left full forward alongside Pat Cleary and Pádraig Horan – a powerful line that made a major contribution to Offaly's 2–11 to 1–12 victory.

Earlier in the year Birr Community College, with Billy Dooley in the attack, won the first of two consecutive Leinster Colleges titles. A year later they went one better and won the 1986 All-Ireland title, beating the famous Cork hurling nursery, North Monastery (or North Mon for short). Billy was also a member of the Offaly minor team that won the county's first ever All-Ireland title at that grade in the same year. The roller coaster was gaining momentum. 'For Offaly to come back after the setback of 1984 and win the 1985 final was very important,' says Johnny. 'There was a lot happening at under-age level and in the Community College, so the All-Ireland win gave it another boost.'

Johnny's own career in the Offaly colours began in 1987 when, as a fifteen-year-old, he joined Billy as a member of the minor squad. It was a group of young hurlers brimming with talent – John Troy, Brian Whelahan, Brian Hennessy, Joe Errity, Adrian Cahill, Johnny Pilkington and Declan Pilkington would share dressing-rooms together for the best part of a decade. They beat a Tipperary team in the All-Ireland final that included Liam Sheedy, Conal Bonnar, Michael Ryan and John Leahy.

It was a defining period for Offaly hurling, according

to Johnny. 'We had an abundance of talent in the county at the time and a major talking point was about who would go on and make it to the next level. You were always watching, wondering who was going to be the next Mark Corrigan (a star forward on the team of the 1980s). We also had a lot of the very experienced players who had been successful in the early 1980s. Having them around helped keep the young lads focused. Having won a few minor All-Irelands it can be hard to manage a group of young fellas. Young guys can get carried away with themselves a bit. Sometimes good minors mightn't make good seniors as has been proven so often; there is a big step up from minor to senior and it is how you manage that transition that is very important. We had a successful conversion from minor to senior at the time and that sustained us during the 1990s.'

Séamus and Kieran Dooley were making their contribution too. Séamus played under-age hurling for the county while Kieran played through four League campaigns and was a substitute for the 1986 Leinster senior final when Offaly lost to Kilkenny. 'Kieran was unlucky,' according to Joe. 'It's a funny thing, but if Johnny and Billy weren't around Kieran would probably have played regularly for Offaly.'

With such talent available from one family, it was no surprise that Seir Kieran were on the verge of a major breakthrough in Offaly. They reached their first ever county senior final in 1985 and over the following fifteen seasons would appear in ten more finals and play two replays, winning in 1988, 1995, 1996 and 1998. 'We treasured everything we won with Offaly but the success of the club meant something different. Our numbers were very small but we were a very close group and very determined. To play in eleven finals in that period was a great achievement,' says Joe.

* * *

What would become a familiar sight in Croke Park for the best part of the 1990s was still a novelty when Offaly won their first ever National League title on 12 May 1991, beating Wexford. Johnny and Joe Dooley started in the forward line that day and were joined during the game by substitute Billy, who replaced Mark Corrigan. But the dominance of Kilkenny in Leinster proved to be a source of frustration for the brothers and for Offaly over the next three Championships. The wait for a third All-Ireland title had stretched to nine seasons by the time the 1994 campaign began. The legendary Limerick player and coach Éamon Cregan had arrived to guide the county and a special chapter of hurling history began to unfold.

Kilkenny were embarking on their own quest for history, having won the 1992 and 1993 All-Ireland titles, and were rated as clear favourites for the 1994 title. Offaly had not shown anything like the sort of form that hinted at what was to come, so the manner of Offaly's victory over Kilkenny at the end of June in the Leinster semi-final, 2–16 to 3–9, took everyone by surprise. The Dooley boys scored 2–10 of Offaly's total, Joe and Billy grabbing a goal apiece, while Johnny's accuracy from placed balls was once again underlined. He was again top scorer with nine points when Offaly won their first Leinster title since 1990, beating Wexford in the final. It was a significant moment for Johnny and Billy, because it completed their collection of provincial honours to add to those of minor and under-21 won in the late 1980s. In the All-Ireland semi-final against Galway, Johnny, Billy and Joe scored 1–10 of Offaly's total of 2–13 to set up what would become one of the most extraordinary All-Ireland finals of modern history.

Much of the focus in the build-up surrounded the involvement of Offaly manager Cregan in the final against his beloved Limerick. That helped divert some of the attention away from the three Dooley brothers who were attempting to emulate the achievements of the Bonnars of Tipperary in 1989 and 1991. But the spotlight inevitably turned towards them in the fortnight before the final. 'It was extraordinary to have three brothers make up one half of a forward line,' recalls Johnny, 'but we never felt any extra responsibility because of that. We were just part of the team. There were some very experienced players there with us like John Troy. I suppose there were days when things were not going well in the forwards and you could imagine what was being said in the crowd; it wouldn't have been too complimentary about the Dooleys. But generally it was okay.'

Joe remembers the initial element of surprise that the three brothers brought to the big games. 'But later I suppose we were marked men. Anyway there is always pressure on forwards and I think it was an advantage that we knew each other's play so well. We had been playing together for so long that it came naturally to us. And blood is thicker than water when the going gets tough.'

Rarely had the going been tougher than on 4 September 1994. What had started out as a very special day for the Dooley family, with three of the boys starting an All-Ireland senior final and Joe scoring an early goal, was not turning out as they had hoped. For much of the game Offaly were flat-footed and uninspired. Limerick's new young forward Damien Quigley tormented the Offaly defence, Limerick provided the key men all over the field and with five minutes remaining they led by five points when the famous free was awarded by match referee Willie Barrett from Tipperary.

'A lot of things go through your mind at times like those,' Johnny explains today. 'The important thing for the free-taker is to block everything out – the noise, the nerves, the various decisions you might make. There was a similar situation in the 2009 All-Ireland final when Kilkenny got their penalty. Henry [Shefflin] could have taken the soft option. But the mentality today is different, you go for your goal. Back then the theory was that you take your points and the goals would follow.

'I made my mind up as soon as Billy was fouled. I thought

I didn't have an option, even though I was being told to go for the point. We were five behind and we weren't going well. If we were going to get back into the game, we needed something to kick us on. I was getting instructions and I knew what the safe option was. But once I decided to go for goal I was determined not to change my mind. You can't have any doubts, otherwise you won't pull it off.

'Another decision I made quickly was that I would stand over the ball as if I was going to hit it over the bar; you get nearly the same power anyway behind your strike whether you stand over it or you take a run at it. But I knew they wouldn't expect me to go for goal the way I was standing. It's just a small thing but it was important for me that day especially. I struck it fairly well. They weren't really prepared and the ball just snuck through. It all happened so fast I hadn't time to be worried. It was a gamble on my part and I was lucky it came off. I know I'd have been in some trouble if it didn't work.

'It's hard to know what happened after the goal. They made mistakes and we took our scores. We might still have lost the game but for Pat O'Connor's goal soon afterwards. To score 2–5 in the last five minutes of an All-Ireland final was incredible. It was a dream finish and Limerick just couldn't respond, they didn't have the time.'

For Joe it wasn't just the circumstances of the victory or the family contribution that stood out for him. 'Offaly had fallen out of the limelight a little by that time. It had been nine years since the last senior title and we had always wanted a third All-Ireland. The third one put us on a different level in the game. It stamped our place in hurling and I think that was important for the supporters and the county, as well as for the players.'

The celebrations in their home parish lasted for months. The sweet taste of All-Ireland glory had barely worn off when the 1994 All Star selection was announced. There was huge controversy nationally, and in Offaly, that Brian Whelahan had failed to earn a selection, as he should have been an automatic choice. In Seir Kieran there were three reasons for immense satisfaction. Kevin Kinahan and Johnny and Billy Dooley were honoured at full back, right half forward and right full forward, joining Eugene Coughlan (1984 and 1985) on the All Stars roll of honour.

Johnny and Billy each picked up a second All Star award in 1995, Joe would join the list in 1998 and Johnny brought the Dooley collection to a total of six in 2000. This reflected Offaly's central role during a period of extraordinary change, colour and drama in the hurling Championship. Offaly's sensational triumph of 1994 was the catalyst for a series of events that altered hurling's landscape for a brief but unforgettable period.

When Offaly retained their Leinster title in 1995 by inflicting an eleven-point defeat on Kilkenny, 2–16 to 2–5, they were installed as hot favourites to go on and win the All-Ireland title again. 'The quality of hurling played in that game was as good as you could get,' Joe says. 'Conditions were bad but the game was played at great speed and there was a lot of skill as well. Looking back now you would have to say that it was one of the highlights of my career with Offaly.'

The All-Ireland final would not fit into such a category. Offaly were expected to win, but the hype surrounding Clare's first appearance in the final since 1914 overshadowed everything. Johnny believes that the Offaly players may have become a little complacent in the build-up to the game. It was a subconscious thing but it mattered. 'We beat Kilkenny well in the [Leinster] final and expectations were very high. There was a lot being said about us being favourites and that can get into the minds of the players and they don't perform the way they would normally.'

Offaly led by two points entering the final five minutes, but a goal by Clare substitute Éamon Taaffe and points from Anthony Daly and James O'Connor, with just a solitary reply from Johnny, snatched the title. 'Definitely the most disappointing day of my life,' was Billy's post-match summing up of the day.

Three years later, in 1998, the two teams would meet again in what turned out to be an epic and controversial series of games during a Championship full of twists and turns that the Dooley brothers agree was probably the best of them all. The GAA had introduced new Championship structures that allowed the beaten provincial finalists in Leinster and Munster re-entry to the competition at a quarter-final stage, through which Offaly became beneficiaries. Injuries, illness, the loss of a manager in the middle of the summer, an unfinished game and the first All-Ireland final involving two teams from the one province contributed to the package.

A broken thumb and a broken cheekbone were just some of the trials faced by Johnny during that eventful season. But Offaly had good reason to be grateful that he was fit for the Leinster semi-final against Wexford, as his late goal rescued Offaly from elimination. Fortunately, that guaranteed them a place in the All-Ireland series because they played poorly in the Leinster final and lost to Kilkenny. The final score read Kilkenny 3–10, Offaly 1–11. D.J. Carey had scored two goals from frees. Kilkenny had not been particularly impressive in victory, but Offaly had given a lacklustre display. 'Physically we were in good shape going into that game, but for some reason our heads weren't right,' says Johnny. The fun was only just beginning.

Immediately after the game Offaly's manager, Babs Keating, was critical of the players when speaking to the media. The headlines the following morning were far from complimentary and the Offaly players were upset with their manager. The row became public. Newspaper headlines exposed the rift between some senior players and the manager. After three days of wrangling, Keating announced his resignation. It seemed that the Championship would end in ignominy. Offaly had to find a new manager quickly and all the obvious candidates were already in positions. County officials were advised to examine the credentials of Michael Bond, a school teacher in Galway who had not been involved at such a high level before. Bond was actually in the United States on the weekend of the Leinster final and unaware of what had happened in the game. The officials met Bond and were impressed, and he was appointed to take charge of the team for the All-Ireland quarter-final against Antrim. 'We certainly became focused after that,' explains Johnny. 'A bit of stubbornness crept in because we had a point to prove, we needed to show a few people that they were wrong in what they had said about us. It helped us develop an even stronger team spirit.'

They beat Antrim by nine points to qualify for the semi-final in which their opponents would be the defending champions, Clare. Offaly produced what the Clare manager Ger Loughnane described afterwards as 'a superb display, absolutely outstanding all the way through'. It took a late James O'Connor point to force a replay. On Saturday 22 August the two teams engaged in another memorable contest. Clare led by 1–16 to 2–10 when the referee, Jimmy Cooney, blew the final whistle. Players on both sides were surprised and many in the stands began questioning the timing. Almost immediately Cooney – who had won an All-Ireland with Galway in 1980 and was on the team beaten by Offaly in 1981 – realised his mistake, but he was shepherded off the field by officials while irate players tried to intervene. Thousands of Offaly supporters held a protest on the field and an inquiry was announced. A day later, another replay was fixed for Semple Stadium, Thurles.

'We got three great games against Clare, the sort of games Kilkenny were not getting, and it really set us up for the final,' recalls Johnny. 'You could feel the momentum building over those few weeks. There was no way you could get that sort of preparation on the training ground. As well, the supporters were really getting behind us. The protest in Croke Park started something with the supporters. There was something different going on that we hadn't experienced before. There was a buzz around the place. At our first training session in O'Connor Park after the replay there was a big crowd and they really got behind us.'

In the committee rooms the Offaly officials noticed a change too as they prepared for the third replay. Never before had there been such demand for tickets. Joe remembers the atmosphere. 'It wasn't just in the ground, it was on the road to Thurles and in the town itself. I don't remember an atmosphere as good in all the years I played with Offaly.' Clearly he was inspired, as he scored five points from play to help Offaly finally squeeze past the champions by 0–16 to 0–13. Facing them in the final was Kilkenny, their conquerors just a few weeks previously.

Johnny lined out at midfield alongside Johnny Pilkington. Joe and Billy flanked Joe Errity in the full forward line. It was a hard, fast, entertaining final, far different to their previous meeting in the campaign. The result was different as well: Offaly 2–16, Kilkenny 1–13. The change in fortunes was extraordinary. Offaly had won the All-Ireland Senior Hurling Championship for the fourth time and Joe Dooley found himself in the unique position of being the only Offaly hurler to win three All-Ireland senior medals.

'I think what made 1998 more special was that it was a much harder Championship to win,' is Billy's view. 'Also, to win a second medal meant a great deal because it showed that we were a reasonably good team. Any team that wins back to back titles must be a good team, but to come back after four years to win an All-Ireland proved that we were a fairly dedicated bunch of players. We were able to enjoy ourselves but there was a discipline about us as well that made us a hard team to beat in the Championship.'

Johnny wonders if the supporters enjoyed the semi-final victory in Thurles even more than the final itself. 'So much had happened before that game; losing a manager, the early finish of the game in Croke Park and the fact that we had to go to Munster and beat a Munster team that were the All-Ireland champions. It was an adventure for them.'

The adventure would have one more twist on the day of the final. The charismatic Brian Whelahan woke up feeling unwell. Johnny explains: 'The rest of us were unaware that he was sick until we were getting on the bus to go to the game. He had the 'flu but wanted to try and start and the management decided he would. But it wasn't going well for him in the backs and he was moved to full forward and went on to score a goal and six points. It was incredible what he did and showed you the hurler he was. We also had great guys to depend on at the back like Martin Hanamy and Kevin Kinahan because you would never have known there was a problem.'

While Offaly remained a major force in hurling over the next two Championships and Johnny had the honour of captaining the team to the 2000 All-Ireland final, the players themselves began to see signs of the end coming for that team after the 1998 final. 'We were beginning to slip,' admits Johnny. 'We were getting a few new players coming through but not enough. Every successful team needs at least two new players every year. We did get the likes of Colm Cassidy and Gary Hanniffy coming through, but to keep everything working you needed people pushing for places and we hadn't enough of that happening.'

Joe, Billy and Johnny Dooley played together for the final time in Championship hurling in the 1999 All-Ireland semi-final when Offaly lost to Cork. Joe and Johnny were part of the team for the All-Ireland final of 2000 when Offaly again played Kilkenny. Few could have foretold at the time just how dominant that Kilkenny team would become. The Offaly players had an inkling as they lost by 1–14 to 5–15, Carey scoring 2–4 and a young Henry Shefflin contributing 1–3. That game marked the end of Joe's remarkably lengthy spell in the Offaly squad that had begun in the autumn of 1982 and during which he played in thirteen Leinster finals. It had been a magnificent career. Johnny began to suffer from a series of injuries, particularly to his left knee, and in March 2003 decided it was time to stop.

All three immediately immersed themselves in coaching. Johnny had a stint with Kildare and then moved to Westmeath where he guided them to two Christy Ring Cup triumphs and a League Division Two title. Currently he is involved with under-age coaching with Tullamore where his young son Jack is following the family tradition. Billy continued playing senior hurling with Seir Kieran until 2009 and has coached club under-21 teams. Joe has returned to the Offaly camp as team manager and is in the process of re-building a team in which his son, Shane, is an integral part.

They agree that the demands on inter-county hurlers today are excessive, and Joe is not convinced that the heavy workload now being placed on young shoulders is improving the game. 'If you look back on some of the games of the 1990s they were every bit as good as games today. The game was just as fast then and there was a lot of skill. There is too much emphasis on weights today.' However, he is enjoying the challenge of team management. Offaly have slipped from the highs of the 1990s and he is anxious that he plays his part in helping them to once again challenge Kilkenny, Tipperary, Galway and Cork at the highest level.

For the moment, Johnny is concentrating on coaching the young boys in Tullamore and takes a keen interest in the game generally. He has strong views about the modern trend of county panels taking action against team managements.

'This management thing is gone a bit ridiculous. I get tired of reading day after day about disputes between players and managements. Players need a bit of a reality check and to start looking at themselves. It can't be the fault of the manager all the time. The whole manager thing is over-emphasised. His job is to direct operations. It is up to the players themselves to make sure that they are putting in the effort, making the commitment and performing on the field. When you are a player you must realise that you are only there for a short time and you just put your head down and get on with it. Sometimes a manager might not be the best, but as a player you know, or you should know, what needs to be done. Players need to take responsibility for themselves.'

He looks back on his time with Offaly with great fondness. 'I had thirteen or fourteen really good years. I played with and against some great players. Every year we togged out we knew we had a chance of winning something, that we were competitive and we could put ourselves in a position where we could win a Leinster or All-Ireland title. We were able to enjoy ourselves but we also knew how to work hard. You look back not just at winning All-Irelands or Leinster Championships, but the team holidays we had, the All Stars tours. There was no financial gain for us but there were other things to enjoy. I wouldn't change a thing.'

He is a great admirer of Kilkenny manager Brian Cody and his ability to keep a group of players performing to such a high level over such a long period. 'It's not easy to maintain that sort of dedication and to keep your feet on the ground. A player can get carried away with himself and not realise he is just passing through. Things might go well for one year but you must never forget you're only a short distance away from the bottom of the pile. Cody has done a brilliant job keeping this group going at such a high level.'

Billy decided to move back to junior hurling this year. There were twelve under-21 players on the Seir Kieran senior team with him in 2009. His own three sons are showing a keen interest in the game. Another generation of Dooleys is ready to serve Offaly hurling.

THE LYONS BROTHERS

Just seven kilometres north of the rattle and hum of the M4 motorway lies an oasis of peace and tranquillity. Rathcore Golf Club has a natural beauty set among the drumlins of Meath that provides an escape from the pressures of everyday life for golfers from all over the Irish midlands and the eastern seaboard. There is a good chance that on a visit at any time of the year some familiar faces from the world of GAA past and present can be spotted, drawn to the course by its strong connection with football.

It is a bright spring morning when Mick Lyons strides purposefully into the clubhouse, the powerful gait unchanged from the days when he ruled Croke Park. There might be a few flecks of silver in the hair but this man has carried the years better than most. The big smile is as warm and engaging as ever, the handshake firm and welcoming. This is his lair now. For the last eight years Mick and his cousin Austin have created this course, far from the hustle and bustle of the football cauldrons Mick occupied for a decade and a half spanning the 1970s, 1980s and 1990s.

From the day he put away his boots as a footballer with Summerhill and Meath, Mick dreamed of mixing his enduring love of sport with his business life. Rathcore is the result. These are not the easiest times for business or golf, but the majesty of the place which is apparent when you drive through the gates and up the sweeping drive towards the first tee, allied to the determination of the man, suggests they will ride out the storm.

Mick endured many stormy days in an immaculate career with Meath during the glory years of the 1980s. More often than not he had an able lieutenant alongside him, his younger brother Pádraig. They survived the hard days together when the Meath football team existed in a nether world, far from the land of silver and gold. And when Meath rediscovered their pride and place among the giants of the game, the Lyons brothers were central to the rejuvenation. They played together for their country as well and tamed the Australians in International Rules football.

Proudly Mick recalls that on one occasion around 1985, when Meath was emerging from football obscurity, the full back line was made up of the three Lyons brothers, Pádraig, Mick and Terry. For three seasons between 1984 and 1986 Terry was on the margins of the team, always waiting for the breakthrough but never quite managing to make it. His glory days would be with Summerhill.

The Lyons boys, and their sisters Mary and Brenda, were brought up in the parish of Oldtown, near Summerhill, on the border with Kildare where Paddy and Mairéad Lyons had set up their home. Paddy, with Mayo blood coursing through his veins, loved football and played with Kilcock, making the Kildare senior team. 'In those days,' explains Mick, 'Kilcock was the major centre of activity. People shopped there, went to church there and many of the people went to school there. My father played for Kilcock, but he also played for Summerhill and there was a time he played for Cappagh.'

The boys' football destiny was decided when they were sent to Coole National School in the parish of Summerhill. Their schooling coincided with the emergence of a very talented Summerhill group of players who would go on and have a major influence within the county and would produce a number of very talented players for Meath. Mattie Kerrigan, a member of Meath's All-Ireland-winning team in 1967, was a major figure in the club and would have a huge influence on the footballing careers of the Lyons brothers. Mick's secondary schooling brought him to Trim, but he was a fully fledged Summerhill player by then.

Football was their first love but they played other sports when the mood, or the influence of television, struck them. The front garden of their home was the playground, where boys from all around gathered to play whatever the chosen sport of the day might have been. 'That's where you learned to look after yourself,' remembers Mick. 'It was a good training ground for the years ahead.'

Mick was attracting notice from an early stage. He

was Summerhill's Young Player of the Year in 1974 and the following year played corner back on the club's junior team that won the Meath Championship. A year later he had joined the senior team alongside his cousin Austin, Mattie Kerrigan and the Gibbons brothers, John and Tom. They won two County Championships and the Leinster Championship in 1977, although Mick's participation was interrupted by injury.

By 1979 the Meath selectors decided it was time to elevate the youngster from Summerhill to their senior team. He started at centre half back. 'I was definitely the worst number six ever,' he laughs. But the Meath experience was hardly uplifting. He had come from a club scene where standards were exceptionally high to a county environment that was almost chaotic. 'The truth is that Summerhill was far better equipped than the county team. Training was more organised, more professional. There would always be twenty or more players at training. When you went training with Meath only about six or seven players might turn up. We trained under lights with the club. There were no lights for the county team. I had to fight harder for my place with Summerhill than I did with Meath.'

Midfield was his position with the club and he loved it. Though he would become a household name as a full back and is regarded as one of the best ever in the position, Mick always enjoyed midfield more. 'Full back was grand but it doesn't have the freedom of midfield. Out there the ball was around you all the time and if you were any good in the air you really got involved in the game.' He even played at full forward for Meath in 1981.

Not that anyone took much notice of positions or of what was happening with the Meath team at the time. A general apathy prevailed. Games were played in front of a few hundred souls. There were no great expectations and they slipped way down the rankings in Leinster. Although the county did produce a number of talented players, there was no one around to mould them into a competitive unit. There was a stagnancy about the Meath county scene that smothered the ambitions of the players. 'If you told anyone at the time that you were playing for Meath they laughed at you,' Mick remembers.

'I spent more time messing about than training with Meath,' he admits now. 'It just wasn't taken seriously by enough of the players or the officials. Our training was poor. Everyone could beat us.' Wexford beat them in the 1981 Championship. The county chairman, Brian Smyth, embarked on a search for a new team manager to replace Mick O'Brien. He faced rejection at every door. 'No one wanted the job and you couldn't blame them,' says Mick. 'We knew Seán Boylan all right but we didn't expect him to get the job. We were surprised when he did get it. We were lucky too. We would never have done anything if it wasn't for Seán Boylan,' he adds forcefully.

'I have no doubt that if things had remained the same in Meath a lot of us would have been gone the following year. Myself, Joe [Cassells], Gerry [McEntee] and Colm [O'Rourke] had been around for a few years and we hadn't won anything and there didn't seem to be any prospect of us winning anything. We wouldn't have kept at it because there was no point. Seán changed all that.'

One of the first things Seán Boylan did when he became Meath manager was to remove Mick Lyons from the squad! 'Yes, he dropped me,' Mick says with a smile. 'He was right too. I wasn't really training. I was doing more socialising than anything else. Seán had to change the way of thinking around the Meath team and anyone who wasn't working hard enough would have to go. The first thing Seán had to do was put a bit of organisation into the squad, make the players disciplined. Getting rid of me was part of that.'

Very quickly Mick learned his lesson. Less than two months later he was recalled to the squad and played at midfield in a League game against Galway. It brought an eventful year to an end for the Lyons family. Pádraig had not played minor football for Meath but enjoyed three years with the under-21s and had been impressive during the 1981 Championship. Promotion to the senior team followed in the autumn. It was the start of an eventful period in their lives that would involve exotic travel to the far side of the world and to the summit of Championship football.

Boylan not only had to change structures, he had to put them in place for the first time. He also had to change the mindset of a county and that was going to take time. When Meath lost to Longford in the first round of the Championship on 16 May 1982, the knives were out. Boylan survived because there was still no one prepared to take on a team that seemingly could not win. But Mick and Pádraig Lyons had played Championship football together for the first time that day. Things could only get better.

'For the first couple of years Seán was putting an organisation together and changing the way we approached our football and how we thought about it,' explains Mick. 'Some were small things but they were important. After training we used to go our own way. There might have been a sandwich, half rotten, available under the stand in Navan, but that was about it. We just rushed home to get fed.'

Early in his tenure, Boylan organised post-training meals in Bellinter House, where training sessions were also held on the twelve acres owned by the religious order, the Sisters of Sion. Not only was the standard of fare welcomed by the players, but the gatherings allowed the development of a team spirit. 'Before that players went their separate ways. You didn't really get to know one another and that wasn't much good when putting a team together for the Championship.

'With Seán we would have a hard training session and then sit down together for a chat. Views would be exchanged. We would talk to each other about what happened in matches or in training. We would talk about how we could do things better. We talked about the opposition and everyone had an opinion. It was all part of the preparation we needed.'

Gradually they began to gel as a group. Boylan intensified the training sessions. The hill of Tara became a punishing ground, the beaches at Bettystown were a form of purgatory, even hell, for players unused to such physical exertions. Mick remembers playing a game against Dublin when Meath competed well for twenty minutes. 'Then they obliterated us. We were not fit enough at all. Seán knew then what he had to do and the hard work really started. But he also drilled into us that if we could get properly prepared in a physical sense, that we had the football in us to compete. And if we could beat Dublin then we had a chance of winning the All-Ireland. Once we realised that and he had everything organised for us, then we really wanted to train and we were prepared to hurt.'

The message was getting through. Pádraig remembers long runs through the land undertaken by himself and Mick during the winter months before training under Boylan resumed. 'It was a great help to have a bit of fitness in the bank before we went back to Seán,' Pádraig says. In the 1983 Leinster semi-final Dublin and Meath drew and Dublin won the replay by a point after extra time. They went on to win the All-Ireland title. A year later the two teams met in the provincial final. The new Meath was gaining momentum. Then Mick Lyons suffered a broken hand in a club game and missed the Leinster final. Dublin won. No one could have foretold that Mick Lyons and Meath would not lose a Championship game again to Dublin until the last year of the decade, when Mick was again an absentee through injury.

'There was something else about Seán that was important,' says Mick. 'He had a group of about twenty-eight players. There were all sorts of different characters. You have some very strong personalities and lads who weren't afraid to express an opinion. You had Gerry [McEntee], Colm [O'Rourke] and Liam [Hayes] who would all have been strong personalities. It wasn't easy to manage a group like that. I wouldn't have liked the job but Seán was very comfortable. He kept it going.

'I was one of the quieter lads in the dressing-room. I didn't want to have to say too much. But Seán would always be at me to express an opinion. He didn't want anyone to be shy. He wanted lads like me to be stronger within the squad. There were plenty of rows, but Seán was happy with that. A row is a good thing because it shows that people care. He never let it get out of the dressing-room. Everything was between us.'

The road to glory would hit a rocky patch in 1985 when Meath were heavily defeated by Laois. Boylan had to survive a vote at County Board level and changes had to be made in the squad. Bob O'Malley and Bernard Flynn were becoming permanent figures, but newer players began to emerge, including Liam Harnan, a cousin of Pádraig and Mick. Terry Ferguson also made the breakthrough along with Kevin Foley and David Beggy. The players were buying into Boylan's plan and by June 1986 they were ready. They beat Carlow and Wicklow on the way to the Leinster final and the start of a massive rivalry with Dublin. On 27 July, Meath became Leinster champions, beating the Dubs by 0–9 to 0–7 with Mick Lyons wearing number three and Pádraig Lyons wearing number four. They celebrated mightily in Summerhill that night.

'One of the things we needed to learn at the time was how to win big matches,' Mick offers. 'All the successful teams know how to close out a game once they get on top. It comes with experience. We hadn't won big games for so long that we didn't have that knowledge.' He recounts one very painful experience to illustrate the step Meath needed to take. It happened during the All-Ireland semi-final against the reigning All-Ireland champions, Kerry. The ball had been driven in high from the middle of the field to the edge of the Meath square. 'It was the sort of ball I would go for instinctively. But this time Joe [Cassells] and Mickey [McQuillan, the goalkeeper] decided to go for it too. We crashed into each other and ended up in a heap on the ground. All I remember is being at the bottom of the pile and looking up and seeing Ger Power with the ball in his hands and no one near him. He just tapped it into the net. I was thinking "how the hell is he not down here in the middle of this pile and not up there looking at us eejits?" You wouldn't have minded getting hurt so much if you had taken him with you. That was Kerry. And we had to learn that when we got in control of a game we had to kill it. A year later we knew how to do it.'

By the end of a very eventful 1986 Meath had learned

some very valuable lessons and were ready to move on to a new level. They were Leinster champions for the first time since 1970; Summerhill won the Meath Championship with Mick, Pádraig as captain and Terry in the team, along with their cousin John. And Mick and Pádraig were selected on the Ireland squad to make a historic first visit to Australia.

* * *

Anything Mick and Pádraig Lyons would have known about the St Colmcille's GAA club in the east of Meath, and bordering Dublin and Louth, would have been learned from their soulmate in the Meath full back line of the 1980s, Bobby O'Malley. To this day they are probably unaware that it was an initiative from that club which propelled them to an experience both rate as one of the most memorable of their sporting careers – the first ever visit by an Ireland team to Australia in October 1986 for the second series of international test matches under compromise rules against the biggest stars of the Australian Rules version of football.

The club proposed to the GAA's annual congress in 1982 that the GAA should examine the possibility of forging a relationship with the Australian Rules Football Association (AFL) 'in order to establish an international series'. The proposal was passed unanimously and a five-man committee chaired by Gerry Fagan (Armagh) and including Dan Hanley (Dublin Colleges), Jimmy Deenihan (Kerry), John Moloney

(Tipperary) and Pat O'Neill (Meath) was formed. A year later an invitation was issued to the AFL to send a team to Ireland in 1984 for the first series of games under negotiated rules.

No one knew quite what to expect when the semi-professional Australians lined out against Ireland for the first time in Páirc Uí Chaoimh in Cork on 21 October 1984. Mick Lyons was named at full back for Ireland and was already known as a footballer who could look after himself. But no one had reckoned on a massive Australian called Mark Lee. In just one example of the incidents which marred the opening game, Lee made a high challenge on Lyons and ended the Meath man's participation in the game. 'I don't remember a lot about it. What I do remember is waking up in the dressing-room and the roof was spinning above me.'

The Australians won that test and a major talking point was whether or not Mick would line out in the second test the following Sunday in Croke Park. 'There was never any question about it,' he recalls. 'I couldn't let that incident affect me. I had to go out and prove something to the Australians and to myself. I had to put things right.' He produced an outstanding display, his high fielding earning him plaudits all over the country and contributing to his status as a national hero.

When Kevin Heffernan was assembling his squad for the return tour in 1986 one of the first players named in his squad was Mick Lyons. Soon after, Pádraig earned his selection. Assembling at Dublin airport in October 1986 for the flight to Perth, the Lyons brothers were joined by their father, Paddy, for the historic month-long tour that would take in Perth, Melbourne, Adelaide and Sydney.

'The day I heard that Kevin Heffernan had picked me on the squad for Australia was one of the best of my life,' admits Pádraig. 'I regarded then and still do Kevin as one of the greatest managers of them all and for him to recognise me as a footballer was a great honour for me. I didn't really expect it at the time and that made it all the better.' There would be drama before departure. Pádraig picked up an injury in the county final and had to pass a medical before travelling. He got the go-ahead, but the injury limited his involvement on the tour.

'It was a massive thing for all of us,' says Mick. 'Growing up you dreamed of playing for your club and you hoped that you would get the chance to play for your county. But you were conditioned that you could not play for your country because there was no outlet. Here was the opportunity that we never expected and it meant an awful lot. To have the chance to go to Australia just added to it. It gave us some idea what it was like to play sport full-time and I loved it.

'Any sportsman will tell you he would love to have a chance to play full-time. For four weeks in Australia we did nothing but train, rest and play, and it was fantastic. To be able to get up in the morning and go out and do something you loved, to be looked after the way we were and to play big matches was just pure pleasure. In that four weeks we were so much fitter just because all we were concentrating on was our football.'

They loved the company of other players – Jack O'Shea, Mick Holden, Joe McNally, Brian McGilligan, Greg Blaney, Damien O'Hagan and Pat O'Byrne among them. There were others with whom Mick and Pádraig would become very familiar in the years to come, including the Cork pair Jimmy Kerrigan and John O'Driscoll. 'For four weeks we had the lifestyle of professional sportsmen and I will always treasure that,' Mick adds. It opened his eyes to new forms of preparation and to how players should be treated.

'We can never have a professional game here because the country couldn't afford it. But that doesn't mean that players shouldn't be treated properly. Seán Boylan changed all that in Meath back in the 1980s, but too many County Boards were slow to move with the times. Players were being asked to give more and more of their time but they were getting nothing back. They weren't getting proper meals or gear or anything like that.

'Players should get jobs; if they can be provided with a car and all that sort of thing, then great. The problem with professionalism is the impact it would have on the clubs. The clubs need money all the time. It gets harder and harder to keep going, especially with all the teams that every club is running now. A professional game would soak up a lot of that money and that would be disastrous for the club. The club is where the player starts. Without the club, you would not have the player to play for the county. The club is already paying the price for putting out a county player because that player is as good as gone from the club for the best part of ten years and those are the best years of his playing life. He comes back to the club then with the best taken out of him.'

Despite further outbreaks of violence in Perth and Melbourne, Ireland proved too strong for the Australians in the three-test series. Victory was secured on a stormy night in Adelaide when Ireland won by fifty-five points to thirty-two. Mick also played for Ireland in the 1987 series. He is, however, worried about the future relationship between the two sports. 'The differences between the two games are just too much. When they catch a high ball, they retreat from it. In Gaelic we don't. It's hard to adapt when you only play every couple of years. And there is a cultural difference. They're professionals, they don't respect amateurism. It's not bad manners, it's just the natural order. And they could not afford to let amateurs beat them and that is why there were some of the problems every time the teams met. I know the crowds are great all the time here, but you wonder if it is doing anything now for football. Back then we did learn a lot from the way they trained and organised themselves and parts of their game have influenced ours. But I don't know if there is much more to be gained from it.'

* * *

Mick Lyons had new responsibilities when he returned to training with Meath for 1987. The quiet, almost shy, lad who liked to keep to himself in the corner of the room was appointed captain of the Meath team. The honour fell his way because Summerhill were the reigning county champions. The manager was happy because he knew Lyons had grown into a leader and the captaincy would help him express himself more in the dressing-room. 'To be honest I would rather not have been captain. But it was a big thing for the club and I was glad of that. But the reality is that it didn't affect me all that much because we had so many leaders in the dressing-room. And on the big days I had plenty to keep me busy. Marking lads like Christy Ryan or Dave Barry you didn't have much time to be worrying about making speeches.'

He would have to make a few speeches during that year, the two most important from the steps of the Hogan Stand as Meath retained the Leinster title and then beat Cork in the All-Ireland final to secure their first All-Ireland title since the team of 1967 that contained so many of the heroes of the Lyons brothers' childhoods. Mick not only provided leadership, but produced one of the most memorable moments of the year with a full-stretch block on a shot by Jimmy Kerrigan that prevented an almost certain goal in the All-Ireland final. Cork were four points ahead at the time. 'I knew a goal would make it very difficult for us. I watched Jimmy coming through and I knew he wouldn't try to go around me that he would shoot. I just had to time it right. Luckily it worked out.' The next score was a Meath goal by Colm O'Rourke. Meath ended up comfortable winners, 1–14 to 0–11.

That final was also the start of a rivalry with Cork that would become bitter over the next four years, resulting in players being sent off and off-the-field problems between the two groups. 'I don't know to this day why it became so bitter. Maybe it was that it was so tense. If we hadn't been around they might have won four All-Irelands and vice versa. Also, they had just come out of the long shadow of Kerry and we had come out from behind Dublin. There was an awful lot at stake. You had two groups of very determined people and we were in each other's way. It was a pity. But we are all friends now.'

Mick had a reputation for being a tough full back and he took as much punishment as he gave. 'Was I a hard man? I don't think so,' he says quietly. 'God, there were some very hard men around at the time, much harder than me. I would give a belt and take one, that's the way football is. It's a tough game but there's a line you don't cross. A lad might do something wrong from time to time but there's rarely anything malicious about it.'

He had a good relationship with referees, even if he incurred their displeasure from time to time. 'I always reckoned you'd know what line not to cross with a referee. He has a very hard job to do on such a big pitch. I never argued with a referee because there's no point. They're not going to change their mind. Have you ever seen a decision changed because a player argued with the referee? And if you accept his decision you might get a break later on.'

The rivalry with Dublin was different. 'When Seán was putting us through torture on the hills or on the beaches on wet, cold and windy winter evenings, the one thing that kept you going, that made all that pain worthwhile, was the thought of a Sunday in July playing Dublin in front of 70,000 people in Croke Park. The build-up to those games was fantastic. The supporters in both counties loved it and there was always a very special atmosphere around the place. Beating Dublin in a Leinster final was just as big as winning an All-Ireland. For lots of supporters it was more important.'

Pádraig agrees: 'There was always a great buzz about the place when you were getting ready to play Dublin in those big games. They were just as special as the All-Ireland finals. There was a different atmosphere about them. We would knock lumps out of each other for seventy minutes and then go off and have a few drinks together. I always thought that side of football was important.'

The 1988 All-Ireland triumph was bittersweet. Following a draw against Cork, Pádraig was dropped for the replay. 'I always felt he was hard done by,' says Mick now. 'He was very quick, very tenacious as a corner back and I thought he deserved a break. His performance in the first half of the drawn game was fantastic.' Despite that disappointment,

Pádraig stuck with the squad and played in the next three Championships, lining out in his customary left full back position in the third game of the famous four-match series against Dublin in 1991. 'I wouldn't change a thing about my time with Meath,' he says happily.

'That season was the most enjoyable of all,' says Mick of 1991, 'but losing the All-Ireland final to Down was probably the biggest disappointment of my football life. The Championship was enjoyable because we were playing football all the time and the training was more a case of resting and getting tired bodies back into shape. People still talk about the four games against Dublin because it was so unusual. But some of the football in those games was terrible.' Boylan's management was put to the test that summer and he came through with honours. 'He took us to Scotland for a two-night break before the last game. We did a bit of training and then he sent us off for the night to let our hair down. The only stipulation was that you turned up for training the following morning. He didn't care what shape we were in. It didn't matter if you came straight from whatever establishment that you had been in for the night as long as you were there. Most of us were sick, dying from the effects of the night, but everyone turned up. He knew we needed that break. It had a big effect.'

Pádraig's inter-county career ended with that series of games. Early in the final game, he suffered a hamstring injury. 'I ruined it,' he says. 'There was talk about surgery but

I was over thirty, had a lot of miles done and I decided not to go there. I knew it was the end with Meath. I tried to play on with the club for a couple of years, but the hamstring was always a problem.'

Mick and Pádraig Lyons settled for two All-Ireland triumphs. By the time their careers ended they had faced Dublin ten times. They lost only twice. On both occasions, 1984 and 1989, Mick was absent through injury.

The brothers, who had gone into business together in Summerhill straight from school, returned to the club and served loyally as players and administrators, coaching various teams up to today. Pádraig's hamstring problems prompted him to try out as a goalkeeper. It prolonged his career until 2001. 'I loved it,' he says. 'I always said that the two most important positions on a team were goalkeeper and free-taker.' For the past five years Pádraig and Mattie Kerrigan have coached the Summerhill senior team. 'We're very lucky. So much great work has been done since the mid-1990s at under-age level in the club that we have a lot of talent to work with.'

Their own children are involved with Summerhill. Mick and Helen have three sons and one daughter, Alan, Kevin, Conor and Michelle. Pádraig and Louise have three daughters and one son, Linda, Sarah, Declan and Joanne. Declan played with the Meath minors in 2009. 'Without support from Louise and Helen we would never have been able to devote so much time to football,' says Pádraig.

THE CARR
BROTHERS

Nestling within eighty acres of lush landscape on the banks
of the River Liffey in Palmerstown, west Dublin, The King's
Hospital is one of Ireland's oldest secondary schools. It has
a proud sporting tradition in rugby, cricket and hockey that
reflects the Church of Ireland ethos that has been maintained
since its foundation more than 300 years ago. From that
description, it is easy to deduce that the school is anything
but a hotbed of Gaelic football and hurling. Yet from its
halls emerged two brothers in the 1980s, who would enjoy
long and successful careers with two different counties in
two different codes and would captain those counties in
All-Ireland finals with contrasting fortunes.

The King's Hospital was not just a school for the Carr
brothers, Tommy and Declan, it was also home. Paddy and
Kathleen Carr had moved to west Dublin from Tipperary
at the beginning of the 1960s in search of employment
and Paddy got a job as works manager at the site which
became the location for the expanding school in the mid-
1960s. Their five children – Rose, Ronnie, Tommy, Declan

and Kieran – attended the school and took a full part in all activities.

Tommy was two years older than Declan but they shared the same interests. They participated enthusiastically in both rugby and hockey during the school week. Then, after rugby training on Saturday morning, they would change gear and head off to either Palmerstown or Lucan Sarsfields GAA clubs to engage in their other passion, Gaelic football, with a little hurling thrown in.

They were both athletic and from an early age were determined to be the best they could at whatever sport they played. With encouragement from their father, football and hurling became their priority. Those who nurtured their talents in the GAA clubs recognised their potential but none could have predicted the careers ahead. Tommy went on to play football for Dublin in three All-Ireland finals, including one as captain, while Declan led Tipperary's hurlers to glory in 1991 when he won his second All-Ireland Championship.

So how did two brothers brought up in west Dublin end up becoming two of the most prominent sportsmen in Ireland with two different teams and in two different codes? At first glance Declan's path looks direct, dictated by the family's return to Holycross in 1980, just after he had completed his Intermediate (now Junior) Certificate. The complex part for him was that in his new school, Thurles CBS, hurling was the only sporting pursuit available and he hadn't played a lot of that in Dublin.

Tommy's route was circuitous, to say the least. He could have played for Galway but turned down the chance. He did play for Tipperary with some interesting team-mates including Nicky English and against some very famous opponents. And by 1985 he had settled back in the county of his birth and played in an All-Ireland final in his first season with Dublin.

It is best to let Tommy explain in his own words how it all happened. 'My father was a man of the land and there wasn't much happening on the land in the late 1950s, so he moved the family to Dublin in 1960 where myself, Declan and Kieran were born. By the time I had sat my Leaving Cert in 1980 my father and mother decided it was time to move back to Tipperary. I left school and joined the Army Cadet School. Declan went back to Tipperary to complete his schooling.'

While training with the army, Tommy attended University College Galway (UCG), where he played both rugby and football. He won two Sigerson Cup titles on a team that included Val Daly, Richie Lee, Peter Lee, Kevin McStay, John Maughan, Gay McManus and Mick Brennan. It was while in UCG that the suggestion he should play for Galway was first made. But summertime visits to the family's new home in Holycross meant that he would play under-age football for Tipperary and eventually graduate to senior level for two seasons, 1983 and 1984. One of his midfield partners during those years with Tipperary was Nicky English, who went on to fame and glory as a hurler. Among their opponents were the famed Kerry midfielders Jack O'Shea and Ambrose O'Donovan.

By 1985 Tommy was posted to Dublin. His plan was clear. He wanted to join a Dublin club and his initial choice was St Vincent's. An army colleague suggested it might not be the best choice because at the time the club did not accept players from outside Dublin. 'I wanted to tell him that I was actually born in Dublin but refrained.' A number of other clubs were mentioned to him. Then another officer intervened and within days Tommy Carr had become a member of Ballymun Kickhams. It was a good choice. Ballymun won the Dublin Championship that year and the legendary Dublin manager Kevin Heffernan spotted the potential of the youngster and invited him onto the panel.

This was a squad full of All-Ireland winners, among them John O'Leary, Mick Kennedy, Gerry Hargan, Mick Holden, Ray Hazley, Pat Canavan, Jim Ronayne, the multi-award-winning Brian Mullins, Barney Rock, Kieran Duff and Joe McNally. A lesser personality might have felt intimidated coming into such company, but Tommy Carr was already displaying the sort of drive and determination that would become his hallmark in a career that would last ten years.

Heffernan would leave a mark. 'Just his name and reputation were an influence,' he recalls. 'With someone like that you knew you would never have to question what he was telling you, the advice he was giving and the way he was coaching. I was very lucky because in Galway Tony Regan had been a massive influence as well. Tony had a massive impact on my career in terms of showing the dedication and commitment needed to play at the highest level. He was an extraordinary character who immersed himself in football. It wasn't easy with Tony and some guys couldn't stick it. But it was worth it for those of us who did stick around. I was fortunate to have two such influential people around me at the start of my career.'

On his Championship debut in 1985, starting at centre half forward, he scored a goal and three points in a rout of Wexford. He was on the score sheet again when Dublin beat Offaly in the Leinster semi-final and Laois in the provincial final. He played in the drawn All-Ireland semi-final against Mayo, but lost his starting place for the final. An injury to Charlie Redmond led to an early introduction, however, and although he did get on the score sheet, the Páidí Ó Sé-led Kerry proved too strong.

It all seemed to happen in a blur. 'It was a hugely exciting time,' he recalls. 'I remember thinking at the time how many All-Irelands we would win. That is where Dublin football was at the time, right at the top. I had grown up with the team of the 1970s and we expected Dublin to win All-Ireland titles every year.'

Back in the Carr homestead Declan's life was much different. Having enrolled in Thurles CBS in September 1980, he discovered that the sporting prowess he had developed with the big ball, round and oval, would not be much use to him. 'I was an average hurler back in Lucan, a better foot-baller. But in Thurles CBS it was hurling or nothing. If you wanted to be involved in sport you had no choice but to play hurling. They played in the morning, at break, at lunch and again after school. And when you went home in the evening you played hurling again.'

While he was naturally fit and well built, Declan knew his skill levels were not sufficient. 'I didn't have the basic skills because I hadn't played enough hurling in Lucan,' he admits. So he resolved to work harder than anyone else. He travelled to school by bus, which arrived an hour before classes began. That hour was spent in the handball alley, striking the sliotar against the wall relentlessly, working on his right side and left side in a bid to make up for lost time. He used every spare minute of the day working on his skills. 'I loved sport. It meant so much to me to be part of the school team so I really did apply myself.'

Within twelve months he had made a huge impression. When preparations for the Harty Cup (Munster Senior Colleges) campaign for the 1981–2 season began, Declan was named captain of the CBS team. Though they lost to North Mon from Cork, Declan Carr had achieved his ambition. Success followed with the Holycross-Ballycahill minor team and by 1985, when Tommy was making his senior debut for Dublin, Declan was a member of the Tipperary under-21 squad that won the All-Ireland title.

Outside hurling Declan did not have a definite career plan and you couldn't live life just as a hurler. He decided to spend a few years working in England where he kept himself in good physical shape, continued to work on his touch with the hurley and sliotar, and kept in contact with family and friends back home, including his older brother. He watched with interest the revolution that began in Tipperary hurling when Michael 'Babs' Keating returned like a whirlwind to the county in 1986, and was back in Ireland, standing on Hill 16, when Tipperary lost the 1988 All-Ireland final to Galway.

'Standing there that day I thought to myself that there must be a place on that team for me,' he says. 'I knew some of the lads from having played under-age with them and I felt with some hard work and with a bit of luck I could make the team. It was well known that Babs was looking for players and willing to give lads a chance. My chance came in a game against Clare towards the end of the year. I can't remember what status it had. Probably not much because some of the lads were taking it easy. I went ballistic. I knew this might be my only chance and I wanted to make an impression. That's what happened. I was selected for the National League of 1988–89 and played in every game, including the final where we lost to Galway.'

On Monday 5 June 1989, Tommy Carr lined out at centre half back on the Dublin football team in the opening round of the Leinster Championship against Kildare. Six days later

Declan Carr made his first Championship start at midfield for Tipperary in the opening round of the Munster hurling campaign against Limerick. It was the beginning of six years of high drama for the Carr family that would include triumph and despair, controversy, anguish and days of great pride.

Dublin won the Leinster Championship and then endured what Tommy describes as 'one of our near misses' when they lost to Cork in the All-Ireland semi-final. They had started in blistering fashion and led by 1–4 to 0–0 after fifteen minutes. But John Cleary quickly netted two penalties for Cork and Dublin were reduced to fourteen men when Keith Barr was sent off. Cork won by four points.

Tipperary won their third consecutive Munster title. 'I valued it because it was my first,' recalls Declan, 'but there was unfinished business for Tipperary. Winning the Munster title in 1987 was huge for Tipperary, so losing the All-Ireland the following year was not seen as a disaster. But we knew and the supporters knew that it was important in 1989 that we would go on and win the All-Ireland. Nothing else would satisfy us. As a Championship it was like a soap opera, there was a different drama everywhere you looked that year. The Munster final against Waterford was a filthy game; then we had the suspension of Galway's Tony Keady for playing illegally in New York (he had not received an official club transfer). We beat them after a very tough game. Then there were reports that Paul Delaney had played illegally in England, so he wasn't able to play in the final. It was incredible stuff.'

They did win the All-Ireland title, but Declan feels the achievement was tainted in some eyes by the fact that it was Antrim they defeated in the final. Antrim had been unexpected finalists having surprised Offaly in the semi-final. 'We couldn't afford to lose that final,' he says. 'It didn't matter to us who we played; at that stage in the development of the team it was crucial that we became champions and we went out to beat them as well as we could. It was said in some places that winning was made easier because it was Antrim we played, but all that concerned us was that we took the next step and became champions. Tipperary hadn't won an All-Ireland for nearly twenty years. That had to be bridged.'

Although neither county managed to retain their titles in 1990, there was little respite for the Carrs. Tommy's profile increased when he was named the new Dublin captain. Declan had different worries. He picked up a leg wound in the Munster semi-final which led to blood poisoning and an extended stay in hospital. He had barely returned to training when he was selected to play in the Munster final against Cork. 'I wasn't fit to play,' he says candidly. It reflected the general preparations for that game which were not as sharp as they should have been. Cork's Mark Foley scored two goals and six points. Tipperary surrendered their Munster and All-Ireland titles. 'We just weren't right that day,' says Declan. 'I felt we were a better team than Cork that year but we didn't prepare right. Beating them the following year proved that I was right.' Declan did recover fully from injury to help Holycross win the Tipperary county title. With the county champions given the right to nominate the captain of the county team, in 1991 Declan was handed the honour.

There was a novelty factor about two brothers captaining different counties in different codes, but events during 1991 added a new dimension to the story. Tommy collected his first major trophy as captain in May of that year when Dublin won the National League title, beating Kildare in the final. What followed in six dramatic weeks between 2 June and 7 July would capture the attention of the entire nation and move sport to the front pages and the opening credits on prime time news. As Tommy led Dublin in an epic four-match opening round of the Leinster Championship against Meath that would attract in total almost 250,000 supporters to Croke Park, Declan was leading Tipperary to another Munster hurling title.

Declan attended the first game between Dublin and Meath on 2 June with members of the family. The following week he was in action himself against Limerick while the first replay went ahead in Croke Park and ended in another draw after extra time. Another period of extra time still could not separate Dublin and Meath on 23 June so a third replay was fixed for Saturday 6 July, the day before Tipperary would play Cork in the Munster final. That Munster final also ended in a draw! It was an extraordinary period that took over the lives of the Carr family as they moved from venue to venue, endured the whole gamut of emotions and watched the two men take centre stage on a national scale.

'We spoke constantly to each other during that period,' Tommy says, 'but I don't think either of us had the sense of occasion that it was. When you are so immersed in the thing, going from match to match, you are unaware of the external issues. To us it was about winning a football match or a hurling match. The drama of it belonged to those looking in. Looking back of course you realise what it meant to people and to our family. And every time those games are shown on TG4 it is amazing the number of texts and calls I get about it. Some of the football was very poor, but the people who were watching were capturing the excitement, the mystery and intrigue which were lost on us as players.

'There were a lot of factors into what made it such an event. A huge, respectful animosity had built up between the two teams at the time. For Dublin or Meath to put one over the other was a massive thing. It was nearly more important for Meath to beat Dublin in the Leinster Championship than it was to win the All-Ireland. It is a massive regret that we lost in the end because there were situations where we could have won it, maybe should have won it. I suppose the fact that people still talk about it shows how much it meant. For me what stands out from my career is that I played in three All-Ireland finals and didn't win any of them.' There was some reward for his efforts at the end of 1991, however, when Tommy won his only All Star award to complement that won by Declan in 1989.

He attended the drawn and replayed Munster finals

and took some solace from Declan's successes. Tipperary won what Declan describes as 'the ultimate All-Ireland' by beating Limerick, Cork, Galway and Kilkenny. 'We made a dog's dinner of the Championship in 1990 and it was important that we came back and won another one. It was proof that we were a decent team. The big game for us was the replay against Cork. We were nine points down halfway through the second half and managed to win by four points. We knew then the All-Ireland was in our own hands.'

A year later Tommy's dreams of All-Ireland glory were shattered when Dublin unexpectedly lost the final to Donegal. Dublin were odds-on favourites to win the game and failed to perform. Some players had been caught up in the hype that preceded the game and were not mentally tuned into the task at hand. Veteran Dublin goalkeeper John O'Leary heaped praise on his captain in the aftermath for his efforts to get the players focused, but that was little consolation. Tommy thought he was suffering with the disappointment of that defeat, but he could not have known what was coming down the line.

Dublin and Donegal met again in the League final in 1993. The first game was drawn and the replay took place in Croke Park on 9 May. Tommy had been named at centre half forward and in the early stages he clashed with Donegal's Brian Murray. Murray was moving away when Carr stuck out a foot to trip him. The linesman alerted the referee and Carr was sent to the line. The action was interpreted as a kick and a three-month suspension was expected. Unfortunately for Carr the GAA had embarked on a disciplinary crackdown that season and had decided to double suspensions for off-the-ball incidents. Carr was banned for six months. His season was effectively over.

A major controversy erupted. The Dublin management team led by Dr Pat O'Neill and the Dublin County Committee felt that a major injustice had been done. Once again Tommy Carr was on the front pages of the national newspapers as appeal after appeal was lodged to have the suspension reduced. He continued training with the Dublin squad in the hope that he would be able to play some part in the Championship. Eventually the suspension was reduced by two months. It meant he would only be eligible to play if Dublin reached the All-Ireland final. They lost the semi-final to Derry by a point.

It was a dark period. 'It was a horrible place to be. What I did was wrong and inexcusable. When I appeared before the committees in Croke Park I was asked how did I think my action looked to children. And I knew in my heart and soul that it didn't look good. I actually don't think it was as bad as it looked. It wasn't vicious or brutal. I'd had my share of skirmishes, that's the kind of player I was. I deserved a punishment, but I didn't deserve six months.

'It was a terrible time. I tried to escape from it all by going to the cinema or a restaurant. I didn't want to talk about it or read about it but I couldn't escape. It was everywhere all the time. The incident itself was shown repeatedly on television and it didn't get to look any better. My close friends and family provided great support, but the more support I got the more I felt I had let people down. Pat O'Neill promised that as soon as the suspension was over I would get my place on the team so I trained every night. Some of the lads thought I was mad. But I was just waiting for the day when I would be released from what I considered a prison. And then they reduced the suspension by just two months which meant I missed the game against Derry. That was wrong and it hurt.'

Effectively it ended his Dublin career. He did play in the following League campaign and was a substitute during the 1994 Championship. But by the time Dublin won the All-Ireland title in 1995, Tommy Carr was watching from afar. Those were the times, he admits, when he hated the GAA. He remembers a newspaper headline at the time that described him as 'the enemy of the GAA'. And he was. But he isn't one who holds grudges. The effects of the year wore off in time. The GAA family embraced him in other ways and it wasn't long before he was back in the centre of the action.

On 8 December 1997 Tommy was appointed manager of the Dublin football team. It was an audacious move for the individual and the county committee. The All-Ireland success of 1995 was almost forgotten in the maelstrom that was the reign of Mickey Whelan in 1996 and 1997.

Dublin had struggled to maintain the momentum of the early part of the decade under Whelan. There was dissent in the dressing-room and Whelan had been subjected to some harsh treatment by the supporters. There wasn't a long queue to take the job.

Tommy explains: 'I always knew I would manage Dublin some day. I wanted to. When the time came I was very young and very naïve. I would also question my sense of timing. I was coming into a team that had crawled over the line in 1995 [to win the All-Ireland Championship] and was actually on the way down. We started disassembling the team. Over a three-year period players like Mick Deegan, Keith Barr, Paul Clarke and Paul Bealin went. That was hard. I had played with them and they had been the heart of the team. But we had to make changes and it took time.'

In four Championship seasons his Dublin teams reached three Leinster finals but lost to Meath twice and Kildare after a replay in 2000. His best memories of the time come from his final year, 2001. Under the new Championship structures, Dublin qualified for an All-Ireland quarter-final meeting with champions Kerry that was staged in Semple Stadium, and were only denied a famous victory by a touch of magic from Maurice Fitzgerald. Dublin were a point ahead when Fitzgerald took a sideline kick 45 metres from the Dublin goal. Kicking the ball from his hands he elegantly sent the ball curling over the bar to earn Kerry a replay which they duly won. Carr reflects: 'I felt that day we were a tight, close team. Although the team did not deliver an All-Ireland I think the Dublin public identified with it. They knew the players were really dedicated. I felt very genuinely about that team and I was heartbroken when they did not achieve what they deserved.

'It is a tough role being Dublin manager. Some managers have received terrible abuse. I was lucky I didn't get any of that. Why? Maybe the public recognised the commitment I gave and the commitment the players gave. It is hard to know how the Irish public feel. Are we sympathetic? Are we giving? Are we cynical? Are we cruel? I think the Gaelic games public, especially when they see something genuine, they respond to it and they knew we were very genuine about what we were doing.'

He sounds frustrated when discussing Dublin. 'Dublin are in this place where everything is set up for them to win something. When I was a player we went through the same thing right up to 1995. There had been near misses – it's about learning the trick of winning, to have a bit more character, a bit more maturity and a sense of what the thing means. Looking back now I can see that we lacked that bit of character and maturity. We didn't lack talent or skill. You could pull out videos of those games over the years and pick out the incidents that cost us those games. It's about maturity. I hate saying that about Dublin teams but it has to be said. I don't believe Dublin are that far off the mark but they need to show a bit more maturity.'

His term as manager ended controversially in October 2001. His name was placed before the county committee for ratification after a period of rumour and counter-rumour about who would stand for the job. There were stories doing the rounds that Mick O'Dwyer had been approached to take over while Tommy was still in the job. Though those stories were denied, they added to the intrigue surrounding the question of his reappointment. Delegates to the Dublin County Board were divided 46–46 when called to vote. The County Chairman, John Bailey, used his casting vote to remove Carr.

He wasn't idle for long. Roscommon came calling at the end of 2002: 'John Tobin approached me and asked me to do it. Initially I said "no" but he was persistent. My wife Mary encouraged me to go for it and I had two tremendous years. We had a great run in the qualifiers when we beat Cork, Leitrim, Offaly and Kildare to qualify for the All-Ireland quarter-finals where we played Kerry. I had great hopes for that game but I'm not so sure the players had the same level of ambition. That is a problem for counties that have not enjoyed success. They are unsure of how to achieve it. It is a question of attitude and belief and I tried to change that.

'In our second year we had some great days. That team had some great characters. Take our goalkeeper Shane Curran. He scored 1–1 against Sligo that year as a free-taker. Again we had a decent run and played Dublin in Croke Park. That was a decent performance and our supporters applauded us off the field. I told the chairman that evening that I was going. But he convinced me to stay. It was a mistake on my part. My heart wasn't in it.'

Early in 2005 there were rumblings of discontent from a small group of players. 'The chairman rang me about it. A few players had issues with me and wanted to meet the board. I said that's it. Maybe I used it as an opportunity to get out. I did have great support from players like David Casey but I knew it was time to go.'

The love affair continues. He became Cavan manager for the 2009 season and despite having to survive a close vote remained in charge for 2010. 'Why am I still involved in the thick of it?' he muses. 'I don't know. People talk about culture and character and all that being in the genes. Maybe that is so; maybe there are psychological things deep down that we can't explain. Am I still chasing the dream? Absolutely. I love the challenge. I still love and enjoy the moment in the changing room when you're walking out, the build-up before the game, the rush of adrenalin when things are going well, working with fellows, seeing them grow up and improve. It is an altruistic thing but there is satisfaction from watching players improve, seeing if you can bring something to the table that wasn't there before. There is also a sense of duty to give something back to the game that gave so much to me. Compared to others I have won nothing, but I have had a great time out of it. I have written newspaper articles, I have worked on radio. It is a privilege to be asked to do those things.' He resigned as Cavan manager in June 2010.

Despite the skirmishes, the controversies and the disappointments, he appreciates today what the GAA is. 'I love it and I hate parts of it, the politics of it. I have never had an ambition to be chairman of a County Board. I don't want to be president of the GAA. Would I like to be involved in management in ten years' time – when things are going well in management I'd say I'd like to stay for another thirty years; when you have a bad day it's like "get me out of here". The GAA is probably one of the greatest networks, brotherhoods, whatever you want to call it, in the world. It's an incredible organisation and I have a greater respect and understanding of it now than I did when I was coming up through it. You go anywhere in the country and you meet people on the one wavelength. It is the same whether you are in the US or Australia or anywhere in the world, you will always find someone who shares your interest. It's an incredible network that is unmatched.'

At the highest level Tommy and Declan played with and against some of the great exponents of the games of football and hurling. Playing for both Tipperary and Dublin, Tommy lined out against Jack O'Shea. 'He was a huge man in every way, a huge athlete, he really had everything.' There were others he regarded as special. 'Peter Canavan had incredible skill levels, so much talent. Larry Tompkins was another. Bernard Flynn was a great forward. All of those guys had super talent but they also had huge application levels which made them what they were.' There is a little regret among the Carrs that they never played alongside one another at the highest level. 'We always supported each other,' says Tommy. 'I was always pumped up watching Tipperary, even last year [2009] in the All-Ireland final. And Declan has been a huge Dublin supporter. If he hadn't played hurling for Tipperary he would love to have played football for Dublin.' Declan has taken on coaching duties as well and has spent two seasons with the Tipperary under-21 hurlers, guiding them to a Munster title in 2008.

Appropriately they did finish their playing careers side by side back where it all began, with Lucan Sarsfields. Tommy was first to return to the old stomping ground when his one-time adversary and good friend from Meath, Liam Hayes, took up a coaching role with the club. The Carr effect would be profound. Lucan regained senior football status in 1995. Declan had moved to the United States for four years but returned late in 1998 and rejoined Lucan. He inspired the hurlers to win the Dublin Intermediate League and Championship. And for a few football games that season Tommy and Declan Carr were team-mates.

THE BONNAR
BROTHERS

Cormac Bonnar was twenty-nine years old when he decided it was time for him to end his hurling career with Cashel King Cormacs. It was 1988 and he was living in Limerick and newly married. He had enjoyed a good innings – twelve seasons in all with the club, All-Ireland under-age medals with Tipperary, great hurling and football experiences in University College Dublin (UCD). He even had a Championship outing with the Tipperary seniors a few years before. That hadn't gone too well. But, all in all, he could reflect happily on his sporting achievements. It was time to move on.

He knew he wouldn't be idle. As a teacher he would be involved with coaching children. That was fairly obvious. And there was a chance he would get involved with a club wherever his career took him. Limerick at that time; who knows where in the future. He was ready to transfer his enthusiasm for playing to supporting his younger brothers as they developed their careers with Cashel and Tipperary.

Colm was five years younger. Cormac had been in the crowd in Fitzgerald Stadium, Killarney the previous summer when Colm had been one of the star turns as Tipperary bridged a sixteen-year gap between Munster Senior Hurling Championship successes after a series of dramatic games against Cork. Colm had lined out alongside another Cashel man, Pa Fitzell, in Tipperary's midfield. The second youngest of the Bonnars, Conal, had been on the Tipperary minor team that won the provincial title in 1987 and had only lost to Offaly in the All-Ireland final by two points.

These were exciting times in Tipperary hurling. Cormac had no regrets that his time had passed. Just one more season with Cashel and that would be it. 'I had had enough, simple as that,' he reflects. 'I had a dozen years at it and enjoyed most of it. There was a lot of travelling back and forth for training and matches and I was getting tired of it.'

Cashel were drawn to play Clonoulty-Rossmore in the first round of the 1988 West Tipperary Championship. With a young Declan Ryan generating much excitement around the county, Clonoulty started as favourites. Cormac had the task of marshalling the new guy. Cashel won against the odds. Among the interested spectators that evening was Theo English, the former star hurler who had become a Tipperary selector with his old team-mates Babs Keating and Donie Nealon two years before and had begun the major reconstruction job necessary in Tipperary.

Theo reported back to his colleagues. They had been searching for new talent all winter and spring. They had come up short against Galway in the 1987 All-Ireland semi-final;

they needed height and physique. Cormac was a defender but they felt he could provide them with the necessary assets in the forward line. He had another attribute Theo admired – pace, and plenty of it for such a big man. They knew he did not have a good experience in his previous incarnation as a Tipperary hurler, but everyone deserves a second chance.

Six weeks before the 1988 Munster final Theo English spoke to Cormac. 'It was a shock at first,' he remembers, 'and I didn't jump at the chance initially. I wondered did I really want it. I had already decided that I did not want to make the commitment to travelling for club hurling and now I was being asked to make a major commitment to Tipperary. I really was unsure. But Theo talked me through it and I agreed to have a look. But once I got back into the squad and saw the potential, felt the atmosphere around the place, I knew I had to have a go. I was delighted and honoured to be back somewhere I never expected to be again.'

Cormac had been on the fringes of the Tipperary team between 1979 and 1983, but injuries limited his opportunities. For the 1982 and 1983 National Leagues he formed a new midfield partnership with Michael Doyle. Then, before the start of the 1983 Championship, he was struck down by injury. In the first round Tipperary played Clare, and Cormac was brought on as a sub in the second half. Ten minutes later he was taken off again. 'It was horrible,' he says candidly. 'It was the hardest psychological blow that any player had to take. It was really tough to accept and I still feel for players when I see it happening.' He didn't make the panel in 1984. The following year he headed for the United States for the summer. His inter-county career appeared to be over.

In July 1988 he came on as a substitute in the second half of the Munster final against Cork. With his first touch of the ball he scored a goal. It steadied the ship because Tipperary had allowed a twelve-point advantage to narrow to two. The Munster Championship was retained and training for the All-Ireland series intensified. The manager, Keating, introduced training matches between the senior team and the county under-21 squad, which included Conal. When the squad was named for the final Conal was given a place in the extended senior squad. Colm started; Cormac appeared as a substitute.

Twelve months later Conal, Colm and Cormac Bonnar played in the All-Ireland senior hurling final together as Tipperary ended an eighteen-year wait to embrace the Liam McCarthy Cup.

* * *

In plying his trade as a block layer, Pearse Bonnar was happy to travel far from his native home in north Donegal in search of employment. Football, sports in general, were his mode of relaxation. He won junior football honours with Red Hugh's of Killygordon in 1947. Maureen, his wife, enjoyed camogie success with nearby Crossroads. She too had an eclectic interest in sports. It was an interest they passed on to each of their thirteen children, providing advice and encouragement while inculcating a strong work ethic.

Their search for stability in terms of employment took them to Cashel, the market town in Tipperary South Riding, which also boasted tourism as an industry. The GAA club was a natural attraction. Football was the dominant game in the town, but Maureen also found an outlet for her camogie skills. They liked all sports and as their children grew they sampled everything.

The eldest son, Kieran, played football before academia claimed him. The girls – Mary, Fionnuala, Philomena, Eithne, Ann, Triona and Niamh – all enjoyed camogie success. Triona was also an accomplished handballer, while Philomena won County Championships in basketball and gymnastics. The boys – Brendan, Cormac, Colm, Conal and Ailbhe – played football, hurling and soccer, and dabbled in a variety of other sports. Conal remembers their leisure time being divided between the major sports as well as badminton, tennis and handball.

At Cashel CBS Brendan and Cormac came under the influence of Br Noonan, who put the structures in place to create a proper hurling environment. This was carried through in the local club where men like Michael 'Monte' Carrie organised coaching and games. Michael O'Grady, who later became a renowned coach throughout the country, was teaching in Cashel at this time and also had a very positive influence on the boys. Cashel had not enjoyed much in the way of success at under-age level, but in 1974 they won a county football and hurling minor double.

'All I can remember,' says Conal, who was born in 1969, 'is from the ages of three and four playing hurling out the back of the house. There were always plenty of people around to play with. It was all we did.' Pearse and Maureen were working hard to feed and clothe thirteen children, and as the family grew they moved into a bigger house in the mid-1960s. 'Kieran, Brendan and Cormac helped out my father a lot with the house. By the time we younger ones came along all the work was done so we had the freedom in the evenings and at the weekend to play sport all the time.'

Cormac, ten years older than Conal, moved away from home in 1977 to study at UCD. Michael O'Grady made the same move and continued to help nurture the talent of the youngster. Cormac won Fitzgibbon Cup medals in 1978 and 1979, but he was temporarily distracted from the game by the presence in the college of some extremely talented footballers. Gerry McEntee and Colm O'Rourke from Meath, Tony McManus from Roscommon, Jimmy Lyons from Mayo and Galway's Morgan Hughes were just some of the star-studded line-up who had already won three Sigerson Cup titles. Eugene McGee coached them. Cormac decided to concentrate on football for the 1979–80 season and lined out at full back in the 1980 Sigerson final, flanked by Roscommon's Séamus Hunt and Joe Joe O'Connor from Kerry. Though they lost the final to UCG, Cormac relished the experience. 'It was fascinating, the next best thing to professionalism I was ever involved in.'

He had missed out on minor representation back in Tipperary, but made the under-21 hurling panel in 1979 when they won the All-Ireland title. 'I hung on to my place for dear life,' he says and worked hard to secure a starting spot in 1980. He was full back when they retained the title, with Pat Fox playing at left corner back. Almost a decade later they would find themselves together again but at the far end of the field.

By then the Bonnars were getting a taste of what the future held for the family. Colm was selected for the Tipperary minors in 1982 and won the first All-Ireland medal of what would become an almost complete collection. He played in the All-Ireland under-21 finals of 1983, 1984 and 1985, when he finally picked up a winner's medal. He had also played minor and under-21 football for Tipperary but displayed the determination and meticulous planning that would mark his playing and coaching career when deciding in 1985 to concentrate on hurling. 'I loved football, I still do,' he explains, 'but I felt then that if I wanted to play hurling at the top level I had to concentrate on it. There were so many good hurlers around at that time that if you started fooling around with football you could soon find that your place was gone.'

Cormac's elevation to the Tipperary senior hurling team

and subsequent unhappy experience mirrored the state of the senior team in the early part of that decade. The long wait for a Munster title was stretching every year as 1971 grew more distant. But at under-age level Tipperary were competitive. Between 1975 and 1985 Tipperary won three All-Ireland minor titles and four under-21 titles. 'What happened at the end of the 1980s was no accident,' insists Conal. 'People seem to think it happened suddenly, but there was a huge amount of success at under-age level leading up to it. You had a big number of players who knew what it was like to win Munster and All-Ireland titles. They had no fears of Cork or Kilkenny or Galway. They had grown up winning. In Tipperary a different club was coming through to win the County Championship every year. It was all healthy.

'When Tipp lost in the Munster Championship in 1986 it was a huge disappointment. The profile of the team needed to be raised. It needed to be made important to play senior hurling for Tipperary again. That's where Babs Keating came in. He was the man to put the structures in place. While the older players at the time were used to losing, the young players knew nothing but winning. Babs had to tap into that state of mind and create an environment where those players would come through to senior level.

'He changed the approach. He set up the first supporters' club in Ireland. He improved the way players were treated. We were the only team wearing suits to the first round of the Championship. We went on team holidays. There were no problems with expenses. We always had enough hurleys and enough sliotars. There was loads of gear for the players. It was important and good to play for Tipperary. And there were sixty or seventy players around that were of a very high standard. Babs helped everything come together.'

* * *

Growing up, Colm Bonnar was accustomed to winning hurling trophies. He was successful with the club and with Cashel CBS. By the age of twenty-one he had acquired a neat collection of All-Ireland medals at minor and under-21 but was denied a medal at junior level in the 1985 final. By the end of 1985 the anticipated promotion to the Tipperary senior team came. It must have seemed like he was entering a different world. There were good players in the dressing-room, but years of defeat, especially the Munster final loss in 1984 to Cork, had cast a dark shadow over Tipperary.

Supporters were becoming increasingly frustrated and even disillusioned. It was hard to understand why Tipperary were struggling with such a continuous flow of talent coming through the under-age ranks. Colm made his Senior Championship debut against Clare in 1986. Tipperary led by nine points at one stage, but they eventually lost by two points. It was a blow which prompted some serious soul searching. Michael Lowry, later to find fame in the political world, was the Tipperary GAA chairman. It was he who made contact with Babs Keating to ask him to become Tipperary's manager.

Changes were immediate. Tipperary reached the semi-finals of the National League in the spring of 1987. Players who had previously been discarded now returned. Pat Fox had been a corner back; in 1987 he was moved to corner forward. Colm Bonnar had played in defence in 1986 but by summer 1987 he was at midfield and would remain in the Tipperary team for the next decade.

The new-look Tipperary, with All Star wing back Bobby Ryan now positioned at full forward, stumbled over Kerry and Clare (after a replay) to qualify for the Munster final, where the opposition was provided by Cork on 12 July. On a sultry day in an electric atmosphere Tipperary let a seven-point lead slip in the second half and had to rely on a free in the final seconds of the game to snatch a draw. But they had survived and lived to fight another day; they had turned a corner. An official attendance of 56,000 was given for the day, but many more thousands gained entry when two gates were forced open. A momentum was building.

The replay was set for Fitzgerald Stadium in Killarney the following Sunday. It was another epic encounter that went to extra time. Again Tipperary had flirted with disaster but emerged intact. The added time would be theirs. With fresh legs they pummelled Cork. Colm galloped around the field bewildering opponents. Michael Doyle scored two goals, Donie O'Connell scored another. Few who witnessed the scenes when Terence Murray of Limerick blew the final whistle had ever experienced such an outpouring of emotion. The youthful captain Richard Stakelum lifted the trophy and declared: 'The famine is over.' The celebrations were wild.

'That was probably the proudest moment I ever had in a Tipperary jersey,' says Colm. 'It is hard to describe the day, to explain the emotions. A generation of Tipperary people had grown up without experiencing the county winning the Munster Championship. There had been so many disappointments. And the games were so tight and there was so much tension. It was a great experience.'

The sequence of games and the celebrations took a toll. Preparations for the All-Ireland semi-final against Galway were adversely affected and still Tipperary had an opportunity to win against more experienced opponents. They lost by six points, but it was a much tighter game than the scoreline suggests. Despite defeat, there was still a feel-good factor around Tipperary. Colm wonders if it might have been a missed opportunity. 'There's no doubt that the effort to win the Munster title took a toll. The celebrations had gone on too long. It was as if winning Munster was the main thing and anything else that came along was a bonus. And that was a mistake.

'Galway had lost the 1985 and 1986 finals and they were under pressure. If we had beaten them in the 1987 semi-final a lot of pressure would have come down on Cyril Farrell [the Galway manager]. Who can tell what might have happened then? Some of the senior players might have gone, players like Conor Hayes, P.J. Molloy, Noel Lane, Brendan Lynskey. And without them you have to wonder how we would have fared against Galway in 1988 when they beat us in the final. The 1987 semi-final was a tight game and it was one of the better hurling games between us. It had none of the enmity that built up between the teams over the next two or three years.

'We had so many great hurlers and we didn't seem to go on and do more. We won two All-Ireland titles but you have to think that we were good enough maybe to win another two more at that time. Galway had a very good side. They won two All-Irelands as well. They were a strong, physical team and they had a brilliant half back line. They played a different style to us, a hand-passing game, and we weren't cute enough to deal with it. There were so many times that if we had just managed to get over Galway we would have achieved a lot more; even the 1993 semi-final was one we should not have lost.'

The arrival of his two brothers on the squad during the 1988 Championship added something of a novelty factor for Colm. 'Our first priority was to look after our own place, but it was good to have the two brothers involved. We are a close family. As well as being brothers we are friends. After games we would seek out each other's company. That made a difference.'

Cormac relished his second chance. His appearance – the helmet with faceguard, the absent teeth, the beard – and his obvious determination made him an instant hit with supporters. He was christened 'The Viking'. 'Those months in 1988 when I was coming on as a sub were a big learning curve for me. I remember coming into the All-Ireland final and the first thing that struck me was the pace of the game. My hurling was not up to scratch that year. It was a big step up from club hurling. So it really took me until the following year to catch up to full standard.'

He worked hard throughout the winter of 1988 on his fitness levels and on his skills, spending as much time as he could in a handball alley. He enjoyed the new physical regime introduced when former international athlete Phil Conway was included as fitness trainer. Team-mates recall gruelling 300-yard sprints repeated a dozen times an evening, with Cormac setting a savage pace.

'I was a back who played with the instincts of a back but my job was to play between Nicky [English] and Pat [Fox] at full forward. I was the one to do the donkey work. I was there to harass, to hook, to chase and to block. My job was to make room for Nicky and Pat to do their thing. If they could get the ball they would score. My job was to help them get it. It was comforting to know those guys and the other forwards could score from any angle.'

The plan was working. The three brothers played together through the 1988–9 League campaign. Tipperary reached the final but were defeated again by Galway. They reached another Munster final and on 2 July 1989 the three Bonnar brothers played Championship hurling together for the very first time. 'Not many players start their first Championship game at the age of thirty,' Cormac chuckles. Uniquely Cormac featured on the front cover of the match programme in his first Championship start, while Colm, then coaching in the Waterford Institute of Technology, was the subject of a special feature in the programme. Nicky English scored thirteen points against Waterford that day, eight of them from frees, as Tipperary won their third Munster Championship in a row by 0–26 to 2–8.

Conal recalls the experience of playing together. 'In the dressing-room it was like being back at home at the kitchen table, it felt like home. It also made it easier for me being so young. Coming in I felt comfortable, this was a natural place to be. It was very enjoyable. We are a very close family so we enjoyed preparing together, enjoyed the games and what came after the games. But we always knew we were part of a team and we were lucky that it was a very close setup. It was special and it wasn't the same playing for Tipperary when they weren't there. You still wanted to do it but you no longer felt like it was home.'

They beat Galway in an ugly semi-final and met surprise opponents in the All-Ireland final, Antrim. Tipperary were raging hot favourites to win. Conal recalls: 'I remember sitting beside John Heffernan on the eve of the final and being a naïve nineteen-year-old getting caught up in the hype about the opposition and saying to him "it's a pity it's not Kilkenny we're playing tomorrow" and he said "go away ye fecking eejit, I wish it was the Isle of Man." We hadn't won an All-Ireland in eighteen years so the only thing about it was to win. And I think Antrim were the second or third best team in the country at the time so they deserved respect. I have as good memories of that All-Ireland as the 1991 win. We had to beat the teams put in front of us and we did that. We started poorly in the final and if they had got a few breaks that game could have been very close. Once we got going we dominated everywhere. Fox got a great goal, Declan Ryan was very much in control at centre forward and when he got his goal it took the pressure off us. We were a team playing under pressure, and when that goal went in we let loose and there was no one better to let loose than Nicky [who scored a record-breaking 2–12].'

Cormac describes the winning feeling as 'phenomenal. It was a proud moment for each of us individually and then collectively as a family. It is an indescribable feeling. For our parents it was a very proud day. They instilled a simple philosophy into us – it was to get out there and do your best. If you have a talent don't sit on it and don't come home thinking you have not given everything. It didn't just apply to hurling. It was a valuable lesson for life. I considered myself very lucky to have come along and been able to latch onto a terrific team.'

The pressures two years later were quite different. Tipperary had surrendered their Munster title to Cork in 1990.

'People were beginning to question our worth, were we as good as people had thought?' Conal recalls. 'We knew we were good enough. The question was did we have the bottle to go out and win another All-Ireland and prove that we were a really good team.' They beat Limerick, then they overcame Cork after a replay. The Galway hoodoo was broken in the All-Ireland semi-final. For the first time since Tipperary's re-emergence they faced Kilkenny. Cormac and Nicky English were injured in the build-up to the final. Both started, neither finished. But Tipperary won a second title. 'We scraped home but it was a huge relief to get that second All-Ireland. That proved how good we were.'

Celebrations were put on hold. The Cashel club reached the Tipperary final. Ailbhe Bonnar had joined his three brothers on the team. Brendan was a selector. Their father looked after first aid. Justin McCarthy had joined as coach and they won the Tipperary title for the first time in the history of the club. They added the Munster title and in February 1992 played in a memorable three-match series against Kiltormer of Galway in the All-Ireland semi-final. Kiltormer eventually won the tie and went on to All-Ireland glory.

Cormac retired in 1993. Colm and Conal continued to play and lined out in the All-Ireland final against Clare in 1997 which they lost by a point. 'We had great chances to win it,' says Colm. 'Everybody remembers the chance Johnny Leahy missed, but there were other chances too. But it would have been an injustice if we had won that one. Clare were well drilled and they got a run at us.' Colm played for one more year. Conal remained until 2000, but injuries were becoming more frequent. He had suffered cruciate, back and hamstring problems between 1994 and 2000 and underwent surgery for his back problem. Just before the All-Ireland quarter-final against Galway another injury struck and he called time with Tipperary. 'There was a small sense of regret that we did not achieve more. We had been so close. But then we were lucky to win two All-Irelands.

'It was a great adventure, not just for the three of us, but for the whole family. They would all meet on the night before big games and we would always meet up with them afterwards. It was like having seven or eight christenings or weddings a year. It was special for my father and mother. It hadn't been easy for them and I think the hurling success was in some way the fruits of their labour.'

* * *

During his thirteen seasons with Tipperary, Conal witnessed big changes in the inter-county scene. 'Preparation has changed dramatically. We brought a new sense of professionalism to it in 1989, the way we were trained and the way we were treated, the equipment – we had everything we needed. We had a professional trainer. But it was still quite social and enjoyable. We had a great time. By the time I had finished it was work. It had moved on to another level. An inter-county footballer or hurler nowadays is almost full-time. You need to be in the gym every day, watching your weight. The social aspect of it is nearly gone. You train and you go home.

'I remember we won the Waterford Crystal League in one of my last games and we were waiting for the bus driver afterwards to come out and bring us home. When I started the bus driver would always have to wait for us because we would be in no hurry, hanging around, maybe having a few drinks. You don't do that any more. That is the way it has to be now to compete at the highest level. Just look at the 2009 hurling final. The intensity of that game for seventy minutes solid was incredible. I know games evolve, but it is so intense now that there is no room for error, you have to be the right weight, you have to have the right body fat, you must have your stamina work done, your speed work, your skill work. You have your psychologists and your various coaches and that is what you need if you are going to compete. Just look at the physique of the players now. Hurling has at least kept the skill level along with the intensity, which is the advantage it has over football and last year's final showed that. Football has the intensity but it has detracted from the skill levels.'

Conal is constantly amazed at how players manage to mix the modern demands with work and believes there are some jobs that will not allow time for inter-county hurling or football. 'If you have a job that requires more than forty hours a week and that doesn't allow the player the flexibility to work around that forty hours then it is almost impossible to be an inter-county player. It is becoming a young man's game. You won't see many self-employed guys playing hurling at the highest level in the future.

'Players are making huge sacrifices and you wonder where it will end. There is talk about pay for play, but very few professional sportsmen do what these guys are doing. The problem here in Ireland is that even if pay for play was introduced the market isn't big enough for a player to earn enough over a ten-year career to provide for himself later in life.

'The GAA has changed; it is no longer just a body set up to promote Irish culture. Its structures are no longer amateur. It has changed a lot. It is now big business, but the people who are creating the business are making all the sacrifices and a solution has to be found. To play at the top level now you have to put your career on hold. But players cannot afford to do that. They must have a career to provide for themselves and in many cases to provide for young and growing families. A lot is being asked of them and the time has come for this to be recognised with some form of payment.

'But that is only part of the solution. There must be an all-encompassing solution in relation to careers. The GAA must become actively involved in helping players in their careers away from the games. The GAA could become a university for inter-county hurlers and footballers, providing greater scholarship incentives, working on CVs, finding work placements, etc. For example, they could work on a pilot scheme whereby their major sponsors would give players six-month work placements. Massive revenue is now generated by the inter-county game. Because players are spending more time training and preparing – sometimes as much as sixty to seventy hours a week, more than they spend on their careers – the GAA is attracting major sponsorship from local and international companies. Gate receipts are higher than ever before. A large section must now be diverted into a scheme to help the inter-county players in terms of enhancing their job prospects and their futures.'

Colm has seen at first hand all the changes. He has spent years working with Waterford Institute of Technology teams, is one of the most qualified hurling coaches in the country, has worked in the inter-county game with Waterford and Tipperary and was appointed Wexford's senior hurling manager in 2008. He returned to inter-county hurling with Tipperary in 2000 and won an All-Ireland Intermediate Championship on a team managed by his older brother Brendan. He played at club level with Dunhill in Waterford until his coaching duties demanded his full attention three years ago. 'I love coaching and working with talented young players, but there is nothing to beat playing. I would have played for as long as I could, but my coaching commitments took over.'

Cormac's teaching career has brought him to Milltown in Kerry where he is now principal of the Presentation Secondary School. He played with Dr Crokes in Killarney and won county titles. He has coached a number of teams and for two years was part of the Kerry hurling management setup. 'We had great times,' he says of his hurling days. 'I was lucky because I was getting to the end of my career when the lads were just starting. I am so glad our career paths crossed. It was a privilege.'

THE McHUGH
BROTHERS

Almost eighteen years have passed but there are moments when one could be forgiven for thinking that time has actually stood still. There are changes around The Diamond in Donegal town, evidence that it enjoyed the favours of the Celtic Tiger before the world economy imploded, but in many ways it is still the same. The façade of the Abbey Hotel is familiar, though inside it has been modernised. This is a busy February lunchtime in 2010, a cold but bright day, as Martin and James McHugh arrive for lunch.

The bar, where food is served, is doing a tidy business despite the tourist season being quite a way off. All that activity stops briefly when the two brothers from Kilcar enter. Everyone acknowledges their presence; a series of 'hellos' and other greetings lead them to an end table where their privacy is respected. Except for the attention of one elderly man. He means no harm, of course, and Martin and James happily engage him in chat. The subject is football. It always is.

They talk about the prospects for the year ahead, albeit briefly. Inevitably, this conversation becomes a reflection.

Nearly two decades on from Donegal's only success in the 1992 All-Ireland Senior Football Championship, memories of the homecoming to The Diamond on the night after the game, the tens of thousands of flag-waving supporters welcoming the Sam Maguire Cup and the thumping sound of Tina Turner chanting 'Simply the Best', remain fresh in every mind.

'Sometimes,' says James, who lined out at right half forward on that famous September day beside his older brother, 'you feel the county is still living on that day. And maybe it's not such a good thing.' But he has a smile on his face. Donegal have not enjoyed anything like that level of success since and has dropped down football's order. But that roller coaster journey to the All-Ireland title and the entire experience has left an indelible mark.

Football was central to the brothers' lives before thoughts of playing for Donegal even entered their minds. It still is. A week on from our meeting and the McHugh brothers are together again, this time watching their sons Eoin (James) and Ryan (Martin) playing for Carrick Vocational School (VS) in the Ulster Under-16 Championship against Cookstown. The opposition coach is Peter Canavan.

Carrick VS has always been an integral part of football in south-west Donegal. 'A real breeding ground' is how Martin describes it. They both recall fondly the inspiration provided by Barry Campbell, now retired, in the school. They won Divisional and County Championships with regularity. They graduated to the county vocational school team. Martin recalls playing in an Ulster VS final, he's not sure which year, when Packie Bonner lined out at midfield; a solid grounding for his future career as one of the Republic of Ireland's greatest goalkeepers.

South-west Donegal was always a hotbed of football. Jim McHugh won a Donegal Championship with Killybegs in 1952 and his sons and daughters were reared on stories of that success and the great rivalries that grew up over the decades between Killybegs, Glencolumcille, Kilcar and other small rural communities. Their uncle, Frankie Daniels Cunningham, was president of the Killybegs club and one of the foremost supporters of the game all his life. 'In places like those,' says Martin, 'you had the pub, the church and the football field. No other game was played.'

They also had big families providing lots of boys to play football. Farming was still profitable, the fishing industry was going well and the fish factories were creating plenty of employment to keep the boys at home. As Martin and James were growing up in the early 1970s, Kilcar enjoyed a period of great success, winning three Donegal Under-21 Championships in a row between 1972 and 1974. For such a small club competing against the big guns from Letterkenny and Ballyshannon, this was a serious message.

During that same period Donegal won the 1972 and 1974 Ulster Senior Championships. Martin remembers travelling by bus to Clones for those finals. In 1974 Michael Carr from the Kilcar club played; Finian Ward from Glencolumcille was at left half back. Danny Gillespie was a sub. 'Michael was a player I really looked up to,' says Martin. 'We used to go training on our own. He was a great footballer but he was also a great athlete and I learned a lot from him.'

Although Martin was making quite an impression with Carrick VS, he failed to attract the notice of the Donegal minor selectors. It seems incredible today that a player who would become the central figure in the county's historic All-Ireland breakthrough never played minor football for the county. 'No, I went off for trials and all of that, but I was never picked,' he says with a smile. 'At the time St Eunan's in Letterkenny and De La Salle in Ballyshannon were the strong schools. I was just a wee lad from Kilcar; I was small so I didn't get too many passes and I wasn't noticed.'

In 1980, the Kilcar selectors decided that nineteen-year-old Martin McHugh was good enough for their senior team. The club won the Donegal Championship for the first time and the wee man kicked ten points in the final. A month later he played in the National Football League for Donegal against Tipperary in Ballyshannon. 'I always remember the Tipperary full back wore glasses. I never saw it before or since. And he was a good footballer too.'

So began a senior inter-county career that would last fifteen seasons and earn him plaudits as one of the outstanding footballers of his generation. 'I was never dropped,' he states before making a mild correction. 'Well, I was dropped once for a game against Sligo. But the game was never played because the goalposts blew down. So I think I can say that I never missed a game for which I was selected.'

The intense club rivalry that was generated throughout the 1980s, as well as ever-increasing inter-county involvement, ensured that football would be central to the lives of the McHugh family. James was elevated to senior level in the club in 1981 and played minor football for Donegal a year later. Martin played his second year at under-21 level in 1982, a significant milestone in the history of Donegal football. They had lost the previous year's Ulster final to an Éamon McEneaney-inspired Monaghan. Team manager Joe Watson stepped aside and Tom Conahan took over. Matt Gallagher, Eunan McIntyre, Tommy McDermott, Brian Tuohy, Anthony Molloy, Donal Reid, Charlie Mulgrew, Joyce McMullan and Paul Carr were just some of the squad members who joined McHugh on the famous journey that brought Donegal its first All-Ireland inter-county success at any grade. 'It was a major breakthrough and it did put us on the map. The county won another under-21 All-Ireland in 1987 and that all contributed to a change in mood in the county.'

The schedule with Kilcar was hectic. James captained the club to their second Donegal title in 1985. They would also win in 1989 and 1993 when younger brother Enda played. 'My father always rated him better that either of us,' says Martin. 'He was a defender, very strong. The fact that he

Distinguished Service: For twenty-seven years between 1964 and 1991 the Henderson name was a constant on the Kilkenny team. Pat, Ger and John won eleven All-Ireland medals between them. © *Ray McManus/SPORTSFILE*

The late Lt Gen. Dermot Earley celebrates his daughter Noelle's elevation to Ladies Football All Star status in 2009, flanked by his wife Mary and daughters Anne Marie and Paula. © *Brendan Moran/SPORTSFILE*

Paul Earley (right) shares a joke with two other legends of Gaelic games, Peter Canavan (left) and Nicky English (centre). © *Brian Lawless/SPORTSFILE*

All Stars: Dermot Earley Jnr celebrates a player of the month award with his mother Mary and father Dermot Snr. © *Brian Lawless/SPORTSFILE*

Seán Lowry, winner of three All-Ireland senior medals with Offaly, pictured during the 1981 final against Kerry. © *Ray McManus/SPORTSFILE*

The Ferbane Clan: Seán, Michael and Brendan Lowry revisit the scene of their greatest triumph as footballers, the 1982 All-Ireland victory at Croke Park. © *Paul Mohan/SPORTSFILE*

With his brother Mick on his left flank, Pádraig Lyons collects the Meath senior championship trophy on behalf of the Summerhill club from County Chairman Fintan Ginnity. © *John Quirke Photography*

A study in concentration: Mick Lyons keeps his eye on the ball in the 1987 All-Ireland final. © *Ray McManus/SPORTSFILE*

Sports Carrs: Brothers Tommy and Declan Carr watch the action from the stands. Tommy captained Dublin in the 1992 All-Ireland football final; Declan went one better a year earlier when leading Tipperary to the hurling title. © *Damien Eagers/ SPORTSFILE *EDI**

Joe, Billy and Johnny Dooley scored two goals and eleven points of Offaly's total in the 1994 All-Ireland final victory against Limerick. © *Ray McManus/SPORTSFILE*

Colm Bonnar won an All-Ireland minor medal with Tipperary in 1982 and finished his career eighteen years later when winning an All-Ireland junior title.
© *Brendan Moran/SPORTSFILE*

The youngest Bonnar, Conal, was at right half back when Tipperary emerged from the wilderness to win the All-Ireland title in 1989.
© *Ray McManus/SPORTSFILE*

Cormac Bonnar was coaxed out of retirement to play a vital role in Tipperary's re-emergence as a major hurling power in the late 1980s. © *Brendan Moran/ SPORTSFILE*

His career was coming to an end in 2000, but Joe Cooney still displayed the style and control that made him a favourite of Galway hurling fans. © *Damien Eagers/ SPORTSFILE*

His adoring fans carry a triumphant Joe Cooney from the field at Semple Stadium after his brilliant individual performance for Galway against Kilkenny in the 1986 All-Ireland semi-final. © *Ray McManus/SPORTSFILE*

Jimmy Cooney, the referee, is escorted off Croke Park after he ended the 1998 All-Ireland semi-final prematurely. He had happier days in the stadium when winning an All-Ireland title with Galway in 1980. © *David Maher/SPORTSFILE*

Martin McHugh evades the attentions of Dublin's Keith Barr as he inspires Donegal to the county's only All-Ireland senior success in 1992. © *Ray McManus/ SPORTSFILE*

James McHugh and Derry's Johnny McGurk exchange pleasantries after the rain-soaked Ulster final of 1993. © *Ray McManus/SPORTSFILE*

Donegal's James McHugh keeps a watchful eye as his brother Martin shoots for goal. © *John Quirke Photography*

Jim McHugh proudly shows his Donegal senior football championship medal, won in 1952 with Killybegs, to his sons James, Martin and Enda. © *Michael O'Donnell*

Gentle Giant: George O'Connor finished his illustrious career with Wexford by winning his only All-Ireland title in 1996. © *Ray McManus/SPORTSFILE*

Wexford's John O'Connor, of whom his brother George said in tribute, 'John had far more skill than I had'. © *Ray McManus/SPORTSFILE*

Tomás, Darragh and Marc Ó Sé pose for the cameras in the build-up to the
All-Ireland final of 2002, the first final that featured all three brothers. ©*Brendan
Moran/SPORTSFILE*

Family Affair: For the first time in the history of the All Stars scheme, three brothers were chosen on the same selection when Marc, Darragh and Tomás Ó Sé were named on the 2007 Football All Stars. © *Brendan Moran/SPORTSFILE*

In Full Flight: Darragh Ó Sé soars into the air to win possession for Kerry against old rivals Cork. © *Brian Lawless/SPORTSFILE*

From Fiji to Na Piarsaigh: Seán Óg, Setanta and Aisake Ó hAilpín celebrate Na Piarsaigh's success in the Cork senior hurling championship in 2004. © *Matt Browne/SPORTSFILE*

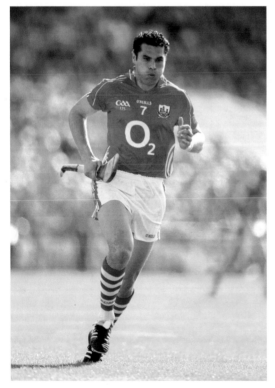

Sean Óg Ó hAilpín on championship duty for Cork. © *Brendan Moran/ SPORTSFILE*

Pascal (left) and Peter Canavan together in triumph after Errigal Chiárain won the Ulster club title in 2002. © *Damien Eagers/SPORTSFILE *EDI**

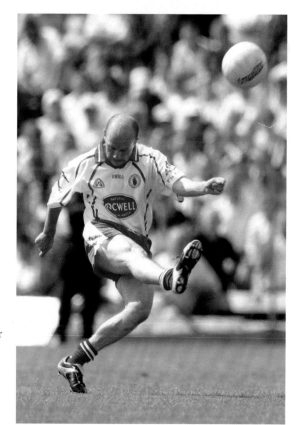

Peter the Great: Peter Canavan in typical pose lining out for Tyrone in the Ulster championship.
© *Pat Murphy/ SPORTSFILE*

Determination: Peter Canavan in action for his club, Errigal Chiaráin. © *Oliver McVeigh/SPORTSFILE*

Bernard (left) and Alan Brogan celebrate Dublin's success in the Leinster football championship in 2007 when both were goalscorers. © *Brendan Moran/ SPORTSFILE*

came after the two of us didn't make it easy. But I always remember the Ulster club final in 1993 when we played Errigal Chiaráin. He was marking Peter Canavan and did as good as job on him as I have ever seen.' Enda also played in the county minor and under-21 teams.

James was taking his time joining Martin on the Donegal senior team. 'I wasn't a great one for winter training and I also broke my ankle twice,' he explains. Martin defends him: 'James was very versatile and that went against him. With the club we played him corner back one day, centre back the next and midfield if we needed him. Then we played him in the forwards. He was so important to the club. There are people here in Donegal who would say he was one of the best club footballers ever in Donegal.'

Martin and James McHugh lined out alongside each other at numbers ten and eleven for the first time in Championship football for the 1990 Ulster Championship. Their parents, Jim and Catherine, watched with pride as the two boys played a leading role in Donegal's win over a highly rated Armagh team in the Ulster final by just a point, 0–15 to 0–14. That day is naturally cherished. Other memories of that Championship bring creases of pain across the foreheads of the two brothers.

The draw pitted Donegal against Meath, the champions of 1987 and 1988, in the All-Ireland semi-final. In terms of achievement there was a gulf between the two teams. But they had played each other in League games and the Donegal players didn't have any fears. Before the day had ended the entire Donegal half forward line of Martin and James McHugh and Joyce McMullan had been replaced. Meath won fairly comfortably by 3–9 to 1–7. 'Definitely one of the worst days in football for me,' is Martin's sad recollection.

'That game affected me more than any other and I'm still not sure why. The game just passed us [the half forward line] by. [Anthony] Molloy had a brilliant game at midfield with [Brian] Murray. They easily won that battle. But for some reason the three of us never got into it. Maybe it was the long ball being driven in from farther out, I don't know. I went home and wanted to lock myself in. We [Martin and Patrice, his wife] were living in a flat at the time and I wouldn't have come out at all but for the fact that our son Mark was born on the Wednesday. I felt I had let everyone down, I had let my family down, the people down. I had let Donegal down. It is hard even now to work out what went wrong. Meath were a really good team, but that wasn't all of it. Kevin Foley marked me that day. I had kicked eight or nine points off Liam Harnan in a League game, which is probably the worst thing I could have done. So Foley marked me. He didn't get much ball, but neither did I so his job was done. We got a lot of stick after that which I felt was unnecessary.'

James believes that Donegal lost their way before that semi-final. 'Donegal's best game was a short passing game, whether people liked it or not. It might not have been attractive but that is the way all the clubs here played and it is what we were used to. For the game against Meath we changed. We played the long ball into Tony Boyle and it didn't work. You have to say too that Meath were a brilliant team. Just look at the full forward line – O'Rourke, Stafford, Flynn. That says it all.'

They thought it couldn't get worse. It did. Donegal reached the 1991 Ulster final and suffered an eight-point thumping from Down. 'We didn't know at the time that this was a really good Down team. That realisation would come later. But coming out of Clones that day I fully expected that it would be the last time I would play for Donegal,' Martin reveals.

'Myself, James, Noel Hegarty and John Joe Doherty left the ground together. As we were walking down the hill towards the town I told the guys, "we should remember this because it will probably be our last time making this journey together as Donegal footballers". This had been our third Ulster final in a row. It was an ageing team and it was hard to see how we could turn it around.'

So how did they do it? 'You would have to say luck had something to do with it as well as ability,' insists Martin. 'I mean we did have the talent, had it for a few years, but we needed some luck. All the successful teams do. And the draw we got for the Championship in 1992 was our bit of luck.'

There was little evidence of a turnaround when Donegal travelled to Breffni Park on 24 May 1992 to play Cavan. It was a tight match which Martin seemed to have won for

Donegal with an angled 50-yard free kick just before the end. He recollects: 'Our preparation was not good enough going into that game and we were lucky to get away with it. We were a point up when Damien O'Reilly fly-kicked a ball that went over the bar. It could just as easily have dipped under the bar and we would have been gone. There was no back door then. We got them back here to Donegal for the replay on a wet day and won easily enough. Then, with all due respect, we had Fermanagh and they were not going too well at the time. But that was a turning point.'

When the players returned to the dressing-room that June evening in Omagh, having beaten Fermanagh, the mood was grim. They had reached another Ulster final but that was no longer a cause for celebration. Deep down the senior players knew that time was running out and they knew they were wasting that time. Donegal were surviving on skill and instinct and that would not be enough if they were to get to the next level. The exchanges between the players were frank, even a little heated. For an hour they sat in the dressing-room while family and friends waited outside wondering what was happening.

'We just knew we weren't training hard enough. Derry had just won the National League, they were probably favourites to win the All-Ireland and it was obvious our preparations up to then were not enough to take on Derry. We needed tougher training and we made that clear. In fairness, our trainer Anthony Harkin took everything on board. We had four weeks to get ready. He went away and came up with a plan, what we called "shock" training. It was done in short, sharp bursts over the next two weeks and then we tapered off building up to the final.'

Derry were the team of the moment. A hot streak had included twelve consecutive victories in League and Championship, which included winning the League title. When John Cunningham was sent off early in the Ulster final and James McHugh had to move from corner forward to corner back, the task was all the harder. But Donegal's pre-match approach was paying dividends. As the second half wore on they looked fresher. The Derry players looked jaded. Donegal won by 0–14 to 1–9.

There were other major events in the 1992 Championship. Clare beat Kerry in the Munster final in one of the biggest shocks in history and would play Dublin in the All-Ireland semi-final. Mayo ended Roscommon's two-year reign in Connacht and set up a date with Donegal. It would not be a game likely to find a place among football's beautiful moments.

'It must have been the worst All-Ireland semi-final ever played,' recalls Martin. 'It was terrible football. We were very nervous going into it. There was this thing about Donegal and semi-finals. We always felt that if we could get through a semi-final we could win a final. It happened at under-21 level. And we knew if we beat Mayo we had a great chance of winning the All-Ireland. I think we were afraid of losing.'

'I don't remember a lot about the game,' admits James, 'but I do remember getting home and people telling me that they had turned it off!'

The negative reaction to that semi-final worked in Donegal's favour. While the county itself was engulfed in a colourful hysteria, with every townland, village and town festooned with flags and banners and bunting, the general consensus in the other thirty-one counties was that the All-Ireland title would belong to Dublin. Nowhere was that more strongly felt than in Dublin itself.

'There's no doubt they took their eye off the ball,' says Martin. 'The hype about them was incredible. People were saying that they would win the All-Ireland final by forty points. That was all based on our performance in the semi-final. That was the mistake everyone made. We had a mental problem with semi-finals and never played well in them. It was not a true reflection of the team. Our job against Mayo was to win a football match, not to entertain or to impress. We did enjoy some luck in the final. Charlie Redmond missed a penalty early in the game when Dublin were going well. But once we settled the game was ours. The best football we played that year was the second half against Derry and the last twenty minutes of the first half against Dublin. It was the best football we ever played as a bunch of players.'

James adds: 'The whole All-Ireland experience is something that will stay with us forever and I am not just talking about the game itself. It is something every county player should be able to enjoy in his life because it develops you as a person. The county was alive in the build-up. It was a fantastic time and to be in the middle of it was a great privilege. And we didn't get carried away with it. For some reason we were so confident going into the final that we hadn't a care in the world.'

'I'll tell you how confident I was,' interjects Martin. 'I had figured out how I was going to get the ball at the end of the game. I decided I would be as close to the referee [Tommy McDermott from Cavan] as possible. That is what I was thinking of before the game. And I was in position, I got the ball and I still have it at home.'

At the end of the 0–18 to 0–14 victory, the players were engulfed in a maelstrom of emotions. The on-field celebrations were manic. Team captain Anthony Molloy's victory speech, his exhortation that "Sam's for the hills", sent tens of thousands of supporters into further extremes of ecstasy. It was a struggle for the players to reach the dressing-room. When they did, a sombre mood prevailed. Rumours began to circulate that Joyce McMullan's brother, Gerard, had died. The celebrations ended. Then Joyce's sister rushed in to assure them that there was no truth in the rumours. The celebrations took on an even greater intensity.

'We stayed at the Grand Hotel in Malahide that night,' says Martin, 'and it was just so good to see so many people so happy. We danced all night. Daniel O'Donnell sang for hours. I couldn't believe the number of people I met that night or over the next few days who told me "I could die happy now". We never realised what it meant to the people. I'll never forget the crowds that welcomed us back on the Monday night. And then on Tuesday we brought the cup to Kilcar. My mother and father met the bus in the town. The pipe band led the parade. It was very special. All the neighbours came out to meet us and we could see how much it meant to them.'

According to James: 'It was a wildly surreal feeling. I remember saying that people in small counties shouldn't be winning things like this. What I meant was that we had grown up watching and admiring the likes of Kerry. We loved our club football and that was where we starred. This was all so new.'

So what had brought about such a change in status? James explains: 'One of the most important things is that you have to believe that you can win at that level. For too long winning the Ulster Championship was all that really mattered here. When you had that won you went down to Croke Park for the weekend. You didn't really think about winning the All-Ireland. But Down changed that in 1991. If Down had not won the All-Ireland in 1991 I don't think Donegal or Derry would have come along afterwards. Down paved the way. We had played Railway Cup football with the Down lads, players like James McCartan and Ross Carr. They helped make the All-Ireland more reachable.'

Martin adds: 'If you had the back door then Down,

Donegal and Derry would have won a lot more. Down had no fear of anyone and that gave us the belief that we could do it as well.'

The celebrations went on, and on, and on. When the 1992 All Stars were announced the names of Martin and James McHugh were among seven Donegal players honoured. It was Martin's second award, having previously been honoured in 1983. Gary Walsh, Matt Gallagher, Martin Gavigan, Anthony Molloy and Tony Boyle joined the McHugh brothers on the All Star rostrum. 'I think the celebrations must have lasted four or five years,' laughs James. 'When we won the All-Ireland we didn't know how to handle it. A year later it was all over for us. We played Derry in the Ulster final in Clones and there was a deluge. That was the saving of us. People wanted the game called off that day but not us. We weren't ready for a final or Derry, and we wouldn't have lived with them in good conditions. The celebrations had gone on too long. It was nobody's fault but our own. The fact that conditions were so bad helped us. It was nearly unplayable.' They lost by two points, 0–6 to 0–8.

Martin takes up the theme: 'We probably should have achieved a lot more, a lot earlier. By the time we won the All-Ireland we were an ageing team. Players were picking up injuries and it was getting harder and harder. Our team was a mix of the under-21 teams from 1982 and 1987, but people forget that we had a lot of players who hadn't been on those teams – James, Declan Bonnar, Brian Murray, Noel

Hegarty, Martin Gavigan, Gary Walsh and Tony Boyle. We had an exceptional team but I think maybe we under-achieved. It was a very competitive period. Down and Derry were outstanding, Meath, Dublin and Cork were also very competitive. But we could have won more.'

Donegal did reach the National League final in May 1993 and Dublin again provided the opposition. The final went to a replay, but Donegal were playing on auto-pilot. The celebrations continued unabated. Not even the prospect of playing in front of 70,000 people in Croke Park against Dublin prompted an early night on the eve of the game. 'It was as wild a craic as you could ever have had,' says James. 'We should all have retired there and then.' Dublin won by 0–10 to 0–6.

By 1994 the retirements were beginning. 'Peter Canavan beat us on his own,' recalls Martin. 'We were lucky we had won our All-Ireland before he came on the scene.' Martin's own future came under scrutiny. The position of manager in Donegal became vacant when Brian McEniff stood aside. Martin wanted the job but he also wanted to continue playing. 'Brian had been player-manager in the 1970s and he was successful. I had been player-manager with Kilcar and we got to three county finals. I always felt it was easier to manage a team when you were on the field yourself, because you could see properly what was going on.'

The Donegal authorities were not prepared to take such a step. P.J. McGowan was appointed. Martin McHugh became manager of Cavan. 'It was a difficult position for P.J. when he got the Donegal job. If I wasn't playing well people would have said I didn't want to play for P.J. If I had played on and he didn't pick me or he took me off it would have been awkward for him and I didn't want that. I couldn't stay.'

Cavan were in lowly Division Three that winter when McHugh first arrived. He knew some of the players and soon came to appreciate the passion for football in the county. 'It is a small county and it hadn't had much success but it has such a tradition. And it has great people,' he says fondly. They won promotion to Division Two in his first season and reached Division One a year later. He was also in charge of the under-21 team and they reached the Ulster final in 1995. They got to the All-Ireland under-21 final in 1996, but lost to a Darragh Ó Sé-led Kerry team.

McHugh's natural enthusiasm was further fuelled by the passion of the people for football. The success of the under-21 team raised expectations. McHugh introduced new, demanding fitness and coaching structures. He set targets and there were no limits. Cavan had not won an Ulster title since 1969. The people craved success and McHugh was determined to deliver. Cavan had been outclassed by Tyrone in 1995, but by 1997 they were ready and defeated Derry in the final by a single point.

Martin's future looked to be in inter-county management. But when he stepped away from Cavan he confined himself to advising colleges and clubs. Family and business took over and only his forays into the media, with a newspaper column and appearances as an expert analyst on television, diverted his attention. But his ambitions have remained.

'I would like at some stage if I keep my health, if my business is going well and my family is looked after to have a go at managing Donegal. It is still an ambition of mine,' he admits. 'There have been opportunities but the time has not been right.

'Actually,' he adds, 'there are two teams that could entice me back into management – Donegal and Dublin. The Dublin job is huge. They are the Manchester United of football. And I love the Dubs, their people have such a sense of humour. They love the craic but they are a very warm people and they love their football.'

Management, however, is extremely demanding. 'There are only a few periods in your life when you can dedicate yourself to managing an inter-county team. That is when you are young and your family is young or when your family is reared and you can devote most of your time to the job. Because it is a full-time job,' he insists.

'I know there is a lot of controversy every year about managers being paid. But it is becoming a major issue and it is something that the GAA must address. Managing an inter-county team takes up all your time. The demands from the media alone are enormous. You spend all your time dealing with so many different things that it is impossible to work an ordinary job at the same time.

'I believe the GAA should take the inter-county manager into the fold. He should be the full-time coach in the county, a director of football who also has responsibility for the county senior team. Not only would this facilitate the manager, it would be an investment by the GAA into football. You would be tapping into the expertise and knowledge of these people for the overall good of the game. If something is not done it will be very difficult to attract the right people to take on the county jobs because they just won't have the time. It is not just about coaching, it is managing individuals, managing their time, planning and organising a daily schedule. It encompasses so many things that it occupies every minute of your day. I enjoy management but it is very time-consuming.

'I hope that one day, I don't know when, I will be in a position to get back into management. I am ambitious and I hope it happens.'

The McHugh brothers are passionate about their club and both are concerned about the future of club football in Donegal and around the country. 'Inter-county football seems to be the focus of all the attention today,' says James, 'to the detriment of the club game. And that means that most of your footballers are suffering some form of neglect. Donegal is not unusual in this regard but during the best months of the year players can be waiting seven or eight weeks to play a game. That is no way to encourage them or to promote football.'

Martin strongly agrees: 'We can't kill the goose that lays the golden egg. We have to be very conscious of the need to facilitate club football in a meaningful way on the calendar. We cannot just stop playing club football because of county football. We will drive players away if they cannot get games and then where will we get the players for the county team?'

He proposes a summertime structure of club and county football on alternate weekends, divided between the provinces. For example, one weekend in Connacht and Ulster would be exclusively for club activity, while in Munster and Leinster inter-county games would be played. The next weekend the schedule would be reversed. 'And every player would play for his club. There would be no exclusivity. You can get injured as easily training as playing and every player loves to play matches anyway. I think this would not only benefit the club game but would also benefit the inter-county game.'

He also proposes that four teams rather than one from every county would qualify for the provincial Club Championship – the two beaten county semi-finalists would qualify for the first round, the two finalists for the second round with the champions guaranteed home advantage. 'Everything must be done to encourage the club game. It's like business; you can't look after 1 or 2 per cent of your customers and ignore the rest.'

He warms to the theme of promotion. 'Look at the amount of time and money that is spent on this Australian Rules thing [International Rules]. If there isn't a fight in it no one is interested. I totally disagree with it. There's nothing in it for us but we [the GAA] spend an awful lot promoting it when we should be promoting our own game. If we put the same energy into football as we do into the Australian thing, football would be much better off.'

They have few regrets. 'When I am with young lads today the one thing that I constantly stress is the importance of enjoying your football,' says James. 'It means nothing if you're not enjoying it. We were very lucky. We had good people looking after us at home, in the schools and in the club. And we had great times.'

The game still defines their days. Martin's eldest son Mark is a student in NUI Galway and made his senior Championship debut for Donegal this year. Martin and Patrice have two other children, Ryan and Rachel. James and Noreen have two children, Emma and Eoin, the latter another promising footballer.

James would love the opportunity to meet more often with those he played with and against. He bumped into his old Derry adversary Kieran McKeever after ten years when they both happened to visit Cassidy's pub in Dublin on the same evening. 'We don't meet except at wakes and funerals,' he says. 'Maybe that is something the authorities could look at.'

One can only imagine the stories that would be told.

THE O'CONNOR
BROTHERS

George O'Connor's eyes are ablaze in wonder. Those big, gnarled hands are gesticulating animatedly. The story he is telling is about hurling in Buenos Aires. He has just arrived back in Ireland after a ten-day trip to the Argentine capital where he conducted a coaching course for a few hundred schoolchildren. 'I was invited by a guy, a man named Mendoza, to visit his children's foundation while I was over there. He looks after disadvantaged kids. There was this one kid there from a deprived background. He hadn't talked for two years. He watched me with the hurley. He didn't understand a word of what I was saying. But when I gave him the hurley and ball he came alive. He took off, just belting the ball with the hurley into the back of a soccer goal with a big happy face on him. That's the power of hurling.'

If hurling ever needs a super-salesman then George O'Connor is the perfect fit. Now in his late forties, he looks as lean as he did when he wore the Wexford jersey for seventeen eventful years. His passion for the game is palpable; he admits he can talk all day about the properties of the game, the advantages it brings to young people, the possibilities for development. He works as a full-time coach now. 'I have the best job in the world,' he declares happily.

He will talk about his long career as both a footballer and hurler with his club St Martin's and with Wexford that ended shortly after George and his younger brother by three years, John, achieved their ultimate ambition of winning an All-Ireland senior hurling title on a memorable day in 1996. But every chapter leads to a diversion. His passion is evident; he cares for society and how the youth of today are being readied for the future. Any sport, but especially hurling, is the proper preparatory tool. Don't get him started on PlayStation and Nintendo or the excesses of the Celtic Tiger years. 'Bringing kids to their Holy Communion by helicopter,' he says in exasperation. 'Were we stone cracked? How stupid it was. We lost all sense of place.' More of that later.

John jokes: 'I don't know what you were talking to him about hurling for, sure he knows nothing about it.' And George doesn't disagree. 'John had far more skill than I had,' he says readily. 'I was an athlete or footballer playing hurling. I could run up and down the field all day. John had great technique.' It was an invaluable combination of attributes, however, that contributed hugely to one of the most emotional Championship experiences of the modern era when Wexford bridged a twenty-eight-year gap to bring the Liam McCarthy Cup back to the county.

It had been the dream of the O'Connor boys when growing up with their older brothers Arthur and James on the family farm in Piercestown to one day emulate the great heroes of their childhood like Tony Doran, Dan Quigley and Séamus 'Shanks' Whelan from their own club who had triumphed in 1968. But they had to experience more than a fair amount of despair and dejection – to the point where they believed the dream would not be realised – before salvation arrived.

Their father Paddy, who won a Leinster Junior Championship medal with Wexford in 1940 alongside a young Nicky Rackard, was a GAA enthusiast who was in possession of something priceless – a ten-year ticket for the All-Ireland football and hurling finals. Each year he would bring two boys to the hurling final and the other two to the football final. 'There wasn't much by the way of holidays then, so that was our big excursion,' George remembers. 'The day of the final always created great excitement. I remember the *Sunday Press* would lay out the teams on the back page in colour. It was the only colour you would see in a newspaper at the time and it made the men look huge. I remember Jim Treacy from Kilkenny, the great Cork players and of course Tony Doran. Going up to Croke Park on that day holding your father's hand you dreamed that one day you would be out there playing.'

Paddy had played a lot of sports in his youth 'all below the radar,' according to George, because of the ban on GAA members attending or playing 'foreign' games. Cricket and hockey had strong followings in that part of Wexford and Paddy played enthusiastically. So too would his sons. Athletics was also popular and the boys would apply the skills learned on the track and field to their hurling and football.

There were signs of early promise at the local St Martin's club. George won county Under-12 Hurling and Football Championships in 1971. 'I found football much easier,' he says. 'If you are athletic at all you automatically have the flexibility for football. There are a few basic skills – the catch, the kick and the hand pass. In those days there wasn't much running off the ball, so catching and kicking were the important skills. Hurling is so different; there are nearly 150 different skills in hurling. People said I was a better footballer and that was because I had the skills from athletics. And I brought some of the football skills to my hurling. I loved catching the ball in hurling. There's no better feeling than bringing the ball down through a forest of hurley sticks. The adrenalin courses through you. The only problem was that sometimes I would forget to bring the hurley up to protect my hand and I took a fair bit of punishment.'

As the 1970s progressed, hurling and football became more and more a way of life. Patricia O'Connor played golf and had a handicap of thirteen. A year or so after she stopped playing the game a friend asked why. 'I have a new handicap,' she replied. 'It's now five – a husband and four sons.' Her support for her sons was unconditional. She watched as fourteen-year-old George won a Wexford Minor Hurling Championship in 1974 with St Martin's, the club going on to win three successive minor titles.

In 1977 George played with Wexford in the Leinster minor hurling final when they lost to Kilkenny; the following year he played in the provincial minor football final when Wexford lost to a Dublin team that would produce future All-Ireland winners like Pat Canavan, Kieran Duff, Barney Rock and Dermot Deasy. In 1979 he enjoyed his first taste of success when Wexford won the Leinster Under-21 Championship, beating Kilkenny after a replay.

John's under-age career had taken a similar trajectory. He was a substitute on the minor hurling team that lost to Tipperary in the 1980 All-Ireland final, he was on the St Peter's College team that lost the Leinster Schools final in 1981 to Kilkenny CBS (who went on to All-Ireland success), and was part of the Wexford minor team beaten in the provincial final by Kilkenny (who went on to All-Ireland success).

George's senior hurling debut with Wexford was in the final of the old Oireachtas tournament in October 1979. The once-prestigious competition had lost much of its lustre, so when Wexford beat Offaly many of the contestants were underwhelmed. 'I remember proudly climbing the steps of the Hogan Stand to collect the cup and I know John Fleming was with me. But when I looked down on the pitch I saw that most of the lads didn't bother coming up. I couldn't understand that because it meant everything to me. I always wanted to be on those steps. I suppose I thought I would be there every year. Little did I know.

'I was so in awe in those days of just being on the Wexford team, just to be able to go back to your home place and say you played for Wexford. I was in awe of lads like Tony Doran, Mick Jacob, Colm Doran, the Butlers, Ned Buggy, Christy Kehoe; these were household names all over Ireland so for a nineteen-year-old to be asked to go out and play with them was something phenomenal. I thought it was only a matter of time before we would start winning things.'

George was also called into the Wexford football team and was a dual player until 1984. They enjoyed relative success, beating Meath in the Leinster Championship in 1981 and gaining promotion from Division Three in 1983. 'Although I enjoyed the football and we had a decent team, it was always playing second fiddle to hurling. We didn't have proper structures and the game was never going to be taken as seriously as hurling.'

His performances for Wexford in the 1981 Leinster Championship – they lost by two points to Kilkenny in the provincial final – earned George his first All Star award. The future looked rosy. 'I would suggest we were naïve not to realise that Offaly were about to make the breakthrough; we thought it would always be Kilkenny or Wexford and that every few years we would get to a final. We're an easygoing people in Wexford; we have the sun and strawberries and it took us a while to accept what was happening, that there was a change in Leinster.'

John, meanwhile, was mastering his craft in Cork as a student in UCC. There he came under the influence of Fr (later Canon) Michael O'Brien and won three consecutive Fitzgibbon Cup medals between 1983 and 1985 alongside players like Nicky English (Tipperary), Richard Browne (Cork), Seán O'Gorman (Cork) and Pat Hartnett (Cork). 'It was a great experience for me because I got up close and personal with the Cork people. You could see the swagger, why they were so successful. They don't suffer from a lack of confidence down there and I learned a lot,' he says. The lessons would prove valuable later in his hurling career.

He laughs when you mention his senior hurling debut for Wexford. It was in a tournament organised to celebrate the centenary year of the GAA in 1984, structured on an open draw basis. Wexford were given an away game against Roscommon. They had just lost a National League final and some of the players, including George, were not required for what was regarded as a routine trip. 'Wexford caught in a spider's web' is how John recalls one newspaper headline that reported one of the biggest upsets in hurling history. 'I think John was one of the few lads who got to bed the night before and he was one of the first taken off,' laughs George.

They did reach the Leinster final in 1984, where they lost to Offaly. They were back in the final again in 1988 and lost to Kilkenny. George explains: 'There were days when we were really downhearted; they were horrible days. You couldn't speak for a week. The hurt when you woke up in the morning in the week after losing a big game was terrible. In the early years just playing for Wexford was enough. But the longer you play the more you strive for. You realise your career is moving on. Every year we felt we had a chance. That kept us going. When Christy Kehoe was our manager we were so close, always at the top and competing well.' Wexford lost the National League finals of 1990 to Kilkenny and 1991 to Offaly. They were taking punishment and coming back for more year after year. Then came 1993.

Wexford reached another National League final. On 9 May in Semple Stadium they played Cork, a star-studded team that had lost the previous year's All-Ireland final to Kilkenny. A crowd of 21,900 were well entertained as the game entered the final two minutes and Wexford trailed by just one point. Larry Murphy snatched the equaliser with a splendidly taken point from the left-hand touchline. Wexford won the puck-out and Martin Storey got possession and was fouled. John O'Connor stood over the ball. 'I was directly behind him,' George remembers. 'His trajectory was spot on. But as the ball lost a bit of speed, a crosswind took it wide.'

In the replay, which also ended in a draw after extra time, John recalls missing a '70', now a 65-metre free. Cork emerged as victors in the second replay. It was a heartbreaking defeat for Wexford, one of the most difficult to stomach. It had an effect on John, though it wasn't long-lasting. 'I did lose a bit of confidence in my free-taking for the next few years because of those misses,' he says. 'But I don't carry around scars. Those things don't bother me too much. You can't beat club hurling to build your confidence back up and by 1996 I was taking the frees again.'

There was more pain ahead in 1993. Wexford met Kilkenny again in the Leinster final. It was a rousing game in which the Wexford players produced one of their greatest efforts of the period. They were a point up as the game entered its final moments, but Kilkenny's Éamon Morrissey scored an equalising point with virtually the last action of the afternoon. 'Psychologically we had no chance the second day,' John says.

When they lost the 1994 Leinster final to Offaly George began to ponder his future. 'I was thirty-four. I had lost something like thirteen finals. I think when Éamon [Morrissey] scored that point in 1993 that I doubted we would ever get a break. We had been so close so often only to see victory snatched away. I was hoping and praying that day for the referee to blow his whistle. I thought it couldn't happen to us again. It was the final straw for me and I started questioning myself. I suppose I had decided that I wasn't going back for more. It was time to stop.

'I got so much encouragement at the time from the people around me, my family and friends. My dentist, Adrian Rogers, had a lot of work to do with my teeth at the time and he told me I should give it at least another year. He wasn't a big GAA man but he knew what it meant to me and gave me the push I needed. My family were also quietly encouraging me. And then Liam Griffin was appointed as the team manager. We spoke. I told him about my doubts. He said I couldn't retire. I had to give him a chance and the decision was taken to give it one more go at least.'

O'Connor had always admired Griffin, a cousin, and wondered how he could be enticed into the Wexford setup. His eventual arrival would have a massive influence, though there were tough times initially when Griffin sought to impose his authority on the squad and had to take unpopular action that would affect everyone – including the O'Connor brothers.

'He dropped John and me,' George says, mockingly incredulous to this day at the apparent audacity of the man whose appointment he had lauded. 'We had tested him and he didn't back off. He had told us not to play a club game. We played anyway and he dropped us. He took the captaincy off Liam Dunne for the same reason. Any time a new manager comes in he will be put to the sword and if he survives then he is right forever. We didn't get away with things that we had done with other managers. Griffin could hear the grass grow. He knew everything that was going on. He laid down his marker and we realised how serious he was and we bought into it eventually.'

'Griffin was ahead of his time,' John agrees. 'He was just so organised. His management embraced everything. We had some good managers before him. Christy Kehoe was brilliant in terms of skills and fitness. But Griffin brought something new to it. He worked on the psychology of it all, he brought in experts and he changed everything.'

George adds: 'He [Griffin] used to get up at 6.00 in the morning to plan the evening's training session. He had thirteen or fourteen people in the backroom team. He was so professional and we didn't realise it. It was done with a minimum budget. If we did something special in training we got our rewards, a pair of boots or a T-shirt. And we appreciated them and we knew we had earned it. People said at the time that there had been better teams than ours in the 1960s and 1970s. But they were missing the point. There might have been better individuals but there wasn't a better team. We were a better team. This was a great team, guys who knew exactly what they were doing, who were tactically very aware, were very fit. Griffin said he could make us the best blockers, the best hookers, the fittest team; they were the attributes he said no one would match and he did it. We were properly conditioned, but he didn't take away our ability to make decisions for ourselves. We could make snap decisions on the field, we could adjust.'

It took Griffin the entire year of 1995 to create the environment he wanted. Results were poor and he had his critics, but the manager had a plan and he was sticking to it. When Wexford beat Kilkenny in the first round of the Leinster Championship by 1–14 to 0–14 on 2 June 1996, the first signs of what was happening on the training pitch were becoming apparent. It was the first victory in the Championship over Kilkenny since 1988 and a county starved of success began to believe that there was potential in this team. The next victory over Dublin was marred slightly by a hand injury sustained by George which meant he was unable to start in the provincial final against Offaly.

John made his first start of that Championship in the Leinster final at left full back alongside Colm Kehoe and Ger Cushe. Wexford and Offaly had played six times in the Championship in their previous sixteen seasons and Offaly had won them all. Offaly had been All-Ireland champions just two years previously and the team was laced with players of great talent. They led by 1–5 to 0–4 after less than twenty minutes. The Wexford players were clearly nervous. They needed a tonic. It came in the form of a penalty which goalkeeper Damien Fitzhenry converted. What followed was a pulsating contest that tested not just the skill but the character of the Wexford team. They showed just how much progress they had made by taking control and scoring a total of two goals and twenty-three points to win by eight points. It was a defining victory.

George was on the bench for the All-Ireland semi-final against Galway but came on after twenty-eight minutes as a replacement for John, who had suffered a head injury. It was a typical semi-final, dour but laced with some good scores from Tom Dempsey and Rory McCarthy. Wexford won by

2–13 to 3–7. They had qualified for the county's first All-Ireland senior final since 1977. The dream was alive.

John was fit for the final against Limerick. George thought he might not start. But when Seán Flood was ruled out through injury George was selected at midfield alongside Adrian Fenlon. The game was a tough, tight affair. Griffin had talked a great deal about the character of his team. That was tested when Éamon Scallan was sent off before half time. 'That was when Griffin's preparations shone through. He had talked about the importance of decision-making on the field, the responsibility of the players,' says George. 'We had to think for ourselves when Éamon went off. We had to react.' They responded positively. Wexford 1–13, Limerick 0–14. Cue wild celebrations.

'The Oxford English Dictionary doesn't have the word to describe what it meant for John and me, for the club, for the county and all the people,' says George. 'I had been at it for seventeen years and won nothing since the Oireachtas final of 1979. There was a sense of peace more than exhilaration. There was a strange sense of calmness. How important was winning? It was great, like getting absolution when in confession. It was fulfilment, the realisation of the dream that took so long. Then when it did happen life moves on. I wanted to go home on the Tuesday to milk the cows. I didn't realise what was happening outside the dressing-room, the immediate squad. It took some time for us to understand that the victory meant so much to the people of Wexford.

I was brought along on a cloud of euphoria. I think we were all struck by the elation of the people, the sense of relief.'

John admits that, at the ages of thirty-three and thirty-six at the time, both he and George felt that they would never win an All-Ireland. Like George, once the title had been won he wanted to move on. 'It was a moment in time. It happened and I will never forget it but I don't want to dwell on it. I don't even like to hear these days about the lads from 1996. I want us to move on in the county, to be talking about the lads of today. A lot of people are working very hard and we need that at under-age level. We need good minor teams every year. We need to get back to winning big games.'

George left his helmet and hurleys in the dressing-room in Croke Park that evening. He played one more club game for St Martin's. John continued playing for a few more years and won a County Championship with the club in 1999, lining out at full forward. Their love of the game never waned. Their children are now playing and John admits it is harder watching them than it was playing.

George worked for many years on the family farm but in recent years has taken on a full-time coaching role in Wexford. His work takes him all over Leinster and beyond, spreading the gospel. His enthusiasm is infectious. He revels in the challenge of visiting schools where hurling is not played and introducing young kids to the sport. He marvels at the reach of the GAA. 'Anywhere you go in Ireland, almost anywhere in the world you will find the GAA. There is always a connection,' he says. His passion for the GAA emerges in a torrent of conversation.

The GAA has enjoyed enormous success, he acknowledges, but he warns against complacency. 'Maybe it is time to re-evaluate what we are all about, what the GAA is doing for young people, the foundation it is giving them going forward in their lives, how important it is that we properly coach the people who are looking after the kids; that we don't willy-nilly send out any person to do the job – they have to be sweet, they have to be kind, they have to be facilitators and they have to be there for the children. Egos and self-interest have to be left at the door.'

Though he enjoyed success himself as a young boy, he is unhappy about the early introduction of competition and the negative effect it can have. 'At ages six to ten the kids enjoy the games immensely, the parents enjoy the games immensely. You meet parents from other clubs, it is social and the spirit is good. Then we introduce under-12 competition and a whole new world opens up. The kids aren't ready for it and the parents aren't ready for it. It is all about winning. Should we be doing that? I don't think so. Once you put a jumper on the ground to mark a boundary there is competition anyway, there is stimulation and attention and that is how it should be. That's the way kids operate. They want competition but not the way we parachute it down on top of them. It affects their skills, their wellbeing and their family. If a mother hears abuse being hurled at her son – we call it negative aggression – she won't want that.

'We need to look after our young people. As a society we lost our way. The Celtic Tiger years, look what it did to us. We had helicopters flying our children to their first Holy Communion. Were we cracked? God help us. How stupid it was. Helicopters and limousines. Where were we going? We needed to get a grip. We lost all sense of place.'

He is not a fan of PlayStation, Nintendo and the modern playthings that occupy so much of young people's time today. 'Playing those games is easy. They don't require organisation. It's just pressing buttons. That's all you have to do to get stimulation. But you won't see a computer make a hurler out of a young lad. The only way to make a footballer or hurler is to get out on the park. And don't text me to say we are going to meet somewhere. Ring me up and say hello. Modern technology is fantastic in its own right. But you can't beat the personal touch, the man-to-man chat, the cup of tea at the end of a training session. We are going too far – it's like the man who can't go out and have a pint in the country. It has nothing to do with drinking and driving. He wants to have his one or two pints and a bit of social interaction and are they going to abolish this altogether? Are we living by extremes?' he asks.

He is not just concerned about the kids. While the elite at inter-county level are well catered for, George wonders if enough is being done for those who wish to play the game on a recreational basis. 'We have people who play for the spoils at the very top and of course that is what everyone strives for. But not everybody gets there. What about the guy who does a hard day's work and wants to play a game in the evening. Is there anything for him nowadays?'

He wants to see an expansion in social hurling so that players of every age and every level of ability have the opportunity to play the game. George recalls some lively midweek evenings around Piercestown and neighbouring towns and villages. 'The rivalry locally was fierce. Junior 'B' hurling was a great example. You had the guy who was only half trained and you had the guy with the beer belly. Then you had the guy playing in goal who was smoking a fag and he'd be coughing and snorting. The sidelines used to be packed. Then a row would break out and there'd be a bit of a shemozzle. They weren't fit enough to fight. The ball would drop in around the goal and some fella would get a stick at it and the ball would end up in the back of the net. And he would end up in the pub that night and he would have the bragging rights. And it was great. We need more of that.

'I remember when it was first suggested we play hurling on the quays in Wexford and we were told it couldn't be done. We said why not; let's have a go at it. Some people said we would lose the ball into the sea or on the road. We needed insurance so we got it. We caged it up and let them off and it's great fun with 400 young people playing there during the summer. Hurling is there to be enjoyed and played. We need to develop our games so that everyone at every age can enjoy them even if they cannot aspire to playing in Croke Park on the first Sunday in September. We need to bring back the magic.

'I am not arguing against the elite; I admire the guys who set the standards at the highest level. They are training to professional levels. Their dedication is amazing. There is no comparison between the game of the 1970s and the 1980s and the game now. If you don't get your first touch now you're gone. And the fitness levels are gone out to the stratosphere. Everything is different, nutrition is better, structures are better and training is much more professional. There are disadvantages because of the pressure on managers and County Boards, especially from a financial point of view. We must keep a balance. It is index linked. It is the dream to play for the county, to play in an All-Ireland. But not everyone will achieve that so they have to be catered for. We need to give the junior 'B' player every opportunity to play the game.'

At the highest level of the game he recognises the enormous demands that burden the modern inter-county hurler and footballer. Some counties are better than others in looking after these players and the GAA need to constantly monitor what is happening. But he warns: 'For the GAA to survive we must hold on to our amateur status. If we went professional we would see the demise of the GAA because it would create false hopes and people would play the game for all the wrong reasons. We play because we want to enjoy the games and want to be part of the community. We would erode one by one all the values we have [by going professional]. Look at rugby. You have the provinces that are successful, but no one is talking about local clubs or their national League. Rugby can survive because it has an international outlet. We do not have that. So we must look after the original philosophy of the GAA which is to cultivate the games and create the environment in which people play them for enjoyment. It cannot be about becoming wealthy or anything like that.'

The O'Connor brothers look to the future. They both yearn for the time when Wexford will have new heroes to replace those of 1996. The longer the county waits the harder it is to make the breakthrough. But they look at the work being done at under-age level in the county and they are re-assured. 'I would love to see Waterford and Limerick coming through to win an All-Ireland as well,' says John. 'The game needs those counties and it needs Wexford. The GAA must be careful to ensure these counties stay competitive.'

He believes the game has changed dramatically from their own playing days. 'Every facet has changed. It is all about the ball now. The skills of the players have improved and the speed of the game has changed. The players are also mentally tougher. When you look at videos of the 1970s and 1980s the games look pedestrian compared to today. This Kilkenny team has brought the game to another level. Their fitness and skill is amazing; they have developed everything to a very high standard – hooking, blocking, aerial catches. The only possible weakness that might creep in is hunger. It is hard to keep going at that level for so long. But there is no sign of that hunger disappearing yet,' he adds.

They enjoy reminiscing because they had good days. There was even something to be enjoyed about the bad ones. But they don't want to dwell on the past. There is too much to look forward to.

THE Ó SÉ BROTHERS

16 February 2010: In the coffee bar of the Imperial Hotel, on Tralee's Denny Street, two legends of Gaelic football meet in mid morning. It has become a ritual in recent years. Darragh Ó Sé represents the current generation for another day at least. Mikey Sheehy represents the Golden Years, 1975 to 1986. They talk football, rugby, soccer, business and politics. And they laugh and joke. Sometimes serious; very often not so serious. On different days some others will drop in. Eoin 'Bomber' Liston is a regular. Seán Walsh too. In the old days they used to meet in Harty's with men like John Dowling. Harty's is gone now, but the tradition is maintained, the baton handed on.

Darragh is enjoying this morning. Tomorrow will be very different. He will be the focus of attention, the talk of the town, the county and even the country. Most people are still unaware of his intentions. On Radio na Gaeltachta the following morning Darragh will confirm to his old friend and team-mate Dara Ó Cinnéide that he has decided to end his inter-county career. The oldest of the three Ó Sé brothers is leaving Kerry's destiny in the hands of his younger brothers, Tomás and Marc, and a host of friends made over the years.

After sixteen years in the Kerry colours during which he has won six All-Ireland Championships and earned a place in football's hall of fame, Darragh still looks fit and healthy. But he has known for a while now that the body is rebelling against the exacting toll of preparing for and playing football at the top level. In recent years he has delayed and delayed his return to the punishing schedule. It gets harder every March when he is supposed to make his return to the training ground. All winter he has mulled over his decision, spoken at length to Amy, his wife, and his family. The time has come.

'I'm lucky, I have had a great career and I can have no complaints,' he says simply. 'The timing was perfect. I came along at the right time to play with and against some of the greatest players ever to play the game – the lads I played with like Maurice Fitzgerald, Séamus Moynihan, Colm Cooper, Michael McCarthy; lads I played against like Pádraic Joyce, Ciarán Whelan, Peter Canavan, Kieran McGeeney. To test yourself out against players of that ability is a huge privilege; it was just a privilege to play for Kerry and I was lucky because I had longevity.'

Across the town, in the local CBS, Marc Ó Sé is also pondering the future without his older brother in the Kerry team. 'It is going to be a massive change for Tomás and myself,' he says a little ruefully. 'He has been such a massive presence in the team. He was such a major figure in the dressing-room and on the field obviously, but he was also one of the great characters. He was mighty craic. In the last few years I travelled to training with him every evening, the two of us and Paul Galvin. The craic started the minute you sat into the car and didn't end. There were evenings when you might not have felt like training, but the thought of the fun we would have would keep you going. We're going to miss him in a lot of ways. But we'll just have to get on with it.'

Tomás absorbed the news at his home on the outskirts of Cork. 'He's the best midfielder I've seen and I'm not just saying it because he is my brother. He will be a huge loss for his leadership alone. Yeah, we'll miss him around the place.'

* * *

Marc Ó Sé was just five years old, but his memories of the arrival of the open-top bus in his home place of Árd an Bhóthair in the west Kerry Gaeltacht in September 1985 are vivid. His uncle Páidí was Kerry's captain that year and stood at the front with the Sam Maguire Cup raised aloft. Little Marc was hoisted from the crowd to stand alongside his uncle and the other great heroes of the golden years. His dreams of one day bringing such joy back to his home place were already forming.

They were a privileged group, the youngsters of the Dingle peninsula. Páidí entrusted care of the famous trophy to the school teachers Maureen Geaney and Seán Keane at

Scoil Caitlín Naofa, Cillmhicadomhnaigh. Each evening as classes ended a pupil would be given the trophy to take home for the evening. 'That was some thrill,' says Marc, a sense of wonder still apparent in his voice. 'People in Kerry were so used to the Sam Maguire coming back at that time that there wasn't much demand for it. Lucky for us.'

Micheál Ó Sé, Páidí's older brother, was a good club footballer who played at junior level with Kerry and shared the family passion for the game. He and his wife Joan loved to see their four sons, Fergal, Darragh, Tomás and Marc out in the garden kicking football with friends and neighbours. 'In west Kerry in those days,' explains Darragh, 'there was no soccer or rugby or any other sport. It was all football. It was boom time for us growing up because Kerry was winning All-Irelands nearly every year and we had Páidí on the team.'

As ambitious as the youngsters might have been, they could not in their more fanciful dreams have scripted the events of the next quarter of a century. But when Kerry re-emerged in the late 1990s as All-Ireland contenders once again, the Ó Sé name would feature more prominently than ever. The statistics are staggering: Darragh won the first of his six All-Ireland titles in 1997; Tomás joined him on the victorious team of 2000; from 2002 to 2009 Darragh, Tomás and Marc would be team-mates in eight consecutive Championships, appear in six All-Ireland finals together (Darragh missed the 2004 final through injury) and would share All-Ireland senior titles in 2004, 2006, 2007 and 2009.

They created a significant bit of history in 2007 when the three brothers from Árd an Bhóthair were named together on the All Stars selection, Marc at right full back, Tomás at right half back and Darragh in midfield. 'You would have to say that for much of our lives we were ignorant of other things happening around us,' says Marc. 'Everything else took second place to football from a very early age. We just loved doing it.'

Encouragement was all around them, though Micheál and Joan insisted that the boys spent sufficient time with their schoolbooks to ensure a solid education. As important as football might be, it would not provide the boys with a living. But evenings always closed with the sound of a thump of a football and weekends were spent training and playing with the club where Liam Ó Rócháin and later the well-known broadcaster and former All-Ireland winner Micheál Ó Sé provided the structures, coaching and advice that would inspire future success. 'Those men provided so much for us. I have great respect for them and everything they did for us' is Marc's tribute.

'When we were growing up we had the Golden Years and our heroes were Páidí and the great players on that Kerry team of the 1970s and 1980s. But Micheál was so enthusiastic about football and about Kerry, and he would tell us great stories about the achievements of men like Mick O'Connell and Mick O'Dwyer, Tom Long and so many others. It gave us a sense of the history and tradition of Kerry football, an understanding of what the game meant to the people in the county.'

Micheál, their father, was not a particularly demonstrative man. He didn't push the boys. 'He was delighted that we played football,' says Darragh, 'but if we decided we didn't want to play he was okay with that. He was always there with a quiet word of encouragement. He wouldn't be shouting it out.' Fergal and Darragh were the oldest, so they got to go to Croke Park to see Uncle Páidí and Kerry. When the boys began to play for Kerry Micheál was always there ready to give advice when needed. Marc attended games with him when Darragh and Tomás were playing for Kerry. 'He was very quiet at games, you knew he was nervous. He wanted the lads to do well not for his sake but for their sake and for Kerry.' One of his proudest days was when An Gaeltacht won the Kerry Championship for the first time in 2001 when the three boys played on the team coached by their oldest brother Fergal.

On 12 May 2002 Micheál Ó Sé travelled to Limerick to watch Darragh, Tomás and Marc play Championship football together for the first time with Kerry. They beat Limerick by 0–14 to 1–7. Just over a month later, on 16 June, he was in Fitzgerald Stadium in Killarney as the three lads played in the Munster final against Cork. The match ended in a draw, 0–8 each. The replay was fixed for the following weekend. Micheál died suddenly on the Tuesday. 'It is sad that he wasn't around for all of the time we played with Kerry,' says Darragh quietly. 'But at least he did see us play for Kerry together.' The Munster replay went ahead the weekend after Micheál was laid to rest. 'We had to get on with it,' says Marc. 'He was a massive influence on us and it was a terrible loss.'

He wouldn't have displayed it publicly, but Micheál Ó Sé would have been intensely proud.

* * *

Darragh was just out of minor ranks when Denis 'Ogie' Moran decided he was ready to play senior football for Kerry. It was 1993 and Kerry's fortunes were low. They had won just one of the last seven Munster Championships. They had been beaten by Clare in the 1992 Munster final. The citizens were getting restless. This represented a famine for Kerry football, an unprecedented period of disappointment. According to Darragh there was no mystery about their predicament. 'We didn't have a strong team at the time. There were some established players, but there were also a lot of young players coming through, a lot of chopping and changing was going on and we couldn't get a settled team. We just didn't have the players to be honest.'

There were welcome distractions. Uncle Páidí had taken over as coach to the Kerry under-21 team in 1993 and by 1995 had assembled a talented bunch. Diarmuid Murphy, Barry O'Shea, Killian Burns, Mike and Liam Hassett, Darragh, John Crowley and Dara Ó Cinnéide were among the youngsters being groomed for the next level. They were learning well and won the All-Ireland title in 1995, the majority of them being eligible for the following season when they retained the Championship. By then Páidí had been elevated to the post of Kerry senior coach.

He had the choice of some experienced campaigners like Séamus Moynihan, Maurice Fitzgerald, Liam Flaherty, Éamon Breen, Stephen Stack and Seán Burke with whom he could mix the pick of the youngsters from the under-21 team. They targeted a Munster title. They won it. And then, as Páidí freely admitted in his biography, they celebrated like madmen. They went into the All-Ireland semi-final against Mayo with Cork still on their minds and were ambushed. More lessons learned.

Marc remembers that day, 11 August 1996, with some fondness, however. It was his first time ever in Croke Park. It was a maiden journey for Tomás too. He was playing for the Kerry minor team in the traditional curtain-raiser. At least the Ó Sé family had one victory to celebrate, though the minors later lost to Laois in the final. It was an appetiser for the Ó Sés for the feast that would follow over the following fourteen years. The next course was served with Darragh winning the first of his All-Ireland Championships in 1997, when Kerry beat Mayo in the final. He remembers: 'Expectations weren't high at the start of that year. There was a new following in Kerry of people who barely remembered the last time the county had won an All-Ireland. We didn't realise how much it meant to the people until we had won it. I remember coming off the field that day and meeting Jack O'Shea and he was happier than I was. He had eight All-Irelands of his own, but he had waited a long time to enjoy a Kerry win as a supporter. That was special.'

He was becoming fully aware of the true meaning of being a Kerry footballer. 'Growing up you know what the county jersey means. It is very special here in Kerry. And when you start wearing that jersey there is always pressure to win. Even when you do win there is pressure. There have been All-Irelands that we have won where we have been criticised here for not playing good football. You try to take no notice of it; it is part and parcel of playing for Kerry. At times you get fed up with it, but ultimately it is vitally important that there is so much interest in football in Kerry. I know in my heart and soul that the interest will never wane and that the pressure will always be there to do well and that is what drives you on. I think that is one of the reasons why we do not lose players. When you walk up the street on any day of the week there is always someone who wants to talk football. Maybe it's the same in other counties, but it's something special here.'

Tomás joined Darragh in the senior squad during the winter of 1997. He recovered from an ankle injury early in 1998 in time to convince Páidí and the selectors that he was ready for promotion. For the opening round of the Munster Championship Tomás was selected at right full back. He was marking Aidan Dorgan of Cork. It was not his greatest experience. By half time he was withdrawn and would spend the rest of that summer on the bench. 'It wasn't the easiest start. I wasn't a natural corner back. I never played in the position again so that tells its own story,' he says with a smile. Some supporters had questioned his right to be selected. Tomás realised he would have to work hard to regain his place and prove it was rightfully his and not the gift of his uncle. A year later he took possession of the number five jersey. He never looked back. No one has questioned his right since.

Marc was chosen for the Kerry minors in 1998 and the three brothers were togged out for the first time together on 30 August that year for the All-Ireland semi-finals. Both the minor and senior teams lost, but the pattern for their adult lives had been set. Their lifestyles became absolutely hectic. The club, An Gaeltacht, decided to field a team in the Kerry Senior Championship, breaking from West Kerry. That added to the demands. Marc decided to take a break from football to concentrate on his studies in 1999.

By summer 2000 Tomás was proving to be just as valuable to the Kerry setup as his older brother. They retained the Munster title with comparative ease but then faced severe tests in the All-Ireland series. An emerging Armagh proved a real threat and only an injury-time pointed free from Maurice Fitzgerald earned Kerry a semi-final replay. The second game went to extra time. Oisín McConville kicked

1–9 for Armagh, Mike Frank Russell scored 2–3 for Kerry. The Kingdom won by 2–15 to 1–15 and qualified to meet Galway in the final. That ended in a draw as well, 0–14 each. The replay was football for the purist, fast and free flowing. Kerry won by 0–17 to 1–10. The medal collection was only beginning.

'I suppose every player will say his first All-Ireland is the most memorable,' says Tomás, 'but for me 2000 was special because of the quality of the football played in the semi-final against Armagh and especially in the drawn and replayed finals against Galway. You had some outstanding footballers on the field in the final – on our side you had Séamus Moynihan, Darragh, Maurice Fitzgerald and Mike Frank [Russell]; Galway had Pádraic Joyce, Michael Donnellan and the Meehans. Those were two good footballing teams.'

By the end of 2000, having watched Darragh and Tomás win their first All-Ireland together, Marc was taking his own tentative steps back into the game with the Kerry under-21s. He had trials with the seniors, flirted on the edges of the squad in 2001 and by the time the National League started in 2002 a third Ó Sé was playing for Kerry.

The eldest brother, Fergal, had played minor and under-21 football for Kerry. He was called for senior trials and enjoyed a few outings in the National League in 1997 but never got the break necessary. That had some benefit for An Gaeltacht. Fergal began coaching the senior team with Séamus MacGearailt. They captured their first county title in

2001 and a second in 2003. The Ó Sés' mother, Joan, spent many Sunday afternoons walking the roads around Árd an Bhóthair, avoiding radio and television, stopping in the local church to light a candle. She doesn't watch her boys playing. She just wants to know they get home safely.

The club scene demanded a lot from the boys. An Gaeltacht won the Kerry Intermediate Championship in 1998. They had a bunch of extremely talented players – the Ó Sés, the MacGearailts and Dara Ó Cinnéide among them. The difficult decision to field a team in the Kerry Senior Championship in 1999 caused controversy and dissent. Some GAA folk in the Gaeltacht were unhappy that an amalgamated team represented the region rather than a number of individual clubs. But they went ahead. The first year was tough. 'We had a lot of injuries,' recalls Darragh, 'and East Kerry gave us a hosing. Séamus Moynihan was outstanding and Johnny Crowley was at his peak.'

A year later they reached the county final, where they were beaten by Dr Crokes of Killarney, a team which contained the combined talents of Pat O'Shea, Connie Murphy, Noel O'Leary and a young kid named Colm Cooper. In their third year playing Senior Championship football An Gaeltacht justified the decision to field their own senior team when they won the Kerry title. 'We beat Austin Stacks in the final and that meant so much because Stacks was regarded as one of the best clubs in the county,' Darragh explains.

'If I have one regret it is that we partied too much after

winning the final. It was a massive occasion for the club, for our families and neighbours, but we lost focus. Instead of looking at the bigger picture, like the bigger clubs would have done, we got carried away. The likes of Stacks or Nemo would immediately have looked at how they were going to take the next step. They would have started preparing immediately for the Munster Club Championship. By the time we started to get ready for it we were too late.' Nemo Rangers beat them in the Munster final and went on to win the All-Ireland club title in March 2002. 'I felt we had our best team in 2001 and if we were to win the All-Ireland that was the season to do it.'

They did reach the All-Ireland club final in 2004, where they lost to Caltra from Galway. Tomás describes that loss as the biggest disappointment of his career so far. 'It is very difficult for a club to win a Kerry Championship and we were probably good enough to win an All-Ireland at that time. It is so hard for a small, rural club to compete at that level. You can only expect to play at that level for a few years and you have got to take your chances. We are back at intermediate level now. That is the lot of small clubs; you don't have the supply of talent that the bigger towns will have.'

Back on the inter-county front, All-Ireland finals were also proving to be frustrating. In 2002 they re-grouped after losing the Munster semi-final to Cork a few days after the Ó Sés had buried their father. In a five-match sequence they trounced Wicklow, Fermanagh, Kildare, Galway and then Cork (by fifteen points) in the All-Ireland semi-final. 'We played some really attractive football, with pace and intensity, and we were strong favourites going into the final. But Armagh were waiting for us. They ground us down,' Darragh remembers.

'We let ourselves down in the second half,' says Marc.

It was a defeat from which they took time to recover. There was criticism of the team, questions about their worth. A year later they lost to Tyrone in the All-Ireland semi-final. Páidí's tenure as manager was coming to an end. 'It was a bad year on the field made worse by the fact that Páidí lost the position of manager,' explains Marc. 'It was very hard on the three of us when he went. But we had to adjust.'

Páidí ended up as Westmeath manager and guided them to a rare Leinster title. Back in Kerry his three nephews were collecting another Munster title, though they needed a replay to beat Limerick. Darragh would suffer an ankle injury in the All-Ireland semi-final that would force him to watch the final from the stands, but Kerry's title chase would surely have been much more difficult but for his performance against Limerick in the drawn Munster final, one of the most memorable of his career. He watched with delight as Tomás and Marc helped Kerry to the county's thirty-third All-Ireland success when they comfortably accounted for Mayo. Tomás' form throughout 2004 earned him the GAA's Footballer of the Year award.

The three played together in the next five finals, losing to

Tyrone in 2005 and 2008, beating Mayo in 2006 and Cork in 2007 and 2009. 'It was said that we couldn't handle the Ulster teams, Armagh and Tyrone especially, but I don't think there was any jinx,' insists Darragh. 'We were well beaten in a couple of games, but there were days when we had our chances and didn't take them. That's what happens in sport. Some day Kerry will beat Tyrone. In the same way Cork will beat Kerry in Croke Park one day. You hear all this talk about bad blood between Kerry and the Tyrone and Armagh lads. There wasn't any. Those teams were fabulous for football. The interest levels they created were huge and they brought great colour to the Championship. I enjoyed playing against them and I have become great friends with lads like Peter Canavan and Kieran McGeeney.'

Marc reckons the 2009 triumph was 'a massive highlight'. He continues: 'I think we would all say that our first final was the most memorable simply because it was the first. But 2009 was special. We had come from a very low point during the season. We hadn't been playing well during June and July. We were well beaten in the Munster final by Cork and we were being written off everywhere. There were times when it seemed that we were on the way out and we just managed to hold on. To turn it around like we did was some achievement.'

Darragh points to the return of Michael McCarthy to the team as a critical factor in the 2009 success. 'Michael was a quiet character, you wouldn't hear much from him, but he was one of the best footballers we had. Just look at what he did in 2009. He came back from two years out of football to play at that level. Very few players would have the ability to come back and do that and to have such a major role in winning an All-Ireland. Just look at the three big games we had in that Championship – Dublin, Meath and Cork in the final – he was one of our top three players in each one of them. It was an amazing thing to do, but he was one of the most natural footballers you could come across. He could be a tight-marking corner back, a centre half back, a midfielder. You could play him anywhere.'

Recalling their run through the qualifier series of games, Tomás is blunt: 'We were very fortunate to survive and if fellas were being honest they would admit that. We could have lost to Longford and we should have lost to Sligo. The funny thing was that we knew at training that we weren't far off the mark, that we were close to hitting our form. We just had to survive long enough to find it.' Tomás himself was the centre of attention briefly when he and Colm Cooper were dropped for disciplinary reasons. 'There was a lot of stuff being said that we were arguing and all that; not true. We dealt with everything quietly and in our own way. There was never much of a problem, just the normal run of things that will happen when you have a large group of individuals together.

'We felt we were getting things right by the time we beat Antrim. But we didn't expect what happened against Dublin [when Kerry enjoyed as seventeen-point victory]. We did play well and got out of the blocks quickly. But Dublin had a big off-day. After what had happened during June and July we were just grateful that we had got through it.'

Tomás suspected on the night of the All-Ireland victory that Darragh might not return for another year. The rumour mill suggested Tomás himself might take a break. But when the squad convened on Portugal's Algarve in April for some warm-weather training the familiar figure had returned. The Ó Sé numbers might be smaller, but there will be additions to this story.

* * *

Darragh Ó Sé reflects on the many changes he has seen since he first pulled on the Kerry jersey way back when the county was struggling to regain its status as a football paradise. Some of those changes are good, some are not so good. 'I always regarded it as a privilege to play for Kerry. I loved winning. And losing from time to time made you appreciate the good days even more. It was tough at times but there was a great social side to it all – team holidays, All Star tours where you would meet with other players from other counties. You would often hear things about me not getting on with the Cork lads and we would have a good laugh about it when we would meet on tour.

'Back in the mid-1990s the media coverage wasn't as big. The increase in coverage was obviously good for the game but it also had a downside. It became very tabloidy and intrusive. They forgot this was still an amateur game. You see people getting in the papers for all the wrong reasons.

'Inter-county football has become a very serious business. The good old days of playing a game and going for a few pints afterwards are nearly gone; they are certainly curtailed. I'm glad I experienced that side of it; meeting lads from the other counties and getting to know them. That is gone to some extent. You don't socialise with other players as much any more and I think that is a poor reflection on us. That should be encouraged in some way. I know and understand the need for discipline and that the demands are greater now. I don't even have the answers as to how you make it work both ways, but it is sad to see it going. I was brought up to play the game hard and fair. You took knocks and you gave them and at the end of the game you shook hands. I think it's a pity that lads don't mix now. I have made great friends with lads from other counties that I still meet up with from time to time.

'The game has definitely speeded up. There has been tinkering with the rules and I understand that there is a constant need to make improvements. But by and large the rules are okay. It is the application of the rules and consistency in application that is the problem. We have too many variables. I also don't think the referees are given enough respect; they need to be treated better across the board by County Boards and at national level. Pay them well, look after them, because they are a crucial part of our game. I was no angel myself in the way I behaved with referees. We all need to play our part. This is a major part of our game that is flawed at the minute. Referees need greater recognition. Referees need an incentive scheme, something for them to aim at. And I would reward them; incorporate them when awards are being given out. We need to make them feel part of the whole thing. We need to create an environment where referees are encouraged to improve their own standards. The inconsistency causes so many problems. No one knows what is right and that frustrates players and then the referees get frustrated.

'The GAA has grown so much. Croke Park has made a huge difference. It's a fantastic stadium and now it has been opened to other sports. We can be very proud of it. It is a fantastic time to be a GAA player. For a lot of the younger guys coming through they are getting a high profile and that is good for them.'

He feels strongly that his friend Paul Galvin has been the victim of some unfair media coverage. He knows footballers are not saints. He has been in his fair share of scrapes during his long career and accepts without rancour the times he has been disciplined. But he feels the treatment of Galvin has been unjust. He explains: 'A lot of our so-called broadsheets have a tabloid mentality. More and more the papers have focused on the private lives of our top players because they believe it sells papers. Paul Galvin sells papers. No one takes into account the effect it has on these lads as individuals, on their families and the communities in which they live.

The way things are reported gives a false impression of what these people are really like.

'Paul Galvin plays on the edge. That is what makes him so exciting to watch. But any incident in which he is involved is blown up, when most of them are innocuous. The coverage is not consistent. You are never told that he is always the first to training, that he puts in the hours and that he is so committed and dedicated. I read some of the stuff and get frustrated because I think "that is nothing like the guy I know". I know that what I'm reading is misleading but some guy in another county might read it and you could forgive them for thinking "what's this headbanger at now?" I would be afraid that there will be major problems down the line because this coverage has gone too far. The media is crucial in terms of creating a profile. That profile helps bring in funding which is important. And young guys can get jobs – even in this economic climate – because of their profile. But the media has to act responsibly and at times it doesn't.'

THE Ó hAILPÍN
BROTHERS

'Is fada an turas é ó Fiji go Corcaigh …' The remainder of the opening line of Seán Óg Ó hAilpín's victory speech on the steps of the Hogan Stand in Croke Park on 11 September 2005 was drowned out by the appreciative roar from the tens of thousands of Cork hurling supporters who had poured onto the hallowed surface to celebrate the county's thirtieth All-Ireland Senior Hurling Championship success.

With an eloquence few could muster in such a cauldron of emotion, the Cork captain spoke *as Gaeilge* for almost four minutes before raising the Liam McCarthy Cup to the skies in triumph. It had indeed been a long journey from his birthplace in the Fiji Islands to Cork and on to Croke Park, but in that moment all the pain, the sacrifice, the life adjustment and the hard work had been made worthwhile.

Seán and Emile Ó hAilpín could never have imagined way back in 1987 when they decided the future for their young family lay in Ireland that their eldest son would become one of the country's most popular sporting heroes and that the name Ó hAilpín would become synonymous with sporting

achievement. The exotic looks, the equally exotic names –
Teu, Setanta and Aisake being the other brothers – added to
the aura, but it was their athleticism, dedication and modesty
that endeared the boys to a nation.

It could not have been foretold either that the eldest son
would become involved in some of the greatest controversies
in Irish sport; that he would find himself at the centre of a
very public and acrimonious debate involving some of the
most powerful figures in the GAA that would help define
the future of the GAA and its players.

In between the various controversies Setanta would enjoy
a year of extraordinary adulation alongside his big brother
before embarking on a professional football career back in
the land of his birth, Australia. The youngest brother, Aisake,
also wore the colours of Cork and tried a professional career,
while the second oldest, Teu, would earn many awards at
club level.

The story of the Ó hAilpín brothers is packed with
drama on and off the field. It is a story of survival, adventure,
despair and ultimately triumph. Acted out on two sides of
the world, it is heroic without any loss of humility. And it
all began on a little island in the Pacific Ocean that few
in Ireland had heard of until the very last decade of the
twentieth century.

* * *

The volcanic island of Rotuma lies almost 400 miles north of Fiji's capital Suva. It is a tiny, 24-square mile speck in the ocean that is home to about 2,000 people, with many more Rotumans spread throughout Fiji, Polynesia, Australia and New Zealand. It was there, on 22 May 1977, that Seán and Emile Ó hAilpín's first son, Seán Óg, was born and would spend the first eighteen months of his life. His father was a native of Fermanagh who had met Emile while working for an oil company on the island.

Emile bore four more children after the family moved to Sydney. Teu (pronounced Deo) was followed by the eldest girl Sarote, then Setanta and Aisake. The sixth and youngest of the clan, Étaoin, was born when the family moved to Cork. Seán Óg recalls a lifestyle in Sydney that was idyllic. His Irish heritage was acknowledged within the family but did not impinge on the life they lived.

He did play a little Gaelic football and all the children attended the annual St Patrick's Day parade in Sydney. Otherwise, they lived like Australians and places like Páirc Uí Chaoimh, Semple Stadium and Croke Park were alien to these sports-mad youngsters. But Seán Óg's dreams of becoming a top rugby league player in Sydney were dashed without warning one evening in late 1987, when his parents informed the family that they were moving to Ireland.

'It broke my heart leaving Sydney,' Seán Óg recalls with candour. 'I was eleven years old then and I already had a life out there. At primary school there was a huge emphasis on sport and I always had a football or a rugby league ball with me when I was on my way to and from school or just out playing. I loved the sunshine, the Australian way of life and I had lots of friends out there.

'We knew there was an Irish connection in the family; that Dad was from Ireland. But Ireland could have been on Mars or Jupiter as far as we were concerned as kids. I used to go with my father to the Gaelic club in Sydney and played some Gaelic football with the other kids around there, but my sports were rugby league and cross-country running. The only time that we recognised the Irish thing really was on Paddy's Day when we would dress up and join the parade in Sydney marching behind the Fermanagh banner. Apart from that we lived a pure Aussie lifestyle.

'In 1987 when my parents announced we were moving to Ireland it ripped my heart. I was leaving behind my sport, the weather, my friends. I was being transported to this foreign place on the other side of the world and I really didn't know what was happening.

'Do I remember my first day? Of course I do. It was a wet miserable February day in 1988, landing in Dublin; we stayed in Dublin overnight and got a train down to Cork. Any rain we had experienced in Australia was a tropical downpour and a couple of hours later the rain had evaporated and the sun was beating down again. Then we came here and it was our first experience of the light drizzle that can go on for a day. And the cold. It was unreal.'

There were other complexities for the children, as Seán Óg explains: 'Cork was a different city then to what it is now. I mean this with the greatest respect, but Cork was a white city. The Ó hAilpín kids had inherited my mother's Fijian features. We were different and it was very obvious to us that we were different in the early days. I don't know how we would have integrated, if we would have been able to integrate, if it wasn't for the GAA.'

Seán and Emile initially set up home in Fair Hill on the north side of the city. Though they later moved to Blarney, the influence of Fair Hill and the GAA community in the area would be profound. The boys attended North Monastery school and joined the Na Piarsaigh GAA club; within both institutions they found a new family and a new sense of identity.

'We are a close family,' Seán Óg recalls. 'When we left Sydney to come here we had no one but ourselves, no relatives or anything like that. We looked for support from each other. When you move a family of five children from one side of the world to the other it is not easy; mentally and emotionally it is a huge thing for young kids. It was hard and the first initial years were torture, getting used to the school system, new kids, a new culture. You felt straight away you were different. Our attitude was "what won't break you will make you" and that was the life. We got used to it. Being different went by the wayside when we started playing for the GAA club and people began to accept us. After a few years we could walk down the street like every other Joe Soap. Only for sport I don't know how we would have integrated as well as we did.'

* * *

'The Mon', as the North Monastery school is popularly known on the north side of Cork city, was founded in the early part of the nineteenth century by the Christian Brothers. It encapsulated all the ideals of the CBS tradition, stoutly Catholic and nationalist, in which the playing of Gaelic games was central to the ethos. Through its history the North Monastery produced many of Cork's greatest hurlers and footballers, most notably Jack Lynch. And it was a group of former pupils who decided during the 1940s to form a new GAA club in the area which they named Na Piarsaigh in honour of Pádraig Pearse.

It was this school, where the curriculum is taught in Irish, that the young Ó hAilpín boys attended when they arrived in Cork in the spring of 1988. From the school they were directed to the club, where a variety of teachers and coaches provided the guidance, encouragement and coaching that allowed Seán Óg and Teu to find their feet in this new land. Setanta and Aisake were six and seven years younger and their transition was less traumatic.

Seán Óg felt comfortable playing Gaelic football. He was naturally athletic and had experienced the game before.

His rugby league skills in terms of handling and running also helped. Hurling was much different. 'I didn't have the skills at all and I was embarrassed to take it up,' he recalls. Although he was fully immersed with football, he was idle during the months when hurling was prominent. One of his first mentors and a man who became a father figure to the youngster, Abie Allen, was persistent. He quietly but effectively cajoled the kid for almost a year before eventually convincing him to give hurling a go.

'Jesus, I was pretty raw at first,' he laughs now in re-collection. 'The lads still remind me to this day about when I started. I was hacking people, double swings and all that. Myself and the hurley didn't go well together. But I was young and willing, and between the school and the club I was exposed to a lot of hurling, I played with a lot of good hurlers and I had a lot of good coaches.'

People like Donal O'Grady, Nicky Barry, Gerry Kelly, Christy Kidney and Billy Clifford, along with Abie Allen, worked with the youngsters. 'I suppose I was a project from the start. My football was flying but my hurling needed an awful lot of work and a lot of patience.' Teu, a year younger, was also learning and in the evenings when they got home they would go straight out to the yard and start pucking the ball around – 'hurling till the lights went out'.

Soon they were fully assimilated into the GAA way of life. Cork football and hurling were the dominant subjects of conversation in the family home. They would watch Tony

O'Sullivan from Na Piarsaigh play with Cork in front of 60,000 in Páirc Uí Chaoimh or 70,000 in Croke Park and meet him the following day at the club. It was inspiring. 'It gave us our dreams watching the likes of Tony, Ger Cunningham, Denis Walsh, Jim Cashman and Teddy McCarthy.'

Their father and mother recognised very quickly the value of the games and the GAA for their young family. 'My parents altered their lives to accommodate our hurling. It must have been hard on the girls because our hurling was so important in the house. I don't remember partying or girls from that time. It was all hurling.'

Less than six years after arriving in Ireland Seán Óg was a member of the North Monastery team that won the Munster Colleges (Dr Harty Cup) title and the All-Ireland Colleges title in 1994. That brought him to the attention of the Cork minor selectors. Bringing home a Cork jersey was a very special occasion for the family. He won his first Munster inter-county title that year with the minors and played in Croke Park for the first time. Cork lost, but it was the start of something very big. A year later he won his first All-Ireland medal with the minors on a team that included Donal Óg Cusack, Timmy McCarthy, Mickey O'Connell and Joe Deane.

Two summers later, in 1997, they were joined on the Cork under-21 team by Wayne Sherlock and Diarmuid O'Sullivan, and two consecutive Munster and All-Ireland titles were captured. Seán Óg had become a part of the Cork senior hurling team in 1996 and at the end of 1998 he was called into the Cork senior football squad. At the same time he was a student in Dublin City University, where he was involved in both the Fitzgibbon Cup and Sigerson Cup teams. It was a roller coaster ride and his brothers lent enthusiastic support. Teu was having an outstanding under-age career with Na Piarsaigh and made Cork minor and under-21 football squads. 'He never got the breakthrough he deserved,' says Seán Óg, 'because he was as good as the rest of us.' Teu continued to play football and hurling, and enjoyed playing in Clare with the Eire Óg club in Ennis and later in London.

* * *

Setanta Ó hAilpín was in his early teens when his big brother first played Senior Championship hurling for Cork on 26 May 1996. The nineteen-year-old Seán Óg came on as a substitute for Mark Mullins, a Na Piarsaigh team-mate, in the opening round against Limerick at Páirc Uí Chaoimh. Young Setanta was already a familiar figure around the Cork squad, always accompanying Seán Óg to training and placing himself behind the goal where he would spend the evening pucking sliotars back into play. The sixteen-point defeat suffered that day against Limerick was an indication of where Cork hurling existed in the inter-county rankings list. They had to wait until the 1998 Championship for a first taste of victory at senior level, when Cork beat Limerick,

THE Ó hAILPÍN BROTHERS

but exuberance triumphed over impatience and the rewards would be reaped in 1999.

Two legendary figures in the history of hurling and football, Jimmy Barry-Murphy and Larry Tompkins, were managing the respective Cork senior teams for 1999. Seán Óg's elevation to the Cork senior football team placed further demands on the time and energy of a young man with an already daunting schedule at club, colleges and county level. Respite came in the form of a first national senior title when Seán Óg lined out at full back on the football team that captured the National League in May 1999. Just two weeks later he made his Senior Football Championship debut in the opening round against Waterford and on June 13 officially became a dual Championship player when lining out for the hurlers against Waterford. With the cooperation of the two team managers, the player performed a delicate juggling act that lasted until the final day of competition in late September.

'Cork had not won an All-Ireland senior title since 1990 and that was a famine for the county, especially in hurling,' he remembers. Expectations were not high in either code at the start of the campaign, but by 4 July Cork had won its first Munster senior hurling title since 1992, when the young team with Seán Óg in the familiar number seven jersey beat Clare by 1–15 to 0–14. Two weeks later he lined out with the footballers as they beat Kerry in the provincial final by 2–10 to 2–4. The pressure was unrelenting. On 8 August, Cork played Offaly in the All-Ireland hurling semi-final, a game rated as one of the best of the modern era, which Cork won by three points. And on 22 August the footballers defeated Mayo to qualify for the All-Ireland football final.

'The build-up to September was massive because of all the hype about me going for two Championships in the one year,' recalls Seán. 'It hadn't been done since Teddy McCarthy had won hurling and football with Cork in 1990. The list of people who had won titles in both games at senior level was small and Teddy was the only one to do it in the one year. He had been one of my early heroes so it was a huge thing to be in a position to emulate him.

'This was my fourth year playing for the hurlers. The first three years were a process of development. When you start playing at that level you are always worrying. When the ball is coming to you, you worry that you will mess it up, you're thinking about things a lot more than is necessary. And when you think too much about things you will mess it up. By 1999 I felt more comfortable in the team. Things began to happen naturally. I was so confident I wasn't thinking about my hurling.'

The hurling final between Cork and Kilkenny on 12 September began a rivalry between two sets of players that would see them dominate hurling in the new century and scrap almost annually for the right to claim the Liam McCarthy Cup. The 1999 final was a classic match-up – Kilkenny's skilful forwards including D.J. Carey, John Power,

Charlie Carter and a young kid named Henry Shefflin, and a powerful Cork defence with Donal Óg Cusack in goal, fronted by Fergal Ryan, Diarmuid O'Sullivan, John Browne, Wayne Sherlock, Brian Corcoran and Seán Óg, who was tasked with marking Carey for the first time at this level. Carey was held scoreless, Cork won by 0–13 to 0–12.

There was no time to celebrate. Training resumed two nights later with the footballers who were due to play a vastly experienced Meath team on 26 September. 'We came up short,' Seán Óg recalls candidly. It was a close game won by Meath, 1–11 to 1–8. That Meath outscored Cork by 0–6 to 0–2 in the final half hour told the story.

Nothing, however, would taint the joy. Eleven years after arriving in Ireland as a frightened young boy from the other side of the world, Seán Óg Ó hAilpín had proven himself one of the outstanding hurlers in the country. In the stands that day and back home on the north side of Cork city and in the Na Piarsaigh clubhouse some tears were shed. The project had been a huge success. Yet the story was only beginning and it had twists and turns to take.

* * *

'Rebel strike throws Cork hurling into state of crisis'. The headline on the front page of the *Irish Examiner* on 30 November 2002 did not come as a surprise to supporters around Cork city and county. For three months towards the end of the year it was clear that the stand-off between the players and the Cork County Board was of a different hue to anything seen before in Gaelic games. Central to that were the very public positions taken by players of the stature of Seán Óg, Donal Óg Cusack and Joe Deane, three of the most popular sportsmen in the county. It was the first battle of what proved to be almost a decade of conflict that led to two more strikes, in 2007–8 and 2009. The issues were complex: the players wanted better facilities, more modern management structures and better expenses. Three times they withdrew their services and each time positions became more entrenched and the divisions became greater.

Seán Óg Ó hAilpín has been talking for a couple of hours. The chat flows freely, tales are swapped and the mood is light. It is springtime 2010 and a new season is about to start. His presence in the foyer of the Silver Springs Hotel has caused quite a stir, though he is the only one around who doesn't seem to notice. Men and women, young and old, steal a glance from time to time but are too polite to interrupt. Two twenty-somethings do ask if he will attend the kick-boxing exhibition later that evening.

'What time?' he asks.

'7.30,' they reply and head off delighted.

Then the conversation turns to the strikes. Immediately the discomfort is obvious. It is not because he is embarrassed or ashamed of what has happened in Cork GAA circles over the last decade. He still believes passionately that the players had a just cause, that there was no other choice but to take the stand they did. It was always a matter of principle. But Seán Óg regrets the hurt caused. The regret is sincere; that is easy to tell from the pained expression on his face. The conversation that flowed so naturally is now halting, he wrings his hands together and does his best to articulate what are very mixed feelings. There is pain, real pain.

'No matter what I do for the rest of my life, in sport or away from sport, there will always be a scar. Those strikes are the scar and we will go to the grave with it,' he says candidly. 'We had three strikes in what was it, eight or nine years, and every one was worse than the other. Did they have to happen? Some people will ask why we wanted to change a system that has brought Cork thirty hurling All-Irelands. But times had changed. We had a group of good, disciplined guys who wanted to compete at the very top and unfortunately we felt the County Board was not giving us the support we needed. We took a stand based on certain principles and no one won. There was no winner.

'I felt a stand had to be made. It had nothing to do with money. I don't care about not being paid as a hurler, but the least the players should expect is to be made feel that they are worth something to the association. When you win they are all over you, they all want a part of you. When you lose they walk all over you as if you don't exist and that pisses me off. It has nothing to do with being paid, it is about looking after your players the very best way you can.

'The Cork County Board was out of date and didn't understand the demands on modern players. It was a clash of cultures. I didn't enjoy any of it; anyone who did must have been mad. I wanted to be playing; I had no wish to get into boardroom battles with the greatest boardroom battler of them all, Frank Murphy. Frank is a shrewd man, an experienced official and a politician. Here we were as players who were used to training and playing with no experience of working the system and we were standing in a room fighting a case; it was daunting to say the least. We didn't want to be there. We were seen as upstarts; people formed their own opinions on us and fair enough. But we didn't wake up one morning and say we were going to take them on and give them a hard time. We didn't do it for fun. It is not good reading on our CVs to be involved with three strikes.

'Gerald McCarthy was caught in the middle of the last strike and became the scapegoat. I can understand people questioning us and being angry with us. Who were we to take on a legend of Cork with seven or eight All-Ireland medals jangling in his pocket? I would be a conservative, a traditionalist. I love hearing stories about teams in the 1950s, 1960s and 1970s, the Christy Rings and all that. It fascinates me, because to understand where you are going in the future you need to know about the past. Because I was involved in the strikes people might regard me as a radical. The way the Gerald thing went made me very sad because Gerald was a player himself. There have to be serious lessons learned. It will take time to heal the hurt. We did things wrong and the County Board did as well. Last winter was a torture; it affected everything, you became almost paranoid just walking down the street. There are people today who won't look at me or talk to me because of my involvement.'

* * *

Solace is to be found in the bosom of the family. In the spring of 2003 Seán Óg was again making the familiar journey across Cork city to training three times weekly. He had a familiar passenger beside him in the car: Setanta. Only this time Setanta was not travelling as a brother, supporter and ball-fetcher. He was a team-mate, potentially at least. The third of the Ó hAilpín boys had been causing quite a stir as an under-age hurler in the county and had played in the All-Ireland minor final of 2001 in which Cork beat Galway.

'Away from hurling we were going our separate ways,' recalls Seán Óg. 'I had moved out of home and I was getting on with my life, getting serious about my career in banking. There is a six-year age gap between us. Setanta was a student in Waterford without a care in the world. But when it came to training with Cork and playing matches we travelled together and it was special.'

Donal O'Grady had been installed as the Cork manager after the turmoil of the strike and knew the Ó hAilpíns better than anyone. At 6 feet 5 inches, Setanta had a physical advantage, but he also possessed speed, balance and natural skill. O'Grady saw him as a target man as well as a score-getter. Playing alongside players of the experience and calibre of Alan Browne, Joe Deane, Ben O'Connor, Niall McCarthy and Timmy McCarthy, Setanta would be a quick learner.

By the time Cork returned to Croke Park as the Munster champions, having dethroned Waterford in the provincial final, the whole country was aware of Setanta. 'Santy's on the run', shrieked Cyril Farrell, the *Sunday Game Live* TV analyst, during the All-Ireland semi-final replay against Wexford. It reflected the growing excitement everywhere about hurling's new superstar.

Although Cork were beaten in the All-Ireland final by Kilkenny, Setanta and Seán Óg had enjoyed a memorable first season together in the Cork jersey. Both were selected as All Stars at the end of the season and Setanta was named Vodafone Young Hurler of the Year. But on the night of the glittering All Stars banquet in early December it was Emile who accepted the award on behalf of her third son. Setanta was on the far side of the world in the land of his birth starting a new adventure.

'It had been a great year but there was no indication until very late that Setanta would get the opportunity to go to Australia and embark on what he hoped would be a profes-sional career,' says Seán Óg. 'It was a fantastic opportunity for him and he has done very well out there. So while having the chance to play together in 2003 was a great privilege, I look back on it with a tinge of sadness because I don't see him coming back now, at least not before I stop playing.'

While Setanta went through the arduous task of adapting to a new game in Melbourne, Seán Óg and Cork embarked on another wonderful odyssey in 2004. It was almost certainly Seán Óg's best year in the Cork jersey and he ended with another All-Ireland medal, his second All Star and won both the Vodafone and Texaco Hurler of the Year awards. But the year was memorable for other reasons too. 'The journey that began in the back yard back in 1990 reached its destination,' is how Seán Óg explains it. Na Piarsaigh won the Cork Senior Championship and Seán Óg, Setanta and Aisake Ó hAilpín were part of the victorious team.

'Setanta had signed a contract with Carlton AFL club that year but was home for a few weeks. The club management convinced him to help us out. He came on in the county semi-final and won it for us. Then he was a great target man for us in the final.'

Seán Óg and Setanta also played together for Ireland in the International Rules series against Australia that autumn. Seán Óg was a mildly controversial selection because he had not been involved with inter-county football for four seasons. 'It came out of the blue. I was reluctant at the start to become involved because I knew there would be hassle and I didn't need it. But Larry Tompkins [a selector with Ireland] convinced me to give it a try. I was embarrassed going to the first trial. I knew there would be people wondering what I was doing there, this hurler. But very quickly I got to know the lads, they welcomed me and I began to feel part of it. Now I treasure it, because beating the Aussies ended a great season on the right note. The fact that Setanta would be playing was a big factor too and it was great to win the series that year. It really made 2004 special for me.'

His views on the series are interesting. 'People knock International Rules and I can see why. Aussie Rules is no relation to Gaelic football. You kick the ball, hand pass it and catch it but that's it. You are trying to marry two completely different sports, two different cultures, different ways of thinking. That is why you get the problems. Having said that, having worn the Irish jersey, having stood for Amhrán na bhFiann in Croke Park, it meant so much and for that reason alone I would be in favour of keeping it going.'

* * *

Aisake Ó hAilpín watched Setanta's early progress in Melbourne with interest. Like all other young men with a talent for sport, he yearned to play full-time. The opportunity arose when Carlton placed him on their 'rookie' list for the 2005 season. Although he did not manage to play a senior game for the club in three seasons in Melbourne, Aisake learned a great deal about conditioning and the lifestyle of a full-time sportsman that would ensure on his arrival back in Ireland a quick return to the Cork hurling squad for the 2009 Championship.

His presence provided Seán Óg with a great tonic. He had endured the traumas of another strike, plus the only suspension of his entire career as a result of what became known as 'Semplegate'. It was a controversial pre-match scrap before the opening round of the Munster Championship between Cork and Clare in June 2007. Seán Óg, Donal Óg Cusack and Diarmuid O'Sullivan were suspended along with four Clare players following a post-match investigation. 'What happened shouldn't have happened,' admits Seán Óg. 'Although how two teams were allowed run onto the pitch at the same time is another issue. I wish it had never happened, because it would be great to look back on your career and have a clean record; I never even got a yellow card and that means as much to me as winning the All-Ireland.'

The Ó hAilpín story continues. On 31 May 2009 Seán Óg and Aisake lined out for the first time together as Cork hurlers in the Munster Championship when they lost narrowly to Tipperary. They played together again when Aisake scored two goals and a point against Offaly in the qualifiers and also in the defeat to Galway. 'Aisake coming back and getting the chance to play together for a few seasons means an awful lot to me,' Seán Óg explains. 'I enjoy training with him, going to games with him and watching him get the enjoyment out of the game that I have had for so long. My brothers, my family, were always my greatest supporters.'

THE COONEY
BROTHERS

The road between Aughrim and Kilreekil is eerily quiet today. The landscape of east Galway has changed. One of Ireland's new motorways has diverted heavy and light traffic off the old two-lane road that linked the two major centres of commercial activity in the midlands and west of Ireland, Athlone and Galway city. Now just the odd car, van or tractor breaks the stillness in the air over the N6. Just a few kilometres to the west lie the neighbouring villages of Bullaun and New Inn, home to the Sarsfields GAA club and some of the best hurlers that Galway has produced over the last three decades.

Jimmy Cooney, the eldest of the Cooney men from Bullaun and second eldest of the clan, farms about a mile from the old family home where Joe, the third youngest brother, has built his own house and now looks after the stock. Their mother Nora still lives next door in the house where she reared fourteen children with her late husband Mick. There are mementos all around to remind them of the glory days of Galway and Sarsfields hurling when the

Cooney brothers were central to the successes. And out in the fields where it all began there are the sounds of a new generation of Cooneys preparing to play their part in the family story.

Thirty years ago in the autumn of 1980, on a never-to-be-forgotten September afternoon in Croke Park, Jimmy Cooney was the first member of the family to play in an All-Ireland final. Three years later the first lines of what would become the legend of Joe Cooney were written when he won an All-Ireland minor title. And in September 2009 the next instalment involving the latest generation began to be crafted when Joseph Junior was part of the All-Ireland-winning Galway minor team.

Bullaun hasn't changed very much in those years. New houses have been built to accommodate an increased population and the national school has expanded with extra teachers employed to cater for higher numbers of pupils. But it retains the tranquillity of rural Ireland, with the hurling field – opened in 1984 when Jimmy and Joe Cooney played together in the Galway colours for the only time – still the hub of activity for the young people.

Mick Cooney played a big part in the creation and development of Sarsfields GAA club. When Mick was playing hurling, Bullaun had supported one team, St Enda's, and New Inn another, St Killian's. But in 1966 they came together and named the new amalgamated unit after Patrick Sarsfield who had fought in the Battle of Aughrim in nearby fields in 1691.

Mick's wife Nora was a Fahy from Craughwell. Her brothers all played football and hurling, Paddy representing Galway in both games.

In the early years Mick served as chairman, secretary, treasurer and team mentor. 'He used to say he served in every position at the same time,' laughs Joe. His sons and daughters all developed an avid interest in the game, an interest that was further fuelled when Jimmy began making an impact with Galway. Throughout the 1970s it seemed that every year the county was on the verge of a breakthrough. Jimmy was selected for the Galway under-21 team in 1977 and was also called into the senior squad that year. Injury restricted his hurling in 1978, but he was back on the Galway panel for the 1979 Championship.

That decade had begun with great hopes in Galway. They won the All-Ireland under-21 title in 1972 with a team that produced a number of players who would make the senior ranks, including Iggy Clarke, Frank Burke, P.J. Molloy and Joe McDonagh. They reached the All-Ireland senior final in 1975 after a famous semi-final victory over Cork, but were not strong enough for a great Kilkenny team. In 1976 they lost to Wexford after a replay in the semi-final. 'When 1979 came around it was felt that we were ready to win an All-Ireland,' remembers Jimmy. 'In fact, it was very nearly the end of that team.'

Galway played in the four major finals in senior hurling in 1979 – the National League final, the Railway Cup final (representing Connacht), the Oireachtas final and the All-Ireland final and lost them all. They were well beaten by Kilkenny in the All-Ireland final. 'People wondered that day, we all wondered, if it was possible for Galway to ever win a senior title,' Jimmy says.

The players gathered before Christmas to discuss the state of play. Cyril Farrell had been appointed coach for the National League of 1979–80 and the Championship. 'There were a lot of guys who had been around a long time,' Jimmy explains. 'You had lads like John Connolly who had given such service to Galway. They had given so much and we wondered could we go one more time. We all agreed to give it one more shot. We couldn't let it go.'

Farrell introduced a heavy training programme. The players responded. 'We worked very hard,' says Jimmy. 'You had to be at your peak just to keep going. But it was worth it.' The turnaround was complete. The despair of 1979 was replaced by unbridled joy. They won the Railway Cup with only Joe Henry from Mayo breaking into the Galway-dominated team. And on 7 September 1980 the All-Ireland victory that had seemed so elusive was finally achieved, Galway's first since 1923. 'It is a day I will never forget and no one from Galway who experienced it will ever forget,' Jimmy says happily.

Joe recalls the final against Limerick. 'I know I was in the stands, but not all of the family could be there. There were so many of us we couldn't get enough tickets. I was looking out onto Croke Park and all I wanted to do was to get a chance to walk on the pitch. I didn't really dream that I would get a chance to play there. It was enough that my brother was playing. A lot of things happened after that, but the final of 1980 is a day none of us will ever forget.'

Conor Hayes, Niall McInerney and Jimmy in the Galway full back line faced the threat of Ollie O'Connor, Joe McKenna and Éamon Cregan. They were three great forwards, McKenna and Cregan having been part of the Limerick team that won the All-Ireland title in 1973. It was a huge tussle. Galway benefited from early goals scored by Bernie Forde and P.J. Molloy. 'But we knew with the talent they had that Limerick would fight back. And they did. There was one huge moment when Conor [Hayes] intercepted a pass. If he had missed it Limerick had a certain goal and that could have changed everything. When Noel O'Donoghue [the referee from Dublin] blew the final whistle I couldn't believe it,' Jimmy says candidly.

'The truth was that in our wildest dreams we didn't think it was possible for Galway to win the All-Ireland. The people had followed us over the years and they had good times, but they didn't think it would happen. And when it did and to see what it meant to them, it made everyone so happy.'

Just a month earlier Jimmy was part of the first Sarsfields team to win a Galway Senior Championship. The club was just fourteen years old and already a major power. When the year ended he was named the All Star corner back. 'It was difficult to take it all in. It just seemed like the good days kept coming and that they would never end.' Jimmy won a second All Star in 1981 after Galway had lost the title to Offaly. After serving a season as Galway's captain in 1982, when they lost to Kilkenny in the All-Ireland semi-final, Jimmy suffered a broken thumb during the 1983 National League. 'I was self-employed, working on the farm and I had had a fair few injuries over the years. I couldn't keep going, taking chances and not being able to work. So I decided then it was time to break from the county team and just play for the club.'

In August 1983 Jimmy wore the number sixteen jersey in the dugout as Galway lost the All-Ireland semi-final against Cork. In the minor game that day seventeen-year-old Joe Cooney wore number twelve as Galway defeated Tipperary. Joe scored five points. Anthony Cunningham scored two goals and one point. John Commins, Seán Treacy, Pat Malone, Gerry McInerney and Tom Monaghan were also in that Galway team. They beat Dublin in the All-Ireland final. Jimmy Cooney left Galway in safe hands. 'Other players emerged in the next two years,' he recalls. '[Michael] "Hopper" McGrath from our own club, Martin Naughton. There was plenty of new blood.'

A glorious era was dawning.

* * *

As Joe Cooney was growing up in Bullaun his father and brothers would often watch him practising against the wall of the house. They noticed the lightness of his touch, the ease with which he could control the ball. Jimmy remembers, 'He was always belting a ball against the wall. It was a sponge ball so it would come flying back at him but he had great control. He was always doing tricks. He had great wrists, just a natural talent. He had touch and control, but most of all he had great vision. He could spot a lad 80 yards away and put the ball into his hand. The one thing was that he was very light and my father was always worried that he would be pushed around. But Joe was well able to look after himself and he didn't have to be physical. He could see everything that was happening around him and he could react to every situation. He had a brilliant sidestep too.'

Joe's progress to the Galway senior team was rapid. He was still in his teens when named as a substitute for the 1984 Championship. Joe watched from the bench in Thurles as Galway suffered a heavy defeat in the All-Ireland semi-final against Offaly, conceding four goals. He was a fully-fledged member of the forward line alongside Tony Kilkenny, Brendan Lynskey, Anthony Cunningham, Martin Naughton and Noel Lane for his first All-Ireland senior final in September 1985 when Galway again lost to Offaly, but this time by just two points. Joe won the first of his five All Star awards that year, the others coming in 1986, 1987, 1989 and 1990.

Cyril Farrell created a new tactical plan for 1986 based on Joe Cooney's talents. He withdrew a player from the full forward line for the All-Ireland semi-final to lure a corner back away to allow Joe exploit the extra space. Kilkenny couldn't cope. The extra space in Semple Stadium suited the plan perfectly. Joe scored two goals and tortured the Kilkenny defence. Galway won comfortably. It created a sensation in the sport.

'It didn't work for the final,' Joe says ruefully. Critics claimed Galway were naïve to think Cork would fall for the same trick and that they should have changed tactics. Joe is not so sure. 'I think their corner back Johnny Crowley had an ankle problem and he just stuck to his position because he wasn't able to move around. We played the ball into where we had planned to create the space and everything fell into his hand. He got man of the match.'

By 1987 there was severe pressure on Galway to deliver. The triumph of 1980 was meant to be a launching pad for a decade of success, but now the romance was being replaced by frustration. Tipperary won the Munster Championship and the All-Ireland series took on a new complexion. Galway were gaining in experience and handled the semi-final against Tipperary well. Now they faced Kilkenny in the final. 'It wasn't a fancy game, it was a hard final,' Joe admits. 'It was a difficult day and Ger Fennelly missed a few frees for them that he would normally put over. But we had a great mix in our team by then. We had stylish players like

Eanna Ryan, Martin Naughton and "Hopper" McGrath. We had ball-winners like Brendan Lynskey who brought the rest of us into the game. We had powerful backs; Conor Hayes and Sylvie Linnane didn't take any prisoners. And we had that half back line of Gerry McInerney, Tony Keady and Peter Finnerty. It was a great line. There were so many players. We had the Kilkenny brothers Ollie and Tony. Steve Mahon and Pat Malone were great midfielders. Michael Coleman then came along. We were a team playing with the rhythm you only get from playing together for a few years.'

It was the same formula that saw them maintain their dominance over Tipperary in 1988 when Galway won a second successive title. It was the beginning of a rivalry that was not always healthy, though Joe contends that it was not as bitter as some would suggest. Contests between them included the 1989 National League final which Galway also won. It was their second League triumph in three seasons. The Galway and Tipperary players met regularly in the interprovincial series, the Railway Cup, when the Connacht team made up entirely of Galway players won four titles out of the five competitions played between 1986 and 1991. Galway and Tipperary played again in the 1989 All-Ireland semi-final, which had been shrouded in controversy over the suspension of Tony Keady for unwittingly playing illegally in an exhibition game in New York. 'Because we were meeting so often the rivalry got a bit out of hand and sometimes it boiled over,' admits Joe. 'But I don't think it was ever too bad. What happened with Tony [Keady] was a pity because he was such a great hurler. But a lot of the challenges in the semi-final that day were more awkward than anything else. And when the game was over it was all forgotten.'

Galway were back in the All-Ireland final in 1990 where they played Cork. For the first thirty-five minutes Joe Cooney produced a virtuoso performance at centre half forward, one of the greatest halves ever produced by an individual in Championship hurling. It wasn't enough. 'Ah, it was one of those days,' he explains. 'All I ever did was to go out and do my best. In the first half that day everywhere I went the ball was there, every time I put up my hand the ball fell into it. In the second half the puck-outs weren't as long, we weren't winning them as easy and it went better for Cork. I remember before half time Jim Cashman kept looking to the sideline to see if he was going to be switched; there was no need to switch him in the second half because the game changed completely. But we could still have won it. I remember Martin Naughton going for a goal. I was waiting for the net to shake and thought "this is it". But Ger Cunningham dived and the ball hit him straight between the eyes. He couldn't have seen it. It went out for a '65' but the umpire didn't signal it. The ball was pucked out and Tomás Mulcahy got a goal at the other end. And that was it.'

Three years later Joe played in another All-Ireland final when Galway lost to Kilkenny. It was his last appearance in a final. He played on until 2000 in search of another title. 'We had a team that was good enough to win a few more titles,' he says, 'but we didn't realise it at the time. Maybe we started taking short cuts. We didn't get cocky, but when you are playing for a long time you might think you are going better than you really are. It was a great time for hurling and you had a lot of teams competing. Ourselves, Tipperary, Kilkenny, Cork, Offaly, Wexford and Limerick were always close. There was never much between any of us. When you are at the top, other teams tend to play above themselves against you so you need to be alert all the time. That's not easy. It's why the current Kilkenny team is so special, because they have stayed successful for so long. Back in 1988 when we won our second title you would never have thought that Galway would still be waiting for another one. We had good teams and we were very close. But I suppose we should be glad we got two.'

* * *

Joe was blessed throughout his career to avoid serious injury. It allowed him to play for sixteen seasons with the county and the best part of twenty years with Sarsfields. 'I always knew that I was lucky playing for Galway because I was going back to play for a very good club team in a very good setup. For other players with Galway it was a much harder slog because their clubs were not as strong.'

Jimmy, Packie, Michael, Joe, Brendan and Peter Cooney were well accustomed to their individual habits, abilities and weaknesses on the hurling field. They had learned at home initially and in the new premises in Bullaun that houses the Sarsfields club. There were Brodericks, Kennys, Kellys, McGraths and many others that made up the tight-knit unit. Jimmy Cooney was club chairman for three years while still playing senior hurling for them during the 1980s and he was also a selector for a few years. It was all hands on deck. Numbers were tight. The spread of talents, both administrative and playing, was wide.

The six Cooney brothers were on board when Sarsfields won the county title for only the second time in the club's history in 1989. They won the Connacht title as well and then played a powerful Ballyhale Shamrocks team in the All-Ireland semi-final in February 1990 in Ballinasloe and only came up short by two points. It was a period of intense competition in Galway club hurling. Kiltormer won the All-Ireland Championship in March 1992 and were fancied to win another Galway title. But Sarsfields emerged as champions and set out in search of an elusive All-Ireland club title. They beat Buffer's Alley of Wexford in the semi-final and qualified to meet Limerick champions Kilmallock in the final on St Patrick's Day 1993.

Packie Cooney was captain and right full back; Brendan was full back and Michael manned the left corner. Joe was at midfield and Peter played at left corner forward. Jimmy was hanging on as a substitute. Kilmallock had outstanding players like Dave Clarke, Mike Houlihan and Pat Tobin. Friends and relations returned to Ireland from all over the world. Families re-united. Arch rivals in Galway even wished them well. 'It was such a unique occasion,' explains Jimmy. 'For such a small club to get to an All-Ireland final was a great achievement. But to go on and win it was incredible.'

Joe remembers running out onto Croke Park that St Patrick's Day. 'Some of us were used to it. Myself and "Hopper" [McGrath] were playing there a couple of times a year. But there were lads with the club who might have been fighting for a place on our team and here they were getting a chance to tog out and run onto Croke Park. That meant so much to them and so it meant a lot to us.' Sarsfields beat Kilmallock by 1–17 to 2–7. 'We were fortunate that so many good players grew up around the parish at the same time. It is difficult for parishes like these to be successful all the time so when the opportunity presents itself you have got to take it. There have been so many strong teams like Athenry and then Portumna. Then you had all the great Kilkenny club teams that came along. For us to be associated with them and to have achieved what we did means a lot to everyone. Hopefully in the future another bunch of players will come along and we can enjoy that level of success again.'

'What struck me about those guys,' says Jimmy, 'is that they were so dedicated. Take a player like Noel Morrissey. If the team was training five nights a week Noel would be out again the other two nights. It didn't matter what the weather was like, he gave everything he had to the team.'

They went on to become the first team to retain the title and Packie was the first man to captain a team to consecutive titles. They beat St Rynagh's of Offaly in the 1994 semi-final and then Toomevara of Tipperary in the final, a game that is still fresh in the mind of Jimmy Cooney. 'That result typified what that Sarsfields team was all about. They were being beaten at half time and Galway teams did not do well in those situations. But they stuck at it. I remember a line ball for Sarsfields under the Cusack Stand. Pádraic Kelly took it and drove it in high. Joe put his hand up through a cloud of hurls and plucked the ball out of the sky. He flicked it to "Bottler" Kenny and he scored a goal. Aidan O'Donoghue then scored a '65' and that was the end. Toomevara were a slightly better team but Sarsfields knew how to win tight games.'

* * *

Jimmy Cooney had been refereeing hurling games before his own inter-county playing career had ended. Living close to the Bullaun pitch, he was readily available to look after under-age games if required. His wasn't a real vocation. He just felt it was the right thing to do to ensure that young lads would get a game in the evening. Work on the farm was typically physical and kept him in reasonably good shape. He was also involved in administration at club level. Part of his role was to encourage others to take up refereeing. The best way of doing that was by example.

When he eventually decided in 1996 that his club days were over – he had played junior hurling for three years – Jimmy found himself elevated to the inter-county referees panel. In the ultra-competitive club environment in Galway he had been a popular and respected referee. That followed him to the inter-county scene and in August 1998 he was given one of the toughest assignments possible in that year's Championship – Clare versus Offaly in the All-Ireland semi-final.

Tensions were high in the build-up to the game. Clare had been involved in a heated Munster final replay against Waterford. Brian Lohan had been suspended following his dismissal. Colin Lynch was suspended for three months after a post-match inquiry and failed in a High Court bid to have the suspension lifted. The Clare manager Ger Loughnane was confined to the stand. At the same time Offaly had been mired in controversy when their manager, Babs Keating, resigned following a spat with the players.

The general consensus after the semi-final, which ended in a draw, was that Cooney had handled it well. There were the usual criticisms: the free he awarded Clare that drew the match was soft; he had not played sufficient injury time. But no one complained too loudly when he was appointed to referee the replay on the following Saturday, 22 August. It is a date he will never forget.

'A nightmare, just one long nightmare that stays with me today,' he states bluntly. Clare led by 1–16 to 2–10 in a titanic struggle. The hurling had been fast and furious, there were some heavy hits and a few that might have earned sterner rebukes from the referee. He chose the discretionary route, believing that a dismissal would have generated a negative reaction generally. But all in all it was a great occasion. Until Jimmy Cooney blew the final whistle. For a second there was a confused silence around Croke Park. And then bedlam. 'I knew in less than thirty seconds what I had done wrong,' says Jimmy. 'I had blown five minutes early. There were two minutes of normal time to play and I had planned on adding three minutes of injury time.'

The players knew he had made a mistake; the defeated Offaly players and their new manager Michael Bond spoke to him. His officials came to him. His thoughts were in a spin. He tried to get them in order, to decide what he should do. He wasn't allowed. Security officials bundled him off the field towards the corner between the Cusack Stand and the canal end where the referee's dressing-room is situated. They shielded him from photographers and he felt like a prisoner.

For hours he was kept in the confines of the dressing-room. He was numb. He got regular updates about what was happening outside, some of them more accurate than others. The Offaly supporters had spilled onto the pitch and were staging a protest. A game between Kerry and Kildare that was due to follow had to be called off because the supporters would not leave the field. 'I even got one report that they were tearing up the pitch. Galway and Derry were due to play in the football semi-final the following day. I had planned to stay in Dublin for that game. Now it was being said the game was in doubt because the pitch would not be playable. I was responsible for all of this. It was a shattering experience.' Of course, the Offaly supporters did no such thing. They protested quietly until told that an official investigation was being held and an announcement would be made.

Jimmy retraces the afternoon. He had intervened in an altercation between two players with about a quarter of an hour remaining. It wasn't much but he needed to bring calm to the situation. He stopped his primary watch. And forgot to restart it. He noticed it some minutes later and resorted to his secondary watch. Add on a bit of injury time and there would not be a problem. Except that he had set the secondary watch for thirty minutes, not thirty-five. That was the calamity.

During the hours he was kept in isolation underneath the Cusack Stand he wrote up his match report and formally submitted it. There was no hiding place from what had happened. He admitted his error.

'I made a bad mistake and I was humiliated. Looking back now we should have acted differently. We should have been able to re-start the game, explain quickly what happened and got on with it. I wish someone had said "hold on, let's see what we can do about this". But I was shifted off the field before we had time to gather ourselves. The hours I spent in that dressing-room were the longest of my life. And the days after that were fairly long as well.'

He worried for his wife, Kay, and the children. He worried about his mother at home and the rest of the extended family. There were tears shed when Kay was eventually allowed to see him. He was due to stay in Dublin but abandoned that idea. There was no way he could be seen in public the following day, especially in Croke Park with Galway playing. Eventually he was escorted out of the room still surrounded by security men talking into walkie-talkies. It would have been funny in other circumstances, but he felt hounded. He could predict the furore that would follow, the negativity and the attention. Kay was flying to Lourdes as an assistant with a pilgrimage so she would be spared the worst of it. 'But the house was a lonely place when I got back to it,' he says.

The nightmare continued for months. The hate mail began to arrive. Then the abusive phone calls. He wanted to protect his young family, but he also wanted to maintain a sense of normality. 'The kids were young and they didn't realise they should hang up when they answered the phone to some lad giving abuse.' At Christmas the calls went something like, 'Are you getting a new watch from Santy?' It went on for a long time and he wondered if it would ever end. Over time it did, but the experience and the reaction of some people will never be forgotten.

There was support too from family and friends; support from people he didn't know but who took the trouble to write and show they cared. That helped him and his family recover. Jimmy didn't quit. He refereed the Galway county final that year. He was also appointed to take charge of the All-Ireland intermediate hurling final between Kilkenny and Limerick. His travails were put in perspective on that day, 10 October. The Limerick hurling manager was their former goalkeeping legend Tommy Quaid, against whom Jimmy had played. A few days before the game Tommy suffered serious injuries in a work accident. He died on the morning of the final.

A torn Achilles tendon finally forced Jimmy to leave the whistle aside. 'But my confidence was gone,' he says. 'I never really recovered. If I made a mistake in a game after that there was always some fella on the sideline shouting at me to remind me of what had happened.'

Joe recalls those days with sadness. 'He didn't deserve it,' says the younger brother. 'The thing is that Jimmy was a really good referee. I'll give you an example of how people thought of him. If we were playing the likes of Athenry they wouldn't have had an objection to Jimmy being the referee.'

* * *

Joe Cooney could have added a few more All-Ireland medals to his collection but he doesn't look back with any regrets. 'When you look back you think of the great fun we had.

There were such characters on that team. You loved going in to training because of the craic. There were so many great players around. We all looked up to Conor [Hayes] and Sylvie [Linnane]. There were great players in other counties; the Cashmans in Cork, the Hendersons in Kilkenny, Brian Whelahan and the Pilkingtons in Offaly. Every county had great players. D.J. [Carey] came along. Every time he got the ball you would close your eyes because you knew he was going to do damage.

'The game was more social then; I think it was more fun than it is now. Today it is win at all costs. We were always bitterly disappointed when we lost. It was serious. But today it has gone over the top.'

In the last two years he has helped out with the Sarsfields under-21 team. But he doesn't have any designs on team management. 'It is cut-throat now. There's too much pressure. If a manager doesn't win titles he is regarded as a failure. It is almost a full-time job now and you need a certain type of personality to do it. Being a selector is fine. Management is different.'

The sporting gene is in the family. Joe's wife Catherine was a talented camogie player and was an Irish schools international in volleyball. Her brother is the All-Ireland-winning footballer Tomás Mannion. Eldest daughter Aoife also attained international status as a schools volleyball player in 2010. Maria is an all-round athlete and the youngest boys are showing promise. Joseph Junior, the eldest and a student in NUI Galway, has developed into a fine wing back. His father doesn't offer too much advice, just a little quiet encouragement. 'You can only tell them so much, they have to learn themselves.'

Jimmy's family is grown up. He is still closely involved with the game and stood for the position of Galway Hurling Board chairman in 2009, losing out to Joe Byrne. 'He's a good chairman and I know Galway is in good hands,' he says. He is disappointed that Galway have not made an All-Ireland breakthrough in modern times. 'The years are pushing on. 1988 is a long time ago now and a lot of young lads in Galway haven't seen the county with a hurling title. Hurling needs it.'

THE CANAVAN
BROTHERS

Mickey Moyna's cars. Peter Canavan chuckles at the memories – all good. The first one, way back in 1989, was some sort of old banger, as he remembers. Gradually over the years the cars got a bit better. The passengers remained constant. Peter and Pascal Canavan, Paul Donnelly, Éamon McCaffrey and Ciarán 'Dinky' McBride. To and from Tyrone training or matches the ribbing was merciless. Pascal was Mickey's chief tormentor, 'the main culprit for Mickey's bad humour' according to Peter. 'It was an exhausting experience getting to a match, worse than even playing. And it was even harder going home. You needed your wits about you as much if not more in Mickey's car than you did on the pitch in a Championship game.'

Thoughts of those journeys over a period of fifteen years and the unflagging loyalty and support of men like Mickey Moyna, of his recently deceased father Seán and of the sacrifices made by his mother Sarah, were part of the combination of factors that invaded the emotions of Peter Canavan on a late September Sunday evening in 2003 when match referee Brian White sounded the final whistle and Tyrone had won their first ever All-Ireland senior football title by beating their great rivals Armagh.

Escaping the embraces of the adoring thousands of supporters that had flooded the playing area, Canavan hobbled up the steps of the Hogan Stand hugging teammates along the way. He thought about what he would say when he accepted the Sam Maguire Cup from the president of the GAA, Seán Kelly. His father, who had died unexpectedly on 4 July that year, a week before the Ulster final, was at the forefront of his mind. Peter would mention Paul McGirr, the young Tyrone teenager who had died while playing for his county just six years earlier. He remembered old teammates, coaches like Art McRory and Eugene McKenna, and others who had contributed to this moment. 'I can't think of a better position or place to be in anywhere in the world than where I am standing now,' he told the crowd as his voice crackled with emotion.

Somewhere and sometime within that splendid cauldron of happiness and celebration, Peter saw his brother. They probably embraced. He doesn't remember for sure. It was bedlam. But for one fleeting moment they exchanged a look that said 'this is what it was all for'. Fifteen years of toil, graft and sacrifice. They had suffered bad defeats and heartbreaking losses together, including the 1995 All-Ireland final. They had shared triumphs with their club, their family and their county. And now Peter held the ultimate prize.

'My only regret,' says Peter now, 'is that Pascal hadn't stayed on with Tyrone to share the All-Ireland victory as a player. We had soldiered together every year since 1990. We had travelled together to every ground in Ulster and most of the grounds in the rest of Ireland for so long and then when Tyrone eventually got the ultimate prize and he was not there was bitterly disappointing for me.'

Pascal, three years older than Peter and an outstanding player in his own right, had made up his mind in the summer of 2002 that his time as an inter-county footballer was done. He was thirty-five. He looked back on a career laced with great successes and a lot of fun. His body was beginning to send messages to his brain that could not be ignored forever. He had been returning to the panel later each year trying to preserve the ageing limbs. 'It was April when I came back in 2002,' explains Pascal, 'and it was getting harder and harder to make up the time. I had injuries, just wear and tear, and I made my mind up that it would be my last year.' He did play in the League final in May 2002 as a substitute and won a national title with Peter. They also captured another Ulster club title with Errigal Chiaráin. It wasn't a bad way to sign off.

Pascal had played as a substitute against Armagh in both a draw and a replay in the Ulster Championship, which Armagh eventually won on their way to All-Ireland glory. He had also appeared against Derry in the qualifier series. The one game he started in 2002 was against Sligo in Croke

Park, a game Tyrone were expected to win handily. Despite the Canavan brothers scoring eight of Tyrone's twelve points that afternoon, they lost by five points. 'I had given it my best shot,' says Pascal. 'I was already having doubts at the start of 2002 about whether I could make a contribution or not. If I had stayed on I would have been hoping that someone else would win an All-Ireland for me. I could not physically have given what was necessary. Time was moving on. It was a young man's game and I had to hand over. Mickey Harte was taking over, it was a new regime and I didn't feel it would be right to try to hang in there when I couldn't give it everything.

'It is hard to describe the feeling of elation to see them winning the All-Ireland the following year. I would love to have been there, to have been part of it. But I have no regrets. I made the right decision.'

The management team made sure Pascal was not removed completely from the squad environment. He was in the changing rooms to celebrate. He travelled on the team bus. It would not have been the same without him. 'Pascal didn't want to be a bit player. He wouldn't have wanted to bluff his way through it if he couldn't give it everything. But he was one player who deserved to win an All-Ireland,' says Peter passionately.

Pascal did play a role in the weeks leading up to the final as a source of encouragement to Peter in his battle for fitness. Other family members, especially Peter's wife Finola, ensured that everything possible was done to create the proper environment and conditions that would allow Peter to recover from an ankle injury sustained in the All-Ireland semi-final success against Kerry. It was the end of a long, arduous campaign during which they had drawn with both Derry and Down in the Ulster Championship before emerging as champions. They had an easy All-Ireland quarter-final win against Fermanagh, before enjoying a comprehensive victory over Kerry in the semi-final. But Peter Canavan played just fourteen minutes of that game, suffering serious damage to ankle ligaments.

On the Friday morning before the final Peter resigned himself to the fact that he would not be able to play. 'It was a strange time. I had really enjoyed the build-up to the final in 1995. It was a great time. But this was different. I was so wrapped up with my injury that I didn't notice what was happening around me. In thirteen years playing Championship with Tyrone I had played in just one final. I figured 2003 would be my last chance and I was frustrated that I would not be able to give it everything.

'My time was consumed by getting my ankle in the best shape it could possibly be. Family and friends drove me everywhere, for treatment, for physiotherapy, for anything that might give me a chance of playing. I wanted to give Mickey [Harte] every guarantee that I could play. It was a decision [to select him] that I did not think Mickey would make because physically I was not able to play.'

Harte had given the decision a lot of thought. He weighed the advantages against the disadvantages. He imagined the impact of not having Peter Canavan in his starting team; how the crowd would react if his name was not called out on the public address system minutes before the start; more important was the reaction of the players to not having their leader and inspiration with them on the field of play. The manager knew the character of the player he was dealing with. They had known each other all of Peter's life. Normally it was not the sort of gamble a manager would even contemplate. But dealing with a talent like Peter Canavan was not a normal situation.

'From the point of view of free kicks I was okay,' Peter says. 'The hope was that we might get a few handy ones. Mickey talked to me on the Friday and he wanted me to start. The plan was to stay on for about fifteen minutes and then Stevie O'Neill, who was flying in training, would come on. But the night before the final Brian McGuigan was feeling unwell so the plan had to be changed. Stevie came on for him during the first half so I had to stay on until half time.'

When Tyrone lined out for the second half Peter Canavan remained in the dressing-room. He had a pain-killing injection and rejoined the substitutes in the stand. With less than ten minutes remaining Harte made the call. As Canavan limbered up gingerly on the sideline the crowds in the Croke Park stands erupted. He jogged back onto the field and his team-mates responded to his presence with a new burst of energy. It was the emotional lift that carried them over the line. Tyrone 0–12, Armagh 0–9.

* * *

Little was known about the kid from Glencull in County Tyrone who arrived at St Mary's teacher training college on the Falls Road in Belfast in the late 1980s. Pascal Canavan didn't have a football pedigree simply because he had not played any organised football. Some years before his older brother Stevie had played with Tyrone's minors and under-21s. Another brother, Barry, played for Tyrone Vocational Schools. But a major split in their club, St Kieran's of Ballygawley, had led to a period of isolation and ineligibility from playing football officially outside the schools environment.

Seán Canavan had been a player, a manager and an administrator with St Kieran's for most of his life. He and Sarah had eleven children. Seán was a butcher who ran the family farm in Glencull. Sarah ran the local post office. Kieran, Barry, Stevie, Pascal, Peter and Joe all played football. Margaret, Agnes, Nuala, Martina and Bronagh played camogie. The youngest members of the clan, especially Peter and Joe, cannot remember the split which happened in 1982 when the Glencull contingent wanted to set up their own club. This created rancour and division. The new club was not allowed to affiliate with the GAA because St Kieran's was already in existence for the area, so its members could not play in official competitions. Stevie Canavan felt his hopes of playing senior football for Tyrone were dashed. He and his brothers watched from the stands as Tyrone won the 1984 and 1986 Ulster Championships.

They organised challenge games, played among themselves on the family farm and remained inspired and motivated by following the fortunes of Tyrone during a period of some success. They were in awe of Frank McGuigan when he kicked eleven of Tyrone's fifteen points in the 1984 Ulster final. They joined in the celebrations as Tyrone reached the 1986 All-Ireland final and were so proud when family friend Paudge Quinn scored the goal that almost beat the mighty Kerry. In the match programme Quinn's club is listed as 'Ballygawley'. His school is listed as 'St Ciaran's'. Spelled locally with a 'K', the school was educating a new generation of young footballers that in 1986 included Pascal and Peter Canavan.

Pascal had departed for St Mary's by 1988 when Peter, his younger brother by three years, captained the Tyrone Vocational Schools team to All-Ireland success. The youngster's talent was beginning to be noticed nationally. But because he was not officially a member of the GAA he could not play for Tyrone's inter-county teams. That was a matter for concern to the Tyrone minor manager, Francie Martin, who decided it was time to be proactive. If Glencull could not be affiliated then Peter Canavan would have to become a GAA member some other way. Utilising a bye-law that allows a player join a hurling club if his own club does not have a hurling team, Peter Canavan was signed up as a player with Killyclogher hurling club. He won an Ulster minor title that summer and a career was launched.

'It was a strange time,' Peter recalls. 'We were reared on football. For nine years the club tried to get affiliated but were refused. So we just played challenge games and trained. It gave us more time to practise the skills, but we were not getting proper competition. I was playing senior football at the age of fifteen and sixteen. It was a difficult time for a lot of reasons. A lot of good players were not getting serious football and were lost to the game. And the community was divided; neighbours weren't speaking to each other. People were so passionate about football and it created divisions. For nine years people paid a heavy price. In the end, the club emerged with a stronger identity.'

In Belfast Pascal found himself a different football family. Players from all over Ulster had gathered. Danny Quinn from Derry. Malachy O'Rourke from Fermanagh. Benny Tierney, John Rafferty and Jarlath Burns from Armagh. Quality footballers and serious students. They won the Sigerson Cup in 1989, beating a UCC team that included a young Maurice Fitzgerald. 'That was my first taste of success at any level and it remains one of the real highlights of my years playing football,' says Pascal.

Back home young Peter was making progress. The Tyrone

under-21 selectors were glad to make use of the Killyclogher connection. And in hallowed halls in the nearby cathedral city of Armagh the problems besetting the communities of Glencull and Ballygawley had been noted. Cardinal Tomás Ó Fiaich sent a new curate to the parish in 1989 with the specific instruction to bring the two sides together. Fr Seán Hegarty was good with people and he was passionate about football. He had managed Armagh and a variety of club teams with relative success. 'He did his job well,' says Peter with a smile. 'He told us what we wanted to hear and he told the other side what they wanted to hear. Fr Seán told the St Kieran's people that we were dying to get back with them. He told us that they were dying to get us back. It wasn't the exact truth, but he got the two sides talking again.' By the end of 1989 the dispute was effectively over and the Canavan boys and girls were officially accepted into the GAA family. Errigal Chiaráin GAA club was officially born in 1990 and the good times rolled.

The Canavans took immediate advantage. Peter had made his inter-county debut in a League game in October 1989 against Mayo. Pascal was selected for the next game against Meath. They played their first Championship match for Tyrone together in the Athletic Grounds in Armagh in June 1990. Tyrone's rise to success was on a slow burner, fuelled by Peter's success in captaining the county to successive All-Ireland under-21 titles in 1991 and 1992. At club level the boys found a new lease of life. Errigal Chiaráin became successful quickly. By 1993, with Stevie, Barry, Pascal and Peter on the team, they became county champions. It was the first success for the parish in sixty-two years. They went on to win the Ulster title.

These were happy times in Ulster football. Down, Donegal and Derry created history by winning three successive All-Ireland senior titles. Tyrone had lost to Down in the 1994 Ulster final. It was progress. In 1995 they reached the final again and beat Cavan. They beat Galway by three points in the All-Ireland semi-final. The community went wild. The build-up was colourful and fun. The players enjoyed every moment. They felt prepared and were without fear. Peter explains: 'Winning the under-21 All-Irelands had changed attitudes. Up to then winning an Ulster title was an achievement and anything else was a bonus. But we had gone down to Croke Park and beaten the likes of Kerry and Dublin, and that was a big boost psychologically. The 1986 team had also inspired us. It had so many great players like [Eugene] McKenna, [Damien] O'Hagan and [Kevin] McCabe, as well as Paudge [Quinn]. We enjoyed getting to the final and everything that came with it.'

The final is memorable too, one of the most infamous in history, for which heartbreak was to be Tyrone's lot. Peter Canavan scored eleven of Tyrone's twelve points. Dublin scored one goal and ten points to win by one point. Peter had made the pass that led to an equalising point, but was penalised for picking the ball off the ground and the point did not stand. Dublin's Charlie Redmond was sent off, but actually played on for a few minutes before referee Paddy Russell insisted on his removal. Peter's performance was hailed as one of the best ever in a final. 'I actually think I played a lot better in many other games, including that year's semi-final,' he insists. 'I got a lot of scores from frees and I would have preferred to have been on the ball a lot more. It was a stop-start game. It wasn't a free flowing game and can't have been a great spectacle for the supporters.'

Pascal says: 'It is only when you look back that you realise how poorly both teams played that day. Peter's scoring was terrific, but our performance overall was not good enough. There was a lot of anger with the referee and a lot of regret. It was understandable at the time. But these things happen. We didn't play well.'

Peter's best memories of 1995 are of the build-up, of the pleasure he got from having his brother on the team and some close friends. Did he pick the ball off the ground? 'No,' he answers emphatically. 'It was a marginal decision but it is one he [the referee] got wrong.' There isn't a hint of anger as he tells it. 'I don't hold a grudge against that man. I said that day and I have said it since that the Tyrone players made a lot more mistakes that day than Paddy Russell did. We didn't do ourselves justice that day. I have never held it against him. There was a lot of controversy at the time and talk about objections but we wanted none of that. They had won on the field of play and that was it.'

He does display signs of annoyance when he reflects on 1996. 'Losing the final in 1995 was heartbreaking but we did bounce back from it. We put two Ulster titles back to back and that hadn't been done since the 1970s. And we played some great football in Ulster that year. We were young and still felt good enough. We thought we were stronger in 1996 and then we took a hammering in every sense of the word from Meath in the semi-final and we didn't recover from that for a long time.

'We had played Meath in a few challenge games and that was a mistake. They knew that if they went out and played football with us that we were younger and fresher. They knew their strength was their physicality and they used it. They used their strength to the full. Gradually they wore us down. I shouldn't have remained on; I had damaged ankle ligaments in a heavy tackle in the first half. Brian Dooher was injured. Ciarán McBride was injured. The manner of the defeat that day was harder to take than any other and it took us years to recover.'

The late 1990s passed them by. A team that should have been reaching its peak was struggling. They lost the competitive edge, became pedestrian. But hope was sparked at under-age level. 'Some of us were wondering about the future,' Peter remembers, 'but the emergence of a new group of young players was the spark. These guys were different. Stevie O'Neill, Cormac McAnallen, Brian McGuigan, Ryan McMenamin all came through. They were seriously good footballers with a great mentality and they were such a disciplined group. I'm not saying we had a problem with discipline. We didn't. But some of us were living in the past, following old routines after games. These new guys were ambitious and they were tight, very disciplined and knowing what they wanted and how to get it. They had a really positive effect on the likes of myself and Chris Lawn. No doubt, they extended my career by a few years.'

* * *

The new kids grew up in a different era in Ulster to Peter and Pascal Canavan. They were historically aware, but had little experience of the troubled times in the 1970s, 1980s and much of the 1990s in the six counties in the north-east of Ireland. They were never subjected to roadblocks and searches, being detained on the side of the road and prevented from getting to training or getting home. They grew up at a time when the politicians were talking and arms were being laid down, fortifications were disassembled and a sense of normality returned to everyday lives.

'We lived it,' says Peter now, 'but we took it in our stride. It was only when people pointed out how different our lives were that we took notice. And looking back now it does seem strange and unusual and we can understand why it was all so off-putting.' He doesn't go into too much detail. It was life. The security forces set up checkpoints. Inter-county footballers felt targeted. No one took responsibility. It was never official policy. But it was too much of a coincidence and happened too often not to be orchestrated in some way.

'Whenever you went out of the house you expected to be stopped. We grew up with it and became accustomed to it. It was second nature. You didn't look up when helicopters flew low overhead because you were used to it. Boys jumping out of ditches didn't alarm you because it happened all the time. You knew when you were going to county training sessions that you were likely to be stopped. Your bag would be searched and your gear thrown around. And coming out of training afterwards they were waiting for you again and went through the same thing all over. I remember lads coming straight to training from the building sites and on the way home they would be held up, left standing on the roadside for an hour before they were let go home. They wouldn't get home until after midnight.

'It is unreal to think that it was allowed to happen. But it didn't prevent us from going out again the next night because we loved what we were doing and we would not be stopped. The people in our communities and all over Tyrone had a great passion for football and we took great pride in representing them. It was annoying that it was happening just because we were training to be inter-county footballers, but we got on with it.'

Having lived through it, he has an ever-greater appreciation for life today. 'Great strides have been made. I remember when I first went to college in Belfast and we were told not to wear our gear on the streets or around the college campus. Now you go to the colleges and the flags and banners are flying and on the streets people are wearing their county colours with pride and without fear.'

As the political situation changed, so did the GAA. The lifting of the ban on members of the security forces joining the GAA and the opening of Croke Park to soccer and rugby caused real anxiety in Northern Ireland. Peter Canavan shared that feeling. 'I remember at the time of the debate about the opening of Croke Park and I said that it would be a sad day for the GAA to see a Union Jack flying over Hill 16. That was how I felt. When it did happen it wasn't gratifying to see it. It wasn't gratifying to see England playing in Croke Park. But it was the right thing for the GAA to do. The majority of people here realised it was the right thing to do, but they were coming from the same position I was, having experienced what we did.

'It wasn't easy and our feelings were being diminished by some people in the south who said that we were living in the past. It was hard to swallow. But opening Croke Park was right without doubt and the association generally has benefited from that decision. It was a courageous step to take. Our games have become stronger as a result. More people around the world are aware of Croke Park now and they have become curious about Gaelic games and that is good for everyone.

* * *

Tyrone may have endured a lean period in the late 1990s, but Peter Canavan was enjoying his elevation to international status. He enjoyed playing with some of the great Ulster teams during the decade, among forward lines that contained some sensational talent. But to get the chance to play for his country and to prepare in an environment as close to professional as a Gaelic footballer can experience meant a great deal to him. He enjoyed the highs of back-to-back test series victories in 1998 and 1999 and endured the lows of defeat and the violence which sometimes occurred during those games and which earned him a suspension. He acknowledges the problems with the game but is a staunch supporter.

'As a Gaelic footballer you watch other Irishmen playing for their country in soccer and rugby and you would love to be in that position. The International Rules series gives us that opportunity. It is the nearest thing we have to an international game and the players value it tremendously,' he insists. 'There is more to it than just the games. It is the training, being involved in a set up that is like being involved with a professional game. We got to see the lifestyle of being a full-time sportsman, training and playing with the best footballers in Ireland, and being well looked after and made feel important.

'My experiences over the years have been largely positive. You have to take the odd hiding now and again but I would gladly do it all over again. The violence in some of the games during that time does leave a stain, but only a small bit. Some of the games in the 1980s were a total disgrace, but I think the authorities are trying everything to get rid of that element from the game. There is now a mutual respect between the two associations and the two sets of players, and as long as that exists we have the basis of a great game. It can't happen every year but I think a bi-annual event is worth holding on to.

'Gaelic games are now played all over the world, but we are nowhere near a situation where you could have competitive games. International Rules gives our players the chance to play for Ireland and that is very important. It also gets people talking about Gaelic football; it gives them knowledge of our game. More people are aware of our game as a result of the series with Australia and that is good. We should continue to promote our own game as well.'

At the same time he was instrumental in the setting up of the players' representative body, the Gaelic Players Association. It was a controversial move that was not readily appreciated by the authorities locally and nationally. They were regarded as rebels who were operating against the spirit of the GAA. Canavan understood the concerns of some people. The spectre of professionalism created fears within the GAA and he recognised that. The GPA was never about professionalism and he always believed it should be adopted as the official voice of the players. 'I just didn't think it would take so long for the GPA to be officially recognised. Now that it has happened it will be good for the players and the association in general.'

He has witnessed the enormous changes that took place in the game during his playing career. The commitment and sacrifice have magnified beyond all expectation. Even since he retired in 2005 he has noticed the increased demands faced by players. This needs to be recognised and addressed. The GPA has to be part of that process. 'The GPA was born out of necessity,' he says. 'We need to look after our players properly. We need to create pathways that will allow our players to train and play, give the commitment that is now required, without having concerns about external issues. All their needs, including medical, must be taken care of. It is not about being paid. No one wants that.

'Of course there are some players out there who would jump at the chance of being a professional. I was never in favour of professionalism. The game couldn't sustain it. The majority of players are realistic that it is never going to happen. Of course players would love to have the lifestyle of a Brian O'Driscoll or Ronan O'Gara. It is a natural instinct. But that is not what drives you to play Gaelic games. If it is what drives you then you can go and play soccer or rugby or something else. GAA players don't look for too much, just basic welfare issues. We need to encourage our players and ensure that they are taken care of. Any youngster who is going to give the amount of time required to play our games at the highest level needs the assurance that he will have access to the best support systems and the best advice.'

* * *

Between 1990 and 2007 Pascal and Peter Canavan played together for club, county and province. Their last game was the Tyrone Championship quarter-final of 2007 when Errigal Chiaráin lost to Dromore. No one was better placed to pass judgement on the talent of the man known nationally as Peter the Great than his older brother. 'It was always very enjoyable playing with him,' says Pascal, 'and with him in your team you always knew you had a better chance of winning. The fact that we were brothers and had played together all our lives obviously helped. He was a special talent and not just because of his score-getting. He had this drive about him. He got the best out of himself, but he also got the best out of others. His motivation techniques were very important. He was a leader on the field and in the dressing-room.'

Though Peter had relinquished the captaincy, his leadership qualities shone throughout 2004. Their young teammate Cormac McAnallen died suddenly in March. Things were put into perspective. Peter and the senior players rallied those around them. They got back to their football and dedicated themselves to winning another Championship in memory of their friend. Peter remembers the 2005 All-Ireland final against Kerry with affection. 'There was a new belief in Tyrone. From scraping on our hands and knees to win an All-Ireland, we had developed the confidence to go out and win a final playing some of the best football against Kerry. We took on Kerry at their own game and beat them. Some of the scores were outstanding that day. It was very gratifying.' In the dressing-room after the game Peter announced his retirement.

He became club captain and with Pascal again alongside him they won the County Championship. Both of them retired from club football in 2007 – and went directly into management. Pascal has been heavily involved in coaching teams at St Kieran's in Ballygawley where he now teaches. Peter had created the coaching structures at Holy Trinity in Cookstown that would bring that school many major successes, including the 2010 All-Ireland Under-16 Vocational Schools title. Pascal, along with Brendan Trainor, coached Mullahoran in Cavan before taking on Kilrea in Derry. He is also involved with the Errigal Chiaráin under-14 girls' team.

Pascal and Una have four daughters, Catherine, Fiona, Emer and Maeve. Peter's plans for some quality time with his family (he and Finola have two daughters, Áine and Claire, and two sons, Darragh and Ruairí) away from football were disrupted when old friends persuaded him to take charge of Errigal Chiaráin in 2009.

So, is he a future Tyrone manager? 'I can't say I have or haven't an ambition to manage Tyrone. I'm not sure. It's definitely not a target. If it was I would have a route marked out as to how I would do it and I don't have that. I don't have any designs as yet and I am certainly not near ready for a jump of that magnitude. Anyway I would be quite happy if the man we have in charge stayed for another ten years.'

THE BROGAN
BROTHERS

Do you remember the summer of 2002? Can anyone forget? Roy Keane and Saipan. A national crisis of quite different proportions to the one currently being experienced, but one which nonetheless divided opinions and from which there was no escape on the airwaves, in the newspapers and in daily debate. The Republic of Ireland eventually got around to playing soccer in Japan, opening their World Cup campaign against Cameroon in the city of Niigata on 1 June. On the other side of the world Alan Brogan, a keen soccer player in his teens, took an interest in the international events but had a series of distractions to contend with at home.

While the nation seemed paralysed by the drama taking place in East Asia, people were actually getting on with their lives, business and sport other than soccer. The provincial football Championships were getting under way. The Dublin football team was scheduled to play in the opening round of the Leinster campaign against Wexford in Carlow's Dr Cullen Park on that Saturday evening. The game had a 5.30 evening start to avoid a clash with the big soccer game. Alan

Brogan was making his Senior Football Championship debut. The return of the Brogan name to the Dubs for the first time since the early 1980s created sufficient stir to qualify for some space in the national media.

As momentous as the occasion might have been, Alan himself had other things on his mind. Then a student at NUI Maynooth, he was due to sit an exam on the day of the game along with team-mate Barry Cahill. The exam was scheduled to start at 2.30 p.m., which would have prevented them from making the journey to Carlow in time to start the game. The university guardians were alerted to the quandary. They met and agreed to a dispensation for the two footballers. Alan and Barry were allowed take the examination together in the morning, but under strict supervision.

'Willie Hughes was a garda sergeant at the time,' recalls Alan, 'and he had won an All-Ireland medal with Dublin in 1983. The deal was that he would escort us for the day, wouldn't let us out of his sight. The other students were sitting the exam at half-past two, so we couldn't have any contact with them. Willie stuck with us until we got to Carlow to play the game.' It was a gesture from the college that is still appreciated eight years later. The game itself is not as fondly remembered by Alan. 'I only played okay. Got a point. Jayo [Jason Sherlock] came on for me and got two points.' Others were more impressed. The manager of the time, Tommy Lyons, stuck with the young prodigy as Dublin embarked on a memorable Championship run that ended in agony in the All-Ireland semi-final when they lost to Armagh by a point. But the Brogan bloodline was back with the Dubs. A new career was born.

In the years since the Carlow game Alan has become one of the most celebrated forwards of his generation and has been joined on the Dublin team by his brothers Bernard and Paul. The younger Brogans have both had to battle with serious injury during their careers. Bernard has already established himself as a footballer and athlete of great power and skill; Paul was recalled to the Dublin squad in 2010 and is being nursed back to full health after a serious knee injury. The three brothers have played together with Dublin in the O'Byrne Cup and will surely share the county dressing-room for a few years to come. Their parents Bernard and Maria still attend every game, lending support. A new generation of the Brogan dynasty is also making the journey to Croke Park and other venues. Jamie, Alan's young son with his partner Lydia (they will marry at the end of 2010), is his dad's greatest supporter these days.

* * *

The Brogan's were Navan Road people and that meant they were Oliver Plunkett's players. It was a junior club in the early 1970s, a time when whatever little limelight shone on Dublin football sent its rays across the northside to the bigger clubs like St Vincent's. You were guaranteed good fun and good mentoring when you played with Plunkett's, but with that came a degree of anonymity that did not enhance a young man's chances of playing for Dublin. Bernard Brogan was a nineteen-year-old student in 1974 when Kevin Heffernan was plotting the Dublin revolution. Heffo heard about this youngster on the Navan Road. He went for a look and liked what he saw. But playing for Dublin at the time wasn't like playing for Dublin today. Bernard was a serious student and was reluctant to make a commitment. However, he quickly learned that Heffo didn't understand the word 'no' and as the bandwagon began to roll in that unforgettable summer, Bernard was jostling for a starting place, recovering from injury and giving Heffernan difficult selection choices. In the Leinster semi-final against Offaly he was going well when he suffered a serious knee injury. It took him seven months to recover.

In his career with Dublin he started as a forward, but it was when he was partnered with Brian Mullins at midfield that Bernard became one of the most respected participants in what has been termed the golden age of Gaelic football. The rivalry that developed between Dublin and Kerry is the most written about in the game and Bernard played a major part in the story. For a period during that era he lived in Kerry and met his wife, Maria Keane Stack from Listowel.

Bernard's brother Jim also broke into the Dublin panel. It is said on the Navan Road and elsewhere in the county that if there hadn't been a corner back as good as Gay O'Driscoll around at the time that Jim would have featured much more prominently for the county. He did play as a substitute in the 1977 All-Ireland final and was at centre half back for the 1978 National League final.

By the end of the 1975 the Mullins-Brogan midfield partnership had been cemented. Though Dublin lost the All-Ireland final to Kerry, they re-grouped and won the 1976 and 1977 Championships. In the midst of that series of matches was the famous 1977 All-Ireland semi-final in which Kerry were again the opponents. Regarded today as one of the greatest games of football ever played, it featured a spectacular goal from Bernard which helped seal Dublin's victory.

It was an era of great midfielders. The All Star list of honours for the period proves that – Liam Sammon, Willie Bryan, Mick O'Connell, John O'Keeffe, Denis Long, Dermot Earley, Paudie Lynch, Colm McAlarney, Brian Mullins, Dave McCarthy, Joe Kernan, Tomás Connor and Jack O'Shea. Bernard Brogan joined the All Stars honours list in 1979. Dublin had lost a second consecutive All-Ireland final to Kerry that year, but Brogan's contribution to their season secured the All Star award for him.

Bernard's career with Dublin had ended by the time he and Maria started a family. Alan was born in 1982, Bernard junior arrived three years later and then Paul followed. As kids they regularly pulled out the old videos and watched the great games featuring their father. They were also fascinated by the videos of Bernard's successful involvement in the television programme, *The Superstars*, in which prominent sportsmen competed against each other in a variety of events. Bernard was national champion in 1979 and competed with distinction in the international series.

From an early age all three boys showed a healthy interest in sport. Bernard and Maria had set up home in Castleknock. The local club was St Brigid's, but it could not be countenanced that the young Brogan's would play for anyone other than Oliver Plunkett's. They attended St Declan's school, where their football education was furthered. And they became very aware from an early stage of the legacy their famous father had left them. Like all sons of famous footballers they became accustomed to the comparisons and the questions. Even today Alan reckons the question he is most often asked concerns his father and whether Bernard's senior's achievements exerted pressure on the shoulders of his sons. 'The thing is,' he explains, 'there was never any pressure from our father. He let us do what we wanted. He encouraged us in every way no matter what sport we decided to play. And he went to every game whether it was Gaelic or soccer. He let us make up our own minds about what we wanted to do and he supported us fully.'

As well as Gaelic football, the boys played soccer for Castleknock Celtic and Bernard senior coached some of the soccer teams. They were good soccer players too. But the lure of Gaelic football proved strongest. Another major influence was the involvement of their uncle Jim with the Dublin football team from 1991 to 1995 as a selector. That had a particular impact on Alan who recalls his uncle getting him access to the Dublin dressing-room in Croke Park after they had won the All-Ireland title in 1995. It gave him an even greater sense of what football and success could mean.

In St Declan's Alan began to attract notice on his own merit, while the Brogan name brought added attention. He played on a decent team that included Barry Cahill, Declan Lally and Kevin Bonnar, all future Dublin players. In 1999 they reached the Leinster Colleges semi-final, but were beaten. Alan was suspended for that game having been sent off in the quarter-final and old teachers still give him a hard time about it when they meet.

The Dublin minor selectors quickly added him to their squad and the team reached the Leinster final, beating Wexford in a replay. Despite losing to Down in the All-Ireland semi-final, after another replay, Alan Brogan had made his first tentative steps in an inter-county football career and the Brogan name was again on the lips of Dublin fans.

Bernard followed his older brother's early forays with Dublin with natural enthusiasm. He was still playing soccer with Castleknock, but watching Alan fuelled his enthusiasm for the Gaelic variety of football. Though he carried his father's famous name, Bernard junior never felt any real pressure. 'Of course, there was a little bit,' he explains, 'but the fact that Alan was there for a few years before I came along took the pressure off me really. It was more difficult for him because he was bringing the Brogan name back to Dublin. People were used to it when I starting playing. It would have been hard for him, but you can see how well he coped. He has been the outstanding Dublin footballer for nearly ten years, always performed on the big day.'

In his second year playing under-21 football for Dublin, 2002, Alan played in his first All-Ireland final. Attitudes to the grade had changed dramatically in the capital since its inception. Strangely Dublin had rarely made an impact at under-21 level since the introduction of the Championship in 1965. Only twice in the history of the competition had they reached the All-Ireland final, in 1975 and 1980. At the start of the twenty-first century there was a greater focus on the under-21 team. A talented group that included Stephen Cluxton, Paul Griffin, Paul Casey, Bryan Cullen, Darren Magee, Conal Keaney, Declan Lally, Tomás 'Mossy' Quinn and Alan won the Leinster title, but lost to a strong Galway team in the final.

Alan had been drafted into the Dublin senior squad at the start of 2002. His first senior game was against Donegal in Parnell Park. He scored a goal and three points. Throughout the season the manager, Tommy Lyons, threw a protective shield around the young player, who could not resist attracting notice with the maturity he was displaying on the field and the consistency of his scoring returns. The World Cup might have overshadowed his Championship debut that summer when just 8,000 supporters turned up in Carlow, but by 23 June the Dubs had packed Hill 16 for a provincial semi-final joust with Meath, the defending champions, played in front of 65,868 patrons. Dublin won by seven points, 2–11 to 0–10. Ray Cosgrove scored 2–3, while Alan scored three points. World Cup! What World Cup?

By 7 July the fever was rising. Dublin and Kildare came face to face in the Leinster final. Just over 78,000 supporters thronged Croke Park. They witnessed a titanic struggle and a goal from Alan that he still regards as one of the highlights of his career. It came in the second half and inspired Dublin's victory. He also scored two points. Cosgrove continued on his scoring spree and contributed 1–3. Dublin won by 2–13 to 2–11. Alan had his first Leinster Senior Football Championship medal and an early taste of a career playing in front of packed houses in the spanking new Croke Park.

They needed a replay to beat Donegal in the All-Ireland quarter-final and went forward to meet one of the new powers of football, Armagh, in the semi-final. It was yet another tight struggle. Alan gave the pass that set up Ciaran Whelan's goal. With less than ten minutes remaining Dublin led by two points. Armagh fought back and scored two points to level the game. With four minutes of normal time left, Oisín McConville fisted a point to give Armagh the lead. Dublin pressed for an equaliser. Cosgrove, who enjoyed a brilliant season for Dublin, narrowly missed a late free. Dublin lost by a point. A total of 387,642 people had passed through the turnstiles that summer to see Dublin play. It would become a familiar pattern over the rest of the decade.

A surprise loss to Laois in the 2003 Championship provided a little respite. Alan was completing his studies and focused on his role as captain of the Dublin under-21s, while continuing to play for the senior team. A comforting presence in the squad was that of Bernard. He had been making an impression at club level, but missed out on playing minor football for Dublin because of injuries. His involvement in 2003 was, he says, peripheral, but it provided him with experience that would be invaluable. Dublin retained the Leinster title and reached the All-Ireland under-21 final where they played Tyrone. Amongst opponents who would become very familiar were Dermot Carlin, Seán Cavanagh, Kevin Hughes and Martin Penrose. Dublin won by five points, 0–12 to 0–7, and Alan Brogan became the first Dublin captain to lift the All-Ireland under-21 trophy.

So young, so much already achieved and with four years of third level education behind him, Alan needed a break. He headed for Australia with Lydia, where he attended the International Rules test in Melbourne and the Rugby World Cup game between Ireland and Australia. The couple travelled, worked for a while and enjoyed life. From time to time the phone rang. Tommy Lyons was keeping a long distance watch on his young player. The longer Alan was away, the more anxious the manager became. Alan kept in shape but the manager wanted him home. In March 2004 the couple returned to Ireland and Alan to football.

Over the next six years Alan experienced some of the greatest highs and some haunting lows on what can only be described as a football roller-coaster. 2004 was a disappointment, when Dublin were surprisingly beaten by Westmeath in the Leinster semi-final and by Kerry in the All-Ireland quarter-final. That led to the departure of Lyons as manager. Paul 'Pillar' Caffrey took over and Dublin won the next four Leinster Championships. But the failure to make the All-Ireland breakthrough was a frustration and Caffrey departed in 2008. Pat Gilroy took over and another Leinster title was bagged. Alan had six in total at the end of 2009, but the lingering memory was of another All-Ireland series disappointment, this one a shattering defeat to Kerry in the quarter-final.

Through those years Dublin was part of some of the most dramatic games in Championship football; the semi-final of 2002 against Armagh was the first. The drawn and replayed All-Ireland quarter-final against Tyrone in 2005, which featured Owen Mulligan's famous goal, followed. They managed to lose the 2006 semi-final to Mayo, lost to Kerry in the 2007 semi-final by just two points and then suffered two heavy defeats in the quarter-finals of 2008 and 2009 respectively to Tyrone and Kerry – both teams went on to win the All-Ireland title.

You remind Alan of his involvement in so many big games

and he responds quietly: 'Yeah, but unfortunately we lost them all. In 2008 and 2009 we were favourites to beat both Tyrone and Kerry just because we had won handy enough Leinster Championships. I don't know how or why we get the label of favourites. Tyrone and Kerry have been the two teams that we have always struggled with during my time with Dublin. I think the only time Dublin have beaten Kerry was in this year's League and I wasn't even playing,' he laughs.

Bernard admits that in terms of his Dublin career he was a late starter. He doesn't make any excuses. A couple of years on the bench he insists were great preparation for his breakthrough in 2007. But a little research shows how injury delayed his introduction to the game at the highest level and then interrupted the progress that his talent and desire ensured would be made. He never played on the Dublin minor team because of injury, his 2004 season as an under-21 was ruined by knee problems. In 2005 he was injury free, won a Leinster under-21 medal and was elevated to the senior squad. But he had to wait almost two full seasons before Paul Caffrey decided that the second Brogan brother was ready for the heat of the Championship.

'I did have a long apprenticeship,' Bernard says with a smile. 'But the time spent on the bench between 2005 and 2007 wasn't a waste. I was with the lads in Croke Park on the big days. I got used to the crowds, to the noise and all that is associated with big days. Some players come to Croke Park to play for the first time and they are affected by the stadium and the atmosphere. When I got my chance in 2007 I had no nerves. I was ready for it.'

He made his Championship debut against Meath in June 2007 as a substitute in the Leinster quarter-final replay against Meath. He was selected to start in the semi-final against Offaly and the provincial final against Laois. Alan scored a goal and a point. Bernard registered the same tally as Dublin won by 3-14 to 1-14. Bernard remained a first choice half forward until Dublin lost to Kerry in the All-Ireland semi-final. Alan won his second consecutive All Star award at the end of 2007. Bernard was a nominee in his first full year as a regular.

Then injury struck again, in 2008. A bad hamstring tear allowed him just a few minutes of action in the Leinster Championship. He returned for the All-Ireland quarter-final against Tyrone and kicked three points. But we hadn't seen the real Bernard Brogan. Followers of club football in Dublin, however, were getting the real thing. Oliver Plunkett's qualified for the Dublin Senior Championship final. Replays and re-fixtures delayed the final and Bernard had to pull out of the Ireland squad departing for Australia for the International Rules series. It was a sacrifice he was glad to make. Club means a lot. The three Brogan brothers and their cousin lined out in the Championship final. Bernard produced a scintillating performance against Kilmacud Crokes and scored ten points, seven from play. It was not enough for victory, but the new Dublin manager, Pat Gilroy, left Parnell Park with a big smile on his face. Gilroy was another St Vincent's man, just like Kevin Heffernan thirty years previously, looking across north Dublin towards the Navan Road and making space for Bernard Brogan on his team.

Ask Alan about the highlights of his career and he quickly mentions the under-21 success and the Leinster Championship successes, before adding 'and then to see Bernard do so well in 2009 against Westmeath and Kildare. That was very satisfying. I always expected him to make the breakthrough and I actually expected it would have come earlier. I always knew he would get his place.'

Bernard started the 2009 campaign injury free and ready to perform. He scored a few points against Meath and then exploded. As Dublin demolished Westmeath he scored 2–8. He added another ten points in the Leinster final as Dublin overcame the spirited and stylish opposition presented by Kildare. As the wheels came off the wagon against Kerry in August, Bernard tried to make a battle of the encounter. It brought the season to a disappointing end, but no one could forget the brilliance Bernard displayed at times during the Leinster campaign.

Trying to explain precisely what happened that day is difficult. Alan tries: 'They're such a good footballing side and they try to play the game like it should be played. We were all built up for a good start and it didn't happen. They got a great start and when it didn't happen for us we were looking at each other with our mouths open wondering what are we going to do now? When you get a bad start like that against a team like Kerry it is very difficult to claw it back. We weren't capable of doing it.'

* * *

Watching the old videos from the 1970s, Alan often wonders what it would have been like to play in that era. 'When a corner forward got around his man in those days he was generally in on goal. Today with the emphasis on defence and half forwards floating back into defence you don't get that sort of space. From that point of view I would have liked to have played in the 1970s,' he says. Bernard quickly adds: 'You'd have got a few more slaps as well.'

The game has changed, even during the years that Alan has played for Dublin. The commitment alone in today's game is extraordinary. Bernard points out that an inter-county footballer or hurler today needs an understanding employer who is prepared to be lenient or at least flexible in terms of hours. Coaching has changed. Alan explains: 'The top coaches have sought knowledge from other codes and brought new thinking into the game.' He is not enamoured with the amount of handpassing in football, which he believes detracts from the game. But he has no complaints about the amount of time that he must commit to playing football at inter-county level. The sacrifices are worth making.

Media commitments have grown, especially as part of the Dublin team. They have been engulfed from time to time in controversy. Alan was suspended as a result of brawling during a League game in Omagh. Bernard was cited after similar incidents against Meath in Parnell Park. But there have been good days as well. They are both connected to sports gear company Adidas. Alan has made a video with the company in which he coaches soccer players Ashley Young, Jermaine Dafoe and Roman Pavlyuchenko in the skills of Gaelic football.

They have also both become followers of the Leinster rugby team and socialise from time to time with some of the players. Jonathan Sexton has publicly credited Bernard for giving him invaluable advice about kicking in Croke Park, especially into the Hill 16 end, prior to Ireland's famous victory over world champions South Africa at the end of 2009. Comparing schedules, the football and rugby players agree that the only major difference between them is that the rugby players get paid for what they do.

Bernard says: 'It would be great to be a professional, of course it would. Imagine being able to get up in the morning and the only thing on your mind is to train for your sport, to go out on the field and kick a ball around for a few hours. Who wouldn't want to do that? But it won't happen in our time. You only have to look at other professional sports in Ireland. The top teams in soccer are bankrupt. The GAA couldn't support a professional sport. Rugby has managed it but they have had their difficulties.'

Alan adds: 'I would love it [to be a professional] but we have to be realistic. I don't know the numbers, but it is unlikely that the GAA could sustain a professional game. All we ask as players is to be properly looked after. Take the current climate. It is important that the GAA doesn't turn a blind eye to what is happening and to the problems facing lots of players around the country. The GAA needs to work in conjunction with the GPA, with the County Boards and with the players to ensure that players are being looked after. Professionalism won't happen in my time. In rugby the top guys are looked after, but it has affected the club game hugely. When I was growing up you knew all about Cork Con and Dolphin and those clubs. Now you don't hear about them at all because all the top players are with the provinces. On the other hand rugby is now a real competitor to the GAA.'

Another Championship season looms as we part. Dublin's long wait for another All-Ireland title continues. Alan has won everything else. 'But I make no secret of the fact that I want to win an All-Ireland, but it is not easy. If you were to ask if I ended up finishing my career without having won an All-Ireland will it be a regret; well it won't live with me for the rest of my days, put it that way. If we win one it would be great but if we don't when I retire I will be happy with what I have.'

Dublin's dream of All-Ireland glory ended agonisingly in 2010 following an injury-time loss to Cork in the semi-final. But Bernard Brogan's compelling brilliance throughout the campaign and Alan's mature leadership were the significant parts of a team-building process that could yet bring Dublin to the Promised Land. The dream lives.

THE DEPARTED

MICK AND JOHN MACKEY

In the timeless and never-ending debate that occupies the thoughts of generations of hurling followers all over Ireland about the greatest hurler of them all, the name of Mick Mackey is one of the first mentioned. But in his lifetime the genial legend often pointed out that during the great years of the 1930s, when Limerick were one of the major powers of hurling, it was his brother John who often produced the brilliant individual moments that helped Limerick win all the major titles.

Together the Mackey brothers from Ahane, sons of 'Tyler' Mackey who had been a Limerick hurling hero in the early years of the century, would spend the best part of two decades hurling together through the fields of Limerick, Munster and Ireland and create records that are hard to imagine today.

They first played together formally for Ahane as minors in 1929. From that day until the end of 1948 the Mackeys won fifteen Limerick senior hurling titles together; they also won five Limerick senior football titles. They shared in three All-Ireland successes with Limerick in 1934, 1936 and

1940, as well as five Munster Championships. They won five consecutive National League titles between 1934 and 1938, John adding a sixth title to his list of achievements in 1947.

Mick Mackey's senior career with Limerick began in somewhat bizarre circumstances. He had made the short journey to the Gaelic Grounds on the Ennis Road on 16 November 1930 intending to be a spectator at the National League game between Limerick and Kilkenny. The home team were short players and persuaded Mackey to play. The emergency role was short-lived and the eighteen-year-old was not required again until his form for Ahane during their first Limerick Championship success in 1931 convinced the selectors he was ready for a more permanent stint.

He made his debut in the 1932 Munster Championship and his display against reigning All-Ireland champions Cork in the provincial semi-final attracted national notice. Cork won that game, but a new star was on the horizon. John was selected at midfield for the National League and Limerick reached the final in 1933 when they lost to Kilkenny. But the Limerick bandwagon was rolling. Thousands attended their training sessions; they won the Munster final against Waterford in the committee rooms after a crowd invasion of the pitch when Limerick comfortably led Waterford. In the All-Ireland final they lost by two points to Kilkenny. Success was just around the corner.

John Mackey produced one of his great performances as Limerick won the National League in 1934. Limerick beat

Cork, Waterford and Galway on their way to another All-Ireland final where they met Dublin. When the match ended in a draw Limerick believed they needed something extra for the replay. They recruited the renowned Cork trainer Jim Barry. John was named man of the match as the Mackey brothers won their first All-Ireland senior medals in the GAA's jubilee year.

Mick was captain for the 1936 Championship. He scored an astonishing five goals and three points in the Munster final against Tipperary as Limerick won by 8–5 to 4–6. They had thirteen points to spare over Kilkenny in the All-Ireland final. The years that followed brought epic clashes with Kilkenny, Tipperary and Cork. Limerick and the Mackey brothers won their third All-Ireland title in 1940. The great Cork team of the 1940s, with Christy Ring challenging Mick for the title of the greatest hurler, ended Limerick's Championship-winning hopes, but some of the battles between them are recorded in the sport's history books as outstanding displays of hurling.

Mick Mackey's personality contributed to his popularity. He loved people and made friends easily. Fame never affected him. He enjoyed nothing more than mingling with supporters after a match, soaking up the atmosphere and talking about the game. Distinguished journalist Raymond Smith wrote about his impact on Ireland and on hurling followers. 'He broke all the accepted barriers of what seemed possible on the field of play. He made men dream dreams in an era when television had not yet arrived in Irish homes and there were no international standards by which to judge in sport; and what spectators saw before them on the field of battle or conjured up in the mind's eye as they listened to a radio commentary by Micheál O'Hehir sufficed to give a depth of satisfaction that young television addicts cannot comprehend today. He was a god to those who worshipped at the shrine of his greatness.

'Mackey rampaging through the centre on a defence-splitting solo run, culminating in the green or white flag waving at the town end or the Killinan end in Thurles represented the fulfilment of the secret ambitions of the poor, of all who knew they would never climb to the top of the table in life itself.'

TOM AND JOHN JOE O'REILLY

In modern football lore the most famous goal ever scored is that which deprived Kerry of five All-Ireland Championships in a row in 1982. But half a century earlier the Kingdom was similarly deprived of five consecutive titles by a last-minute goal. It happened in the 1933 All-Ireland semi-final against a Cavan team for whom a youthful Tom O'Reilly from Cornafean was enjoying his first Championship season. And it was the start of a golden era for Cavan football during which 'Big' Tom would be joined by his brother John Joe as Cavan embarked on a wonderful journey that would eventually lead to the Polo Grounds final of 1947.

Tom O'Reilly was just eighteen years old when the Cavan selectors decided he was ready for the demands of Senior Championship football in 1933. Kerry were the dominant force and the general expectation was that they would remain on course for another All-Ireland success when they travelled to Cavan for the semi-final. The teams were level as the game entered the final minute when Vincent McGovern punched a goal to give Cavan a 1–5 to 0–5 victory.

It was the catalyst for a decade and a half of football achievement. Tom was centre half back on the team that won the county's first ever senior title when beating Galway in the final. He won his second All-Ireland two years later and by 1937 had been joined on the Cavan team by his younger brother John Joe. For the next ten years they would line out alongside each other for Cavan. Tom was captain from 1937 to 1945 during which they lost three All-Ireland finals, including a replay against Roscommon in 1943. He was still a squad member when John Joe was the captain and inspired the county's All-Ireland success in 1947.

In his book *The Football Immortals*, first published in 1968, Raymond Smith put into context the O'Reillys' place in football history. 'The O'Reillys were to Cavan football what the Mackeys were to Limerick hurling and the Rackards to Wexford. Seven brothers, Michael, Brian, Tom, John Joe, Vincent, Frank and Séamus, and four of them wore the county colours in senior grade, John Joe becoming a legend in his lifetime. He had about him that mystique that developed around the name of Bobby Rackard after the 1954 All-Ireland final, but it rested not only on individual performance on the field of play but on the qualities of the man – qualities like complete sportsmanship, an ability to inspire and bring out of others the very best that they could give and a style of play that had its lustre in defeat as much as in victory.

'All these and more he had and gave to Cavan and it is not surprising then that Joe Stafford, Mick Higgins and the others should first talk about his abilities as a leader before they talked about his prowess as a centre back. I unhesitatingly pick John Joe O'Reilly as my ideal of the great footballing captain.'

Cavan enjoyed an astonishing period of dominance in Ulster. Between 1931 and 1949 they won seventeen of the nineteen provincial Senior Championships, the exceptions being Monaghan's success in 1938 and Antrim's win in 1946, and the O'Reilly brothers were involved in fifteen of those successes. In that time Tom won nine Cavan Championship titles with Cornafean and was captain on seven of those occasions. John Joe had joined the Defence Forces in 1937, which meant he had to leave Cornafean and play his club football with the Curragh. The brothers shared success together on the Ulster teams of 1942 and 1943 in the Railway Cup, then a fiercely contested event.

John Joe's status as one of the greatest ever centre half backs was constructed gradually in the period up to 1947. Events that year would add to the legend, none more so than the staging of the All-Ireland football final in the Polo Grounds in New York. The idea was hatched by Kerry exile John 'Kerry' O'Donnell and Canon Michael Hamilton, the man who eloquently proposed to the GAA's annual congress that year that the final be played in New York as a gesture of support for the GAA in the United States.

In his account of the events of 1947, published fifty years later, the late Mick Dunne, who had covered Gaelic games for half a century with the *Irish Press* and RTÉ, reproduced some of Canon Hamilton's rhetoric which convinced the GAA that it was a good idea. 'Another reason for our motion,' the Canon said to delegates at congress, 'is more sentimental but no less cogent – it is to give many thousands of our exiled brethren – who could otherwise never hope to see one – the thrill and joy and exaltation of an All-Ireland final. I could not attempt to express what an All-Ireland would mean to our exiles. There are hundreds and thousands of them awaiting the decision of congress and if that decision is in their favour there will be a wave of joy and happiness in the homes of our exiles not merely in New York, but north to Chicago, south to Florida and west 3,000 miles to San Francisco.'

It got even more colourful. 'This is the year 1947, the centenary of that dark and dismal period, when hunted by the spectre of famine and pestilence, the great exodus of our people found a friendly welcome and warm hospitality on America's shores. The enemies of Ireland boasted that the Celt was going – going with a vengeance – and they gloated over the prediction that the time was coming when an Irishman would be as rare in Ireland as a Red Indian on the shores of Manhattan. We need no vindication from that wishful thinking but by sending out the best of our athletes, the flower of our manhood, to contest the All-Ireland in New York, we give a magnificent demonstration of the unbroken historical continuity and the insuppressible [*sic*] tenacity of our race.' Such tugging at the heartstrings kept the proposal alive. Eventually, a week later the GAA's Central Council agreed by twenty votes to seventeen to allow the football final to be played at the Polo Grounds.

Cavan encountered some resistance from Monaghan in the Ulster Championship before winning in a replay. They comfortably beat Tyrone and then Antrim to qualify for an All-Ireland semi-final against their great rivals, Roscommon. A record crowd of 60,075 attended the game and saw Cavan enjoy a narrow win by 2–4 to 0–6. The journey to America by boat and air was immediately planned. The final itself against Kerry was almost overshadowed by the pageantry involving visits to the mayor of New York and to St Patrick's cathedral.

The game started badly for Cavan and after just fifteen minutes they trailed by 0–1 to 2–2. But then John Joe's leadership came into focus. He rallied his team-mates and slowly they began chipping away at the lead. By half time they led by 2–5 to 2–4 and at full-time Cavan were the champions by 2–11 to 2–7. A year later John Joe joined an elite band of men who were presented with the Sam Maguire Cup on two occasions, when Cavan retained the title by beating Mayo. He was also captain in 1949 when Cavan lost to Meath.

Hailed 'The Gallant John Joe', he was celebrated in song and there was shock not just in Cavan, but all over Ireland and indeed in the United States, when it was announced by the Defence Forces on 21 November 1952 that John Joe O'Reilly had passed away after an illness. He was named in 1999 as centre half back on the GAA's Team of the Millennium. 'Big' Tom entered politics towards the end of his playing career before concentrating on business. He died in 1995.

JIMMY AND PHELIM MURRAY

It was very late in the evening on Saturday 23 September 2006 as a cavalcade made its way from Athlone to Roscommon. The lead vehicle was the bus carrying the victorious Roscommon minor football team from the scene of their All-Ireland final triumph after a replay against Kerry played in Ennis. Friends and family were ahead of them in the company of over 10,000 supporters awaiting their arrival in Roscommon's town square. But the loved ones and the others would have to wait just a little longer. There was one stop they had to make, one that would provide them with the final crowning glory. They were bringing the cup home to Jimmy Murray, known to generations of Roscommon people simply as Jamesie.

A little frail at the age of eighty-nine, he hadn't been able to attend the game. But he had watched on television and the light in his eyes shone brightly. He didn't expect them to call. Jamesie was too humble for such notions. But no one else doubted that the visit would take place. It didn't have to be planned. It was just done.

Local lad Michael Miley, Roscommon's goalkeeper that day, and team manager Fergal O'Donnell, a native of nearby Roscommon town, brought the cup to Jamesie. Tears of joy were shed. After years of frustration and often despair shared by all Roscommon supporters, Jamesie Murray had reason to celebrate. And his smile was more valuable than any trophy.

Knockcroghery isn't much bigger now than it was in the second decade of the twentieth century. Murray's public house and grocery was at the centre of the village having been opened by John and Susan in 1915. Two years later the first of their ten children was born. They named him James. Everybody knew him as Jamesie. Their fifth child and third son was Phelim. Together they would help create a special part of Gaelic football's history in what is recalled today in the village and county as 'the glorious forties'.

There were hints of what was to come for Roscommon and the Murrays at the end of the 1930s and early 1940s.

Roscommon won the All-Ireland Minor Championship in 1939 and Phelim was a member of the squad. The county team was regraded to junior status, however, and they won the All-Ireland Junior Championship in 1940 with Jamesie playing at midfield alongside Éamon Boland. Phelim was a substitute. They were beaten by Galway in the 1941 and 1942 Connacht finals before they made the big breakthrough in 1943. For the first time since 1914 they won the Connacht title. They beat Louth in the All-Ireland semi-final and prepared to meet Cavan in their first ever final. Phelim started at right half forward with Jamesie in his now customary position at centre half forward and team captain.

Jamesie described the occasion of the final to the broadcaster and author Brian Carthy in his book *Football Captains*: 'As a young fellow in our own back yard I had imagined leading the parade. I loved looking at newspapers on a Monday morning after a final just to see a photograph of the parade. I always thought it would be wonderful to march behind the band at Croke Park. Now I was doing it and better still I was captain of the Roscommon team in their first ever All-Ireland. It was a great feeling. Then other thoughts crossed my mind and I wished I was away from the pitch and sitting in the stand. I looked up at Micheál O'Hehir in the commentary box and I imagined he was saying something like "here comes Roscommon led by the fair-haired Jimmy Murray". It brought my mind back to my native village, Knockcroghery, and I tried to envisage what my father and mother were doing. I knew my mother would be praying and I could imagine all the crowd in the kitchen listening to the radio and I said to myself "we have to do something for those people". It made me feel good and fierce determined to do or die for the sake of Knockcroghery more than anything else. I had a great village feeling.'

He was sentimental. This was the realisation of a childhood dream. But Jamesie Murray was also very tough mentally. His leadership was based on massive commitment and courage. He demanded the same from his team-mates. The final ended in a draw, 1–6 each. Roscommon won the replay two weeks later by 2–7 to 2–2.

They began the defence of their title in less than impressive fashion in 1944 when they were fortunate to escape with a draw against Sligo in the opening round of the Connacht campaign. Phelim was switched to defensive duties and Jamesie returned from injury in time to lead the team to a comfortable final win over Mayo, a feature of the game being Phelim's two points from '50s'. They beat Cavan easily in the All-Ireland semi-final to qualify to meet Kerry. Jamesie later said: 'To beat Kerry in the final was a wonderful thing. I have always said that no team can be regarded as champions until they beat Kerry.' Roscommon duly did so by 1–9 to 2–4. Jamesie Murray became the first man to captain a county to consecutive Championships. Only a handful have followed him – John Joe O'Reilly of Cavan (1947 and 1948), Seán Flanagan of Mayo (1950 and 1951), Enda Colleran of Galway (1965 and 1966), Tony Hanahoe of Dublin (1976 and 1977) and Declan O'Sullivan of Kerry (2006 and 2007).

By this time Phelim had moved to Dublin and UCD, with whom he won a Sigerson Cup in 1944. After qualifying as an engineer, he continued to live in Dublin and would retire from inter-county football at the age of twenty-six. He was still around, however, for one of the most famous All-Ireland finals, the two-game saga with Kerry in 1946. In the drawn game Roscommon were leading by 1–7 to 0–4 with less than five minutes remaining. Jamesie had to receive attention on the sideline for a facial injury and watched with something approaching horror at the events taking place.

Later he recalled: 'I had lost a fair amount of blood and I imagine I looked a messy sight. One of the St John Ambulance men got to work cleaning the blood from my face. He said he wanted to make me presentable when I received the cup. Thousands of other people, including myself, thought Roscommon had won. What happened is history. Kerry scored two late goals to draw the match and they went on to win the replay. The extraordinary thing is that I came back into the game after Kerry scored the second goal. I can't remember how it happened but I definitely got back on the field and even got one chance to score a point, but I missed. It would have made history for me and for Roscommon if I had scored.

'Of course that was my greatest disappointment in football and the thought of that day still hurts. We felt terrible. I knew coming off that day that we should have won the game and when you feel like that it is very hard to win a replay. I don't like making excuses for losing but I think we were a very tired team in the replay. Collective training [with squads coming together for a week and sometimes two for full-time training] at the time was allowed and in 1946 we had seven spells of training, nearly two weeks each time, and it was just too much. The hunger was gone.'

Jamesie remained closely involved with the GAA for the rest of his life with St Dominic's and Roscommon. He was the county's Central Council delegate for a time and served in various roles with the club. His public house, his home for his entire life, became a shrine and attracted visitors from all over Ireland and abroad. During a fire that extensively damaged the premises, Jamesie risked his life to save the match ball from the 1943 final which is still displayed proudly by his son John.

An inspiration to generations of young footballers, he was the perfect host and many a great day ended with his version of 'The West's Awake'. He took up golf and played into his eighties. He died in January 2007. Phelim died in 2005.

NICKY, BOBBY, BILLY AND JIMMY RACKARD

Nicky Rackard was already a ten-year veteran of Championship hurling when Wexford reached the Leinster senior hurling final in 1951. It was their second consecutive final but only their third since Nicky had first established himself in the team in the early 1940s. His best years should have been behind him. In fact, they were only starting.

As he led the team out for the provincial decider against Laois he was joined by three of his brothers. Jimmy played in goal, Bobby started at centre half back and Billy lined out at left half back. Nicky had spent the best part of his career at midfield, but was now settling in at full forward where he would play out the remaining years of his time with Wexford.

Victory over Laois, bringing Wexford their first Leinster senior hurling title since 1918, began a period of success that is still heralded in Wexford and beyond. Not only was a new force emerging, but they were playing a different brand of hurling, moving the ball through the air and keeping it off the ground. It didn't always make them popular with the traditionalists, but it brought them unprecedented success and encouraged others to change their tactics.

Jimmy did not hold his place, but Nicky, Bobby and Billy played in their first All-Ireland final that September and would become three of the best-known players in hurling over the next decade, during which Wexford won All-Ireland titles in 1955 and 1956 and played in some of the most memorable games in the history of hurling.

Although beaten in the provincial finals of 1952 and 1953 by Dublin and Kilkenny respectively, Wexford were continuing to build. By 1954 it seemed as if they were ready to finally end the long wait for All-Ireland success. They beat

Dublin comfortably in the Leinster final and then scored an extraordinary 12–17 in an annihilation of Antrim in the All-Ireland semi-final, with Nicky contributing seven goals and seven points.

The final against Cork was one of the most memorable of the period. When Wexford lost their brilliant full back Nick O'Donnell to injury early in the second half Bobby, who was giving a masterclass at centre half back, was switched to number three. With just minutes remaining Wexford led by two points. Then Cork's Johnny Clifford, later an All-Ireland-winning coach, took advantage of some hesitation in the Wexford defence to pounce on a loose ball and score the decisive goal.

Nicky Rackard admitted in interviews after the game that he believed then his chance of winning an All-Ireland title was gone. In the twilight of his career he had played in two finals and lost both. A year later, however, he realised his dream. Bobby, Billy and Nicky starred in the All-Ireland final success over Galway, 3–13 to 2–8, Nicky's goal at the start of the game providing the inspiration for a famous victory.

He considered retiring after the final. But there were those who claimed that Wexford could not be regarded as true champions until they had beaten a Munster team in an All-Ireland final. So they gathered themselves again for another campaign and duly reached the final, in which Christy Ring was aiming to win a record ninth medal in the colours of Cork.

His task seemed hopeless when Wexford led by seven points during the second half. Inspired by Ring, however, Cork gradually reduced the margin and Ring hand-passed a point to give them the lead ten minutes from time. Wexford fought back to go two points ahead. Then, with minutes remaining, Ring bore down on goal. His shot was goal-bound, but Wexford goalkeeper Art Foley stuck his hand in the air and saved. In the next attack Nicky smashed the ball into the net. The All-Ireland title was returning to Wexford.

Nicky and Bobby retired in 1957, the latter following an accident at home. Billy continued to play and won a third All-Ireland title in 1960, retiring in 1964.

Nicky worked as a vet in Wexford for many years and suffered from alcoholism. But by the 1970s he had overcome the problem and became a prominent figure with Alcoholics Anonymous. The brothers shared a deep passion for horses and horse racing.

LAR AND DES FOLEY

Around the farmlands of Kinsealy in north County Dublin in the 1940s and 1950s the people had an ecumenical view of sports. Officially the GAA's 'ban' on its members playing sports other than Gaelic games was in place, but the locals here played what they liked. In the Foley household some played soccer, others played football and hurling. In some cases they played all three. Lar and his younger brother Des played football and hurling. With work on the farm they didn't have time for anything else. That was good news for their club, St Vincent's, and for the Dublin football and hurling teams of the late 1950s and 1960s.

From their earliest days with Dublin under-age teams in the mid-1950s, to the conclusion of their club careers at the start of the 1970s, the Foley brothers would write a very special chapter in Dublin GAA history. They played in the 1961 All-Ireland hurling final when Dublin lost narrowly to Tipperary and were back in Croke Park two years later as the Dublin footballers won the All-Ireland senior title when beating an up-and-coming Galway team.

They played interprovincial hurling and football with Leinster, and Des created history in March 1962 when he played in the Railway Cup finals in both codes on the same day. He played at midfield alongside Dublin's Mick Kennedy as Leinster beat Munster in the hurling final and then lined out with the footballers, with Lar at full back, as they beat a star-studded Ulster team.

The heady days for the Foleys began in 1955, when Lar won the first of two All-Ireland minor football medals with Dublin. They beat Tipperary in the final and the following year Des had graduated to the team of which Lar had been named captain. They defeated Leitrim in the final and Lar was selected on the St Vincent's senior team. They were beaten in the county final by Erin's Hope, but Lar and Des would share in some remarkable successes with the club in both football and hurling between 1957 and 1972. St Vincent's won twelve Dublin football titles and four hurling titles in that period.

With Dublin they were back in Croke Park on All-Ireland football final day in September 1958. This would be a unique day for the Foley family. Des became the second brother to captain the Dublin minor team to All-Ireland success and Lar won his first All-Ireland senior medal when he lined out at right corner back on the team that beat Derry. Lar had already won his first national title at senior level earlier in the year when Dublin captured the League title with victory over Kildare.

There were signs of growing prosperity for Dublin hurling during this period. In 1958 they had lost to Kilkenny by just one point after a replay. They were beaten by Kilkenny in the 1959 provincial final and lost to Wexford in 1960, as Wexford marched to a famous All-Ireland victory. Even with that record of improvement, there was little expectation outside the team that they would make the breakthrough in 1961. Wexford were strongly fancied to at least retain their Leinster Championship and all the talk was of a re-match with an outstandingly talented Tipperary team. But in a sensational Leinster final Dublin beat Wexford by 7–5 to 4–8.

With Galway now playing in the Munster Championship, the Leinster winners went straight through to the All-

Ireland final. Five players from the St Vincent's club lined out for Dublin against Tipperary – the full back line of Des Ferguson, team captain Noel Drumgoole and Lar Foley, Shay Lynch at left half back and Des Foley at midfield. Hurling's first televised All-Ireland final would prove to be heartbreaking for Dublin. Lar's sending off along with Tipperary's Tom Ryan did not help the cause, but they also missed a number of good chances and lost by just one point, 1–12 to 0–16. Dublin did reach the 1963 and 1964 Leinster finals, but a great opportunity to win an elusive All-Ireland title was lost.

Hurling was their first love, but football would provide them with a measure of compensation for the 1961 defeat. In the 1962 Leinster Championship Dublin re-emerged from under the shadow of Offaly to regain the Leinster title, but lost to Kerry in the All-Ireland semi-final. A year later they returned to the semi-final stage and a meeting with the outstanding Down team of the period. In an interview later with Raymond Smith, Des Foley described their victory. 'That success was the making of us,' he declared. 'It may not have been a great team from a footballing point of view, but no Dublin team had greater heart or spirit. They trained very hard and showed tremendous fire in all their games.'

Dublin met an emerging Galway team in the final. Mattie McDonagh remained from Galway's 1956 All-Ireland-winning team, but he was surrounded by a group of younger players who would go on to record football history by winning three titles in a row between 1964 and 1966. But before that they had to face Dublin. Des Foley, captaining the team at number eight, pointed out later that the real turning point of the game was Gerry Davey's goal nine minutes into the second half. Galway had led by 0–6 to 0–4 at half time, but that goal changed the pattern sufficiently and Dublin held on to win by 1–9 to 0–10.

Dublin's decline in both codes through the rest of the 1960s did not mean any great rest for the Foley brothers. The St Vincent's football team of that decade is regarded as one of the greatest club teams of all time, while the hurling team was also enjoying great success in the county. The introduction of the All-Ireland Club Championship as an official competition in 1971 came as the two men entered the final years of their careers as footballers and hurlers. But they did play in the 1973 All-Ireland club football final, when St Vincent's lost after a replay to Nemo Rangers of Cork. That St Vincent's team included youngsters such as Gay O'Driscoll, Bobby Doyle, Tony Hanahoe, a teenage Brian Mullins and a certain Jimmy Keaveney, who would all enjoy great success during the 1970s.

Des was elected as a Fianna Fáil TD for Dublin County in 1965 and held the seat until his resignation five years later. Both brothers remained closely involved with St Vincent's and Lar managed the Dublin senior hurling team from 1989 to 1993, a period in which they reached two Leinster finals, losing the 1991 decider by just two points to Kilkenny.

EPILOGUE

One of the major changes in Irish society in the period covered by these stories is the demise of the large family. It has not yet fully impacted on sport, but it will certainly be very rare in the future for three brothers to feature on an inter-county football or hurling team. The impact at club level will be even greater and the days of six and seven brothers featuring on a club team are also coming to an end.

However, just a brief glance through the inter-county list for 2010 shows that brothers are continuing to make a contribution to the rich history of Gaelic games. At least two sets of twins competed again this year in the football and hurling Championships – the McMahons, Joe and Justin, of Tyrone and the O'Connors, Ben and Jerry, of Cork. Elsewhere, the Kernans of Armagh are entering their peak years, while Dublin's hopes of football glory rest significantly on the shoulders of the Brogans, Alan and Bernard.

The brothers featured in these pages are a representation of a unique facet of Gaelic games. There have been, are now and will be in the future, others whose achievements should be recorded for posterity and pleasure – when time and space permit.

INDEX